The **Princeton** Review

500+ PRACTICE QUESTIONS FOR THE NEW

SAT®

The Staff of The Princeton Review

PrincetonReview.com

Penguin Random House

The Princeton Review
24 Prime Parkway, Suite 201
Natick, MA 01760
E-mail: editorialsupport@review.com

Published in the United States by Penguin Random House LLC, New York,
and in Canada by Random House of Canada, a division of Penguin Random
House Ltd., Toronto.

ISBN: 978-1-101-88175-0
ISSN: 2376-7316

Editor: Aaron Riccio
Production Editor: Jim Melloan
Production Artist: John Stecyk

Printed in the United States of America on partially recycled paper.

10   9   8   7   6   5   4   3

2015 Edition

Editorial

Rob Franek, Senior VP, Publisher
Casey Cornelius, VP Content Development
Mary Beth Garrick, Director of Production
Selena Coppock, Managing Editor
Calvin Cato, Editor
Colleen Day, Editor
Aaron Riccio, Editor
Meave Shelton, Editor
Orion McBean, Editorial Assistant

Random House Publishing Team

Tom Russell, Publisher
Alison Stoltzfus, Publishing Manager
Melinda Ackell, Associate Managing Editor
Ellen Reed, Production Manager
Kristin Lindner, Production Supervisor
Andrea Lau, Designer

Acknowledgments

Project Managers

Claudia Landgrover
Kathryn Menefee

Authors

Aaron Lindh
Amy Minster
Alice Swan
Brian Becker
Lisa Mayo
Elizabeth Owens
Erik Kolb
Zoe Gannon

Reviewers

Cara Fabre
Cat Healey
Spencer LeDoux
Joelle Cotham
Shannon Thompson
Steve Voigt

National Content Director

Jonathan Chiu

Contents

Part I: Orientation 1

1   Your Guide to Getting the Most Out Of This Book 3

2   What You Need to Know for the New SAT 7

Part II: Writing and Language 15

    What Can You Expect to See on the Writing & Language Test?....... 16

3   Writing and Language Drills 23

4   Writing and Language Answers and Explanations...................... 49

Part III: Math 67

    What Can You Expect to See on the Math Test?........................ 68

5   Heart of Algebra Drills... 73

6   Heart of Algebra Answers and Explanations......................... 93

7   Problem Solving and Data Analysis................................. 111

8   Problem Solving and Data Analysis Answers and Explanations 133

9   Passport to Advanced Math.. 147

10 Passport to Advanced Math Answers and Explanations 165

11 Additional Topics 183

12 Additional Topics Answers and Explanations 191

Part IV: Reading 197

    What Can You Expect to See on the Reading Test? 198

13 Reading Drills 201

14 Reading Answers and Explanations............................... 237

Part I
Orientation

1 Your Guide to Getting the Most Out Of This Book
2 What You Need to Know for the New SAT

Chapter 1
Your Guide to Getting the Most Out Of This Book

What Is The Princeton Review?

The Princeton Review is the nation's most popular test-preparation company. We offer courses and private tutoring for all of the major standardized tests, and we publish a series of books to help in your search for the right school. If you would like more information about how The Princeton Review can help you, go to PrincetonReview.com or call 800-2-Review.

WHAT'S INSIDE

Hello, and welcome to *500+ Practice Questions for the New SAT*! You've most likely picked up this book because you heard that the SAT is being redesigned, and you want to get a first look at what to expect. Congratulations: It's never too early to begin your test prep, and this is a good first step toward mastering the redesigned SAT. We're delighted that you've chosen us for your needs!

In these pages you'll find more than 500 questions to help you prepare for the redesigned SAT. These questions showcase all the features of the new SAT, including its retooled subject areas: Writing & Language, Math, and Reading. Working through these problems in conjunction with our detailed, technique-filled explanations is a great way to familiarize yourself with the challenges of the redesigned SAT.

HOW TO USE THIS BOOK

These drills are divided into each of the three tests: Writing & Language, Math, and Reading. If you want to focus on one particular test, there's no need to work through the other material: the table of contents can direct you to your test of choice and all the drills you can handle! The Math test is also divided into four sections: Heart of Algebra, Problem Solving and Data Analysis, Passport to Advanced Math, and Additional Topics. These subsections reflect the different Math question types that you'll encounter on the redesigned SAT, and we've designed multiple drills to help you master each type.

The Optional Essay

Keep an eye out for future publications from us with full-length practice tests that include essay prompts. This book is designed to introduce you to many of the fundamental concepts that will be necessary to successfully attack the new SAT questions. As the essay is optional—check in advance whether the colleges you are applying to expect it— we have chosen to focus on other preparations.

The questions are broken into drills, which allows you to practice on your own schedule and comfort level: as much or as little as you need at a given time. Taking a drill or two a day is a great way to build your SAT expertise over time, while taking several drills at once can help you prepare for the somewhat-taxing experience of taking the full-length test. We recommend you do both!

Once you've finished a drill, don't just close the book. Be sure to read over the detailed explanations following each drill to see what questions you missed and what you can improve upon next time. As with all other Princeton Review prep materials, these explanations showcase our powerful SAT strategies and techniques. Even if you answered a question correctly, our explanation might show you a way to solve it faster and more accurately!

WHEN YOU TAKE A DRILL

Here are some suggestions for working through this book:

- Keep track of your performance. Remember that the purpose of all the work you're doing now is to achieve a certain result when you take the actual SAT, so all of this will be for nothing if you don't remember it. Use this opportunity to self-diagnose your weakest areas and figure out the techniques and skills you need to work on.

- Focus on the areas where you need improvement, and practice until you improve! By all means, work through all of the problems in this book—the more you expose yourself to these questions and the overall rhythm of the test, the more prepared you'll be. But start by going over the sections that you feel least comfortable with; you want to give your mind as much time as possible to adapt to what you're learning.

- The redesigned SAT, like the old SAT, is a timed test. You may be a star test-taker when you have all the time in the world to mull over the questions, but can you perform as well when the clock is ticking? Timing yourself on the drills will ensure you are prepared for the constraints of the actual test.

Filling In Answers

On the actual SAT, you will have to fill in your answers on a separate scantron sheet. However, because this is a book of drills, and because we'd rather have you focus your energy on the questions themselves, our directions recommend that you mark your answers directly in the book. (You can also use scrap paper, if that's more comfortable for you.)

Remember that this book is for your personal use; as long as you are able to self-diagnose by checking our answers and explanations against your own, you can mark it up however you please. You may even want to consider the sorts of marks to make if you want to return to check a question or remember to bubble in a question that you skipped.

That said, you should be aware of how to fill in a Student-Produced Response question (that is, a grid-in). We have used small icons to represent these questions in the book, like the one in the sidebar here. Here is how you would actually fill it out on a scantron sheet:

Directions: A Student-Produced Response question requires you to solve the problem and enter your answer by marking the circles in the special grid, as shown in the examples below. You may use any available space for scratch work.

Answer: $\frac{7}{12}$

Write answer in boxes. → Fraction line

Grid in result.

Answer: 2.5 ← Decimal point

Answer: 201
Either position is correct.

Note: You may start your answers in any column, space permitting. Columns not needed should be left blank.

- Mark no more than one circle in any column.
- Because the answer document will be machine-scored, **you will receive credit only if the circles are filled in correctly.**
- Although not required, it is suggested that you write your answer in the boxes at the top of the columns to help you fill in the circles accurately.
- Some problems may have more than one correct answer. In such cases, grid only one answer.
- No question has a negative answer.
- **Mixed numbers** such as $3\frac{1}{2}$ must be gridded as 3.5 or 7/2. (If [3 1 / 2] is gridded, it will be interpreted as $\frac{31}{2}$, not $3\frac{1}{2}$.)

- **Decimal Answers:** If you obtain a decimal answer with more digits than the grid can accommodate, it may be either rounded or truncated, but it must fill the entire grid. For example, if you obtain an answer such as 0.6666..., you should record your result as .666 or .667. **A less accurate value such as .66 or .67 will be scored as incorrect.**

Acceptable ways to grid $\frac{2}{3}$ are:

STAYING AHEAD OF THE REDESIGNED SAT

Because the first official test date for the Redesigned SAT is in 2016, it is possible that the College Board will continue to make slight changes and tweaks to the way the test is presented. The **PrincetonReview.com/SATchanges** page of our website will always feature the most up-to-date information. You can also attend free events at the Princeton Review—both in-person and online—to learn more about the redesigned SAT and the other college prep resources we offer. Search on our website for events taking place near you.

GOOD LUCK!

We know that the redesigned SAT might seem intimidating, but you're already headed in the right direction. And we'll be with you every step of the way.

Chapter 2
What You Need to Know for the New SAT

What Does the SAT Test?

First off, while the SAT may be changing, we at The Princeton Review understand that certain fundamentals of a test always stay the same. As you begin your prep, it's useful to remember that the SAT is not a test of aptitude, how good of a person you are, or how successful you will be in life. The SAT simply tests how well you take the SAT. And performing well on the SAT is a skill, one that can be learned like any other. The Princeton Review was founded more than 30 years ago on this very simple idea, and—as our students' test scores show—our approach is the one that works.

In other words, no matter how well you want to do on the SAT, no matter how much pressure you might be feeling, you don't need to let the test intimidate you. Just remember:

- **It doesn't measure the stuff that matters.** It measures neither intelligence nor the depth and breadth of what you're learning in high school. It doesn't predict college grades as well as your high school grades do, and many schools are still hesitant to use the score from your essay in their application decisions at all: that's why it's now optional. Colleges know there is more to you as a student—and as a person—than what you do at a single 3-hour test administered on a Saturday morning.

- **It underpredicts the college performance of women, minorities, and disadvantaged students.** Historically, women have done better than men in college but worse on the SAT. For a test that is used to help predict performance in college, that's a pretty poor record.

Who Writes the SAT?

Although colleges and universities are the primary users of SAT results, they're not the ones who write it. That's actually the job of Educational Testing Service (ETS), a nonprofit company that specializes in writing tests. You probably know them best for their work on the SAT and GRE, but they also write for groups as diverse as butchers and professional golfers. (Who knew?)

ETS is often criticized for the SAT. Many educators have argued that the test does not measure the skills you really need for college, as we mentioned above. In 2005, this led them to overhaul the entire test, shifting from a 1600 to 2400 point scale—the test with which you're most likely familiar. Beginning in 2016, that test will have changed again. The important takeaway here is that the people who write the SAT are professional test writers, not necessarily professors or superhuman geniuses, and if you understand what they're testing, you can beat them at their own game.

Changes	The Current SAT	The Redesigned SAT (coming spring 2016)
SECTIONS	3 sections • Math • Critical Reading • Writing Skills	2 sections • Math • Evidence-Based Reading and Writing

SCORING	Composite score (600–2400)
	
	• 3 section scores (200–800)
		Total score (400–1600)
		
		• 2 section scores (200–800)
		  • 3 test scores (10–40)
		    • 7 sub-scores (1–15)
		  • 2 cross-test scores

LENGTH OF TEST (WITHOUT BREAKS)	3 hours, 45 minutes	3 hours (without essay) 3 hours, 50 minutes (with essay)
ANSWER CHOICES	5 answer choices per question	4 answer choices per question
INCORRECT ANSWER PENALTY	1/4 point off for each incorrect answer on multiple-choice questions	No penalty for incorrect answers
FORMAT OF TEST	Paper and pencil only	Paper and pencil AND a computer-based option

READING AND WRITING	• Two sections:
	
	  • Critical Reading
	  • Writing Skills
	
	• Vocabulary tested by sentence completion questions; famous for "SAT Words," often considered obscure
	
	• Passage-based questions, with passages drawn from random topics
		• Two tests:
		
		  • Reading Test
		  • Writing and Language Test
		
		• No more sentence completions; focus on multiple-meaning words
		
		• Passages will draw from significant historical or scientific documents – may include informational graphics, such as charts
		
		• The reading passages will include complex structure and vocabulary
		
		• Passage-based grammar – including punctuation

What's New on the SAT (and What's Eliminated)
In a nutshell, while the current SAT is 3 hours and 45 minutes of testing time, the new SAT will be 3 hours and 50 minutes— and only 3 hours without the optional essay.

MATH	Covers:	Focuses on:
	• Arithmetic • Algebra I • Geometry • Some Algebra II	• Application-based, multi-step questions • Higher-level math, including trigonometry • One "extended-thinking" grid-in question (worth 4 points); • Core math competencies (translating math into English and English into math) • A deep understanding of the theories behind mathematical principles, such as building equations
CALCULATORS	Calculators permitted in every math section	Calculators only allowed in the longer of the two math sections
THE ESSAY	Required first section of the test (25 minutes, timed) Students respond to a short prompt by providing personal opinion with supporting evidence	The essay is optional (50 minutes, timed) Students will be provided a substantial passage (600–700 words) and will then be asked to analyze how the author built their argument; students will need to understand the techniques authors used to write persuasively

The More You Know…
These changes may be intimidating, but adopting a careful approach after mastering your fundamentals will help you to do well on the new SAT!

In addition to the obvious changes listed on the table above, such as the shift from five answer choices to four, the RSAT suggests that it has increased the complexity of questions across the board. For the Reading and Writing & Language sections, this refers in part to the way in which all questions are now connected to full passages, which are themselves aligned with what introductory college courses and vocational training programs offer. This means that there's an increase in History and Science-based reading material, if you're wondering what sort of texts you might want to familiarize yourself with. More importantly, there are no more fill-in-the-blank Sentence Completion questions, nor stand-alone sentence-editing questions: instead, students will be tested on their ability to demonstrate a full understanding of the source's ideas.

While it's hard to predict when and where breaks between sections will be provided, it's a good guess that the Writing test's four passages, for which 35 minutes are allotted, will be presented in one go, as will the Reading test's five passages, which are designed to take a total of 65 minutes.

The math has also shifted, and not just in the number of questions (from 54 to 57). The actual scope of the content now focuses on a more specific set of problem-solving and analytical topics, and includes higher-level content (like trigonometry). Students are also likely to encounter more grid-in questions, and will face topics that are both specifically geared to test a student's ability to use a calculator and for which calculators are not permitted.

While higher-level math may sound scary at first, that also means the scope of the test is on a narrower swath of subjects. In other words, there are fewer things to study, which gives you more time to really master these subjects. (And that's where we at The Princeton Review come in.)

The Math Test will be divided into two sections, one with the calculator, with 37 questions over the course of 55 minutes, and one without, with 20 questions administered in 20 minutes. Because of the tight time limit, particularly in the non-calculator section, it's important that you review the explanations for the problems in this book that you solved correctly, as you may discover techniques that help to shave seconds from your solutions. A large part of what's being tested is your ability to use the appropriate tools in a strategic fashion, and while there may be multiple ways to solve a given problem, you'll want to focus on the most efficient.

When Is the SAT Given?

The schedule for the SAT changes from year to year, but it's always found on the College Board website at **www.collegeboard.com**.

Try to sign up for the SAT as soon as you know when you'll be taking the test, especially if you're planning to take the first iteration of the new SAT in Spring 2016, or the last iteration of the old SAT before that, as those are likely to fill up very quickly. If you wait until the last minute to sign up, there may not be any open spots in the testing centers closest to your home, and there's nothing like making a longer commute to an unfamiliar area to throw off your test-taking day.

Additionally, if you require any testing accommodations (such as extra time), the College Board website provides more information about the qualifications required. You don't want to leave anything to chance in the approval process, so make sure you leave at least six months between your application date and ideal testing time so that you can lock it in and spend more time focusing on your school assignments and SAT preparation.

...The Less to Study
While higher-level math may sound scary at first, continued practice can drastically reduce the math complexity for many questions.

Stay on Schedule
Take advantage of "super-scoring" on the SAT in which colleges will take your best subject scores, regardless of test date. Taking the SAT a couple of times can boost your college application portfolio.

Scoring on the SAT

Another major difference has to do with the way that the test is scored. While the return to a 1600 point composite score, now referred to as a total score, isn't new to the SAT, the inclusion of subscores and cross-test scores is. The intent of these scores is to help students and teachers better understand what specific skills and topic areas need to be improved (as opposed to just "Math" in general). In addition, wrong answers will no longer be penalized, so you're advised never to leave a question blank – even if that means blindly picking a letter and bubbling it in for any uncompleted questions before time runs out.

As always, you'll want to check with colleges to see what sort of scores they're most interested in, but so that you're aware, here are the extra categories that are now reported:

An **Analysis in History/Social Studies** and **Analysis in Science** cross-test score is generated based on questions from all three of the subject tests (Math included!) and these assess the cross-curricular application of the tested skills to other contexts. Relax! This doesn't mean that you have to start cramming dates and anatomy—every question can be answered from the context of a given reading passage or the data included in a table or figure. The only changes have to do with the content of the passages and questions themselves.

Additionally, the Math test is broken into several categories, as we've done in this book. The **Heart of Algebra** subscore looks specifically at how well students understand how to handle algebraic expressions, work with a variety of algebraic equations, and relate real-world scenarios to algebraic principles. **Problem Solving and Data Analysis** focuses more on interpretation of mathematical expressions, graphical analysis, and data interpretation. Your ability to not only understand what a problem is asking, but to represent it in your own words, will come in handy here. Finally, **Passport to Advanced Mathematics** questions showcase the higher-level math that's been added to the test, from quadratics and their graphs to the creation and translation of functions.

(We've also included an **Additional Topics** section that's filled with what you might consider wild-card material. Although these questions might not correlate directly to a subscore, 6 of these miscellaneous types will show up on the redesigned test, so you should try to prepare for all of them. At the very least, being able to solve these problems will help to flex other muscles in your brain, and that sort of elasticity always comes in handy on a lengthy exam.)

Because the English portions of the text are passage-based, we chose not to break out the drills by subscore. However, you'll find that our questions in those sections align to these topics. On the Reading test, the **Command of Evidence** subscore measures how well students can translate and cite specific lines that back up their interpretation, while **Relevant Words in Context** ensures that students can derive a proper and specific definition from the words in a passage. The Writing test additionally measures **Expression of Ideas**, which deals with revising language in order to make more logical and cohesive arguments, and **Standard English Con-**

ventions, which assesses a student's ability to conform to the basic rules of English structure, punctuation, and usage.

That said, the big numbers are still the main composite scores—what The College Board now calls total scores—the Reading and Writing & Language sections are tallied together to arrive at a score between 200 and 800, and the Math sections are tallied in the same way. That means the final scores are now between 400 to 1600, with the optional essay reported separately.

Process of Elimination (POE)

Given that there's no longer a big bad guessing penalty, and that the number of answer choices has been reduced from five to four, it's now very much to your advantage to answer every question. If you can eliminate some of the wrong answers, the odds grow ever more in your favor. In other words, you can answer some questions without knowing the correct answer, so long as you can identify the obviously wrong ones. For instance:

1. The capital of Qatar is

   A) Paris
   B) Dukhan
   C) Tokyo
   D) Doha

Paris and Tokyo are likely to be familiar answers to you, ones that you know are the capitals of other major countries (France and Japan). Just like that, a question with four answer choices becomes one with only two options, and while you certainly don't want to gamble your college futures on the constant flipping of a coin, this technique can help you out in a pinch.

Moreover, because the Reading and Writing sections are now largely based on context, you can almost always go back to the passages after narrowing down the choices. A choice that didn't leap out before may suddenly become obvious when given a second look. As another example:

2. The Sun is

   A) a main-sequence star
   B) a meteor
   C) an asteroid
   D) a white dwarf star

A first glance through the passage may stress that the Sun is a star, eliminating (B) and (C). Reading through a second time, looking specifically for terms like "main-sequence" or "white dwarf" may give you the extra information to solve a problem that you otherwise know nothing about.

Part II
Writing and Language

What Can You Expect to See on the Writing and
Language Test?
3   Writing and Language Drills
4   Writing and Language Drills Answers and Explanations

WHAT CAN YOU EXPECT TO SEE ON THE WRITING AND LANGUAGE TEST?

The SAT Writing test has changed significantly. If you're familiar with the ACT, then you know what to expect, but if you're not, the news is good! Traditionally, the SAT has featured three question types: Improving Paragraphs, Improving Sentences, and Error ID. Those designations are gone, and now you've got a single task: make a passage better. The passages will be the length of a short essay and all the questions will be distributed across four passages.

A Sample Passage

Here's a sample of what a new passage will look like:

[1] Studying grammar rules ❶ <u>seem</u> to be a thing of the past. [2] Instead, most English classes are ❷ <u>focus</u> on reading and writing today, with the implicit claim that one learns to write by writing. [3] Also implicit in this claim is the idea that grammar no longer has the practical, ❸ <u>objective or, egalitarian</u> cachet that it once did. [4] "Proper speech" does not exist in and of ❹ <u>itself: proper</u> speech, instead, is the province of those who consider themselves proper. [5] The age of diagramming sentences and laboring over the difference between direct and indirect objects is gone. ❺ ❻ [6] <u>For all that people complain about it, what is the difference between "who" and "whom" anyway?</u>

1. A) NO CHANGE
   B) seems
   C) will seem
   D) seemed

2. A) NO CHANGE
   B) being focused
   C) focused
   D) having focus

3. A) NO CHANGE
   B) objective or egalitarian,
   C) objective, or egalitarian,
   D) objective, or egalitarian

4. A) NO CHANGE
   B) itself proper
   C) itself, proper
   D) itself proper,

5. The best placement for sentence 5 would be

   A) where it is now.
   B) after sentence 1.
   C) after sentence 2.
   D) after sentence 4.

6. Which of the following questions would best conclude the paragraph by summarizing one of its main points?

    A) NO CHANGE
    B) Who is to say, after all, that the speech of a particular race, class, or region is any "better" than any other?
    C) Kids hate learning grammar, and teachers hate teaching it, so why bother?
    D) Why is grammar so difficult for native English speakers?

APPROACH THE QUESTIONS

Think of this as a peer-editing exercise. You're editing a classmate's paper. As you do so, keep two things in mind:

> On the questions that don't have stems, check the differences among the answer choices. This will tell you what the question is testing.
>
> On the questions that do have stems, read as literally as you can. This section of the test is not interested in reading comprehension, so look for cues in the language or punctuation to point toward the correct answer.

CHECK THE ANSWERS

The SAT can test any of about 40 different grammar concepts, and usually the test writers don't state explicitly which concept they're testing. SAT isn't quite nice enough to say things like "Use commas correctly here!" or "Should this be in the present tense or the past tense?"

However, SAT tells you more than you may realize. If we look only at the answer choices from the first question above, we'll see a certain pattern:

1. A) NO CHANGE
    B) seems
    C) will seem
    D) seemed

In this case, every answer choice contains the conjugation of a single verb, *to seem*. Accordingly, these answer choices are hinting that we'll need to choose the correct form of this verb. We can empty our minds of all the comma and punctuation rules because we know that this question is not asking about them.

That said, let's look at the third question.

3. A) NO CHANGE
    B) objective or egalitarian,
    C) objective, or egalitarian,
    D) objective, or egalitarian

This time, the words aren't changing at all, but the commas are! So this time, we know that the question is asking about where the commas go. We can ignore the words and just focus on the punctuation.

These tips are intended for the Writing test. The Reading test requires different skills, and while both are based on passages, each test has its own unique approach.

This may seem like an obvious point, but on a test with so many questions asking about so many things, you need something to help anchor your approach. Checking the differences among the answer choices provides exactly that anchor.

Don't Think: Read the Cues

For the questions that do have questions, however, don't look for implicit meanings. The questions will typically tell you exactly what to look for. We will look more at the questions from the passage below, but for now, look at this question from another passage entirely.

15. Which of the following provides the most specific information regarding the range of Montaigne's subjects?

    A) some of the best-loved essays in the history of French literature
    B) topics that are still of interest to twenty-first century readers
    C) a variety of subjects relevant to a sixteenth-century gentleman
    D) everything from gallstones to great historical events

In this case, the answer MUST be (D) because it is the only one that provides *specific information regarding the range of Montaigne's subjects*. The others are grammatically correct, and possibly relevant in other contexts, but they don't fulfill the question's basic requirements.

Sometimes these very specific cues can appear in the answer choices as well. Consider this question, also from another passage.

22. Which of the following alternatives to the underlined portion would be LEAST acceptable?

    A) However,
    B) Nevertheless,
    C) Therefore,
    D) Even so,

Notice that each of these answer choices provides some transition word. Choices (A), (B), and (D) are contrasting transitions, and (C) is a continuing transition. Since there is only one answer per question, the only one that can possibly work here is (C) because it's the odd one out.

Words, Punctuation, Questions

The SAT's questions can be broken down into three main categories, of which there are two each in the previous paragraph. Let's see that paragraph and question set again.

There can only be one correct answer per question. If two choices seem like they are both correct, they are probably both wrong!

[1] Studying grammar rules ❶ <u>seem</u> to be a thing of the past. [2] Instead, most English classes are ❷ <u>focus</u> on reading and writing today, with the implicit claim that one learns to write by writing. [3] Also implicit in this claim is the idea that grammar no longer has the practical, ❸ <u>objective or, egalitarian</u> cachet that it once did. [4] "Proper speech" does not exist in and of ❹ <u>itself: proper</u> speech, instead, is the province of those who consider themselves proper. [5] The age of diagramming sentences and laboring over the difference between direct and indirect objects is gone. ❺ ❻ [6] <u>For all that people complain about it, what is the difference between "who" and "whom" anyway?</u>

1. A) NO CHANGE
    B) seems
    C) will seem
    D) seemed

2. A) NO CHANGE
    B) being focused
    C) focused
    D) having focus

3. A) NO CHANGE
    B) objective or egalitarian,
    C) objective, or egalitarian,
    D) objective, or egalitarian

4. A) NO CHANGE
    B) itself proper
    C) itself, proper
    D) itself proper,

5. The best placement for sentence 5 would be

    A) where it is now.
    B) after sentence 1.
    C) after sentence 2.
    D) after sentence 4.

6. Which of the following questions would best conclude the paragraph by summarizing one of its main points?

    A) NO CHANGE
    B) Who is to say, after all, that the speech of a particular race, class, or region is any "better" than any other?
    C) Kids hate learning grammar, and teachers hate teaching it, so why bother?
    D) Why is grammar so difficult for native English speakers?

Words

Remember to check the answer choices before you get started. When you do so for the first two questions, you'll find that these are testing the use of *words*.

1. A) NO CHANGE
    B) seems
    C) will seem
    D) seemed

2. A) NO CHANGE
    B) being focused
    C) focused
    D) having focus

As mentioned above, question #1 has four answer choices that vary the conjugations of the verb to *seem*. We will therefore need to use the context to find the one that works. First, all the surrounding verbs are in the present tense, so (C) and (D) can be eliminated.

Then, the subject of the verb is *studying* (not *rules*!), which is singular, and requires the singular verb *seems*, or (B).

As for question #2, this one is changing forms of the verb *to focus*. Choices (B) and (D) are unnecessarily wordy, so they can be eliminated. Then, we have to choose between the present tense *focus* and the past *focused*. Don't trust your ear! These words sound awfully similar, so follow the rules. The word has the helping verb *are* in front of it, so it must be the participle *focused*, (C).

Punctuation

Your ear is a valuable tool, but it won't get you all the points you need. Your ear may help you to spot errors, but make sure you can cite the rules that make something correct or incorrect.

SAT can also test your knowledge of punctuation. Use the same method that you used for the Words. Punctuation is a bit tougher because you can't always hear the different punctuation marks. (Say the previous sentence out loud. Could you hear the apostrophe in *can't*?)

So let's look at some of the ways that SAT can test punctuation.

3. A) NO CHANGE
    B) objective or egalitarian,
    C) objective, or egalitarian,
    D) objective, or egalitarian

4. A) NO CHANGE
    B) itself proper
    C) itself, proper
    D) itself proper,

In question #3, notice how the words are not changing, but the commas are. In this case, the words are part of a series—*practical, objective, or egalitarian.* It doesn't actually matter all that much if you don't know what the words mean in this case because you don't have to decide between them. All you've got to do is put the commas in the right place, as only (D) does. Place commas after every item in a list, but don't insert new commas unnecessarily!

In question #4, the words are again identical, but this time, you have to choose between a colon and a comma. Notice that the ideas on both sides of the punctuation (*"Proper speech" does not exist in and of itself and proper speech, instead, is the province of those who consider themselves proper*) are complete, so a comma is insufficient to separate them. From the available answers, only a colon will work, as in choice (A). If you thought this could be a period or semicolon, you're right! But this is why we check the answers first: if we fix things in our heads, we may not fix them in the way that SAT wants or makes available.

Questions

About half the problems on an SAT Writing and Language test will have question stems. With these, read as literally as you can, and do exactly what the question asks. Let's see the two from the passage above.

5. The best placement for sentence 5 would be

   A) where it is now.
   B) after sentence 1.
   C) after sentence 2.
   D) after sentence 4.

6. Which of the following questions would best conclude the paragraph by summarizing one of its main points?

   A) NO CHANGE
   B) Who is to say, after all, that the speech of a particular race, class, or region is any "better" than any other?
   C) Kids hate learning grammar, and teachers hate teaching it, so why bother?
   D) Why is grammar so difficult for native English speakers?

For question #5, read as literally as possible! Sentence 5's main idea is that the age of learning grammar has passed. Which other sentences discuss similar things? Sentence 1 states a similar idea, and sentence 2 begins to show how things are changing. As a result, sentence 5 should go between these two sentences. The links are very literal: [1] *a thing of the past*, [2] *the age... is gone*, [3] *instead... today.* No reading comprehension or deep thought necessary here! Just follow the words!

For question #6, again, read as literally as possible. We want the question that summarizes the paragraph's main point. The paragraph has so far discussed how grammar is no longer frequently taught because of the emphasis in English classes on other things. The paragraph then goes on to talk about how "proper" speech is a hotly contested category. The concluding remark should include something about both of these ideas: (A) is too specifically focused on grammar, and (C) and (D) focus on topics not mentioned elsewhere in the passage. Only (B) remains, and notice how "better" is being used to echo the word "proper" in the previous sentence.

Conclusion

As you work through the exercises in this book, pay close attention to the explanations. They will provide detailed reasoning for each answer choice's correctness or incorrectness.

In general, remember the two big precepts: *look for what's changing* and *read as literally as possible*. The first step in particular will anchor your strategy and will at least give you something specific to think about as you try to work the questions. You'd be surprised how often the right answer emerges from eliminating all the wrong ones!

Chapter 3
Writing and
Language Drills

Writing & Language Drill 1

For each question in this section, circle the letter of the best answer from among the choices given.
Questions 1-11. Read the following passage carefully before you choose your answers.

A Familiar Voice From Across the World

Even among those who know twentieth-century literature ❶ <u>well. Japanese</u> literature in this period can be a bit of a blind spot. Only two Japanese authors, for instance, have ever won the Nobel Prize in Literature, and today, it can be difficult to find books by ❷<u>those authors, Kenzaburo Oe or Yasunari Kawabata</u> in print. It is difficult to know how to explain this lack of cross-cultural knowledge.

❸ <u>Whatever the cause may be,</u> there is a wealth of fascinating material from Japanese novelists, poets, and playwrights. One of the most curious of Japanese cultural figures, Yukio Mishima, wrote in all three of these media, and worked in many more besides. Known to contemporary Japanese readers not only as a great novelist, but also as a political extremist, ❹ <u>actor, and bodybuilder,</u> Yukio Mishima offers a fascinating combination of many strains in Japanese culture.

From a very young age, Mishima was pulled in many different directions. He fell in love with both contemporary French and German poets and with Michizo ❺ <u>Tachihara, who was born thirty years before Mishima and died before the war.</u> While the literature of the East and West combined in his head, Mishima's father disapproved of the boy's "effeminate" interests, and Mishima was forced to write in secret for many years lest his father find his ❻ <u>manuscripts, tearing it up.</u>

When Mishima was 18, during World War II, he received a draft summons from the Imperial Army. On that day, however, Mishima had a cold, and the doctors declared him unfit for duty, ❼ <u>naming</u> his slight wheeze as tuberculosis. After this disappointing error, Mishima devoted himself more intensely to his studies and eventually obtained a government position, all while writing in secret at night. ❽ <u>Mishima's first novel, *Thieves*, was published shortly before he was rejected by the Imperial Army for service in World War II.</u>

The many influences in Mishima's life combined and intersected until the end. He wrote 34 novels and many short stories, ❾ <u>Mishima starred</u> in some well-known Japanese films, and became a public persona as both a model and a bodybuilder. At the same time, however, his political views were radicalizing, and in 1967, with a small militia that he had founded, Mishima attempted ❿ <u>to overthrow and remove from power</u> the Emperor of Japan, whose views he saw as too liberal.

While Mishima's life may have ended in tragedy, and while his reputation in Japan may be a checkered one, he is, ⓫ <u>nonetheless,</u> a fascinating figure. Moreover, the many confused influences that inform his work make him a wonderful entrée to a world of Japanese culture that has been curiously isolated from our own, despite its many surprising correspondences.

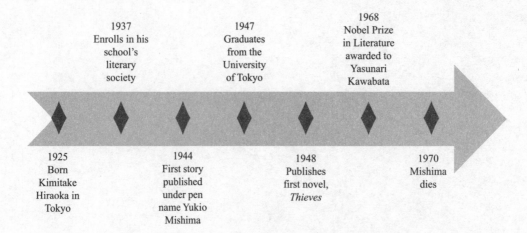

1937
Enrolls in his school's literary society

1947
Graduates from the University of Tokyo

1968
Nobel Prize in Literature awarded to Yasunari Kawabata

1925
Born Kimitake Hiraoka in Tokyo

1944
First story published under pen name Yukio Mishima

1948
Publishes first novel, *Thieves*

1970
Mishima dies

1. A) NO CHANGE
   B) well; Japanese
   C) well, Japanese
   D) well, but Japanese

2. A) NO CHANGE
   B) those authors, Kenzaburo Oe, or Yasunari Kawabata
   C) those authors Kenzaburo Oe or Yasunari Kawabata
   D) those authors, Kenzaburo Oe or Yasunari Kawabata,

3. Which of the following introductions to this paragraph best addresses the uncertainty expressed in the last sentence of the previous paragraph?

   A) NO CHANGE
   B) Obvious to anyone who's looking for it,
   C) As in Europe or the United States,
   D) Amid this economic and political conflict,

4. A) NO CHANGE
   B) actor and bodybuilder,
   C) actor, and, bodybuilder
   D) actor, and bodybuilder

5. Which of the following true choices best helps to establish a contrast with the earlier part of the sentence?

   A) NO CHANGE
   B) Tachihara, a master of the classical Japanese poetic form, the waka.
   C) Tachihara, who is less known to Western audiences than Mishima himself is.
   D) Tachihara, who had also been a great reader of the German poet Rilke.

6. A) NO CHANGE
   B) manuscripts, tearing up in the process.
   C) manuscripts, tearing them up.
   D) manuscripts and tear them up.

7. A) NO CHANGE
   B) eying
   C) guessing
   D) misdiagnosing

8. Which of the following sentences contains accurate data based on the graph?

   A) NO CHANGE
   B) Mishima's first novel was published the same year that fellow Japanese author Yasunari Kawabata won the Nobel Prize.
   C) Mishima's first novel was published when he was only 23 years old, and by 24, he was a sensation in the Japanese literary world.
   D) Mishima was very involved in literary societies in school, and his first novel was published before he graduated from University.

9. A) NO CHANGE
   B) starred
   C) and starred
   D) starring

10. A) NO CHANGE
    B) to remove from his position as Emperor
    C) to throw over and usurp
    D) to overthrow

11. Which of the following alternatives to the underlined portion would NOT be acceptable?

    A) furthermore,
    B) for all this,
    C) nevertheless,
    D) still,

Questions 12-22. Read the following passage carefully before you choose your answers.

Finding a Way

Have you ever wondered how it is that when you enter, say, an airport, you seem to know exactly where to go? You might get your gates mixed up; security might be a huge hassle; and you might find the waiting areas mind-numbingly boring. Still, ⑫ going to the airport is frustrating, whether you're heading from your car to the ticketing agent, from the ticketing agent to the gate, or from the gate to the baggage claim. While we may take these paths for granted, they are typically there by design, ⑬ an environmental graphic designer.

Environmental graphic designers guide us through what is called our "built environment," the buildings and structures that ⑭ we occupy every day. Environmental graphic design draws on many fields, including graphic design, architecture, industrial design, and landscape architecture. Because it navigates through so many different fields and styles, its nickname, "wayfinding," speaks ⑮ decibels. It's because of skilled environmental graphic designers that we can ⑯ enter and step into just about any home, store, or business and feel, "I know where I am." In fact, it's only when the wayfinder has failed—when, for example, we can't find the bathroom in a restaurant—that we notice it at all. Our paths through the built environment have been laid out for us in ways that we're never supposed to notice.

⑰ Atlanta's airport provides a notable instance. All airports are full of signs—you can park here, but you can't park here; your gate is this way; drop your bags here—but Atlanta's has surprisingly ⑱ lesser. Instead, our experience of Atlanta's airport has been largely determined by these wayfinders. When you walk in the door, the subtle design of the lights and floors ⑲ lead to the gates. A long sight line shows you where you need to go rather than directing you there with signs. The angles of the ticket booths lead to the airport gates by suggestion. ⑳

Atlanta's airport is just the beginning. The work of environmental graphic designers is all around ㉑ us, still, the profession is working toward more significant recognition. There are no degree programs in environmental graphic design yet, ㉒ but organizations like the Society for Environmental Graphic Design are growing rapidly. In an age where workers are being encouraged to specialize more and more to fill particular niches, environmental graphic design is a breath of fresh air: "experience," after all, can't be narrowed down to a single discipline. It takes an imagination that can take in the multiplicity of the human experience.

一段落信息表达，署了修卷类问题

12. Which of the following best supports the ideas presented at the beginning of this paragraph?

    A) NO CHANGE
    B) it's pretty rare to get lost inside an airport,
    C) it's a lot more fun to take the train,
    D) I always prefer to drive when I can,

13. A) NO CHANGE   → design的同格
    B) that of an environmental graphic designer.
    C) those of environmental graphic designers.
    D) environmental graphic designers.

14. A) NO CHANGE
    B) occupying
    C) you occupy
    D) one occupies

15. A) NO CHANGE
    B) a lot.
    C) volumes.   speak volumes 意味深长
    D) loudly.   具有含义

16. A) NO CHANGE
    B) establish a presence by entering
    C) enter and go into
    D) enter

17. Which of the following most effectively introduces the topic of this paragraph?

    A) NO CHANGE
    B) Signs block up the scenery and break one's mind.
    C) Air travel is a major hassle these days.
    D) Wayfinding is becoming a major in Georgia.

18. A) NO CHANGE
    B) less.
    C) few.
    D) a few.

19. A) NO CHANGE
    B) have lead
    C) leads
    D) led

20. Which of the following statements would best summarize the information given in this paragraph?

    A) We all know what it's like to get our tickets and then have no idea where to go.
    B) The subtle cues do all the work of signs without cluttering your field of vision.
    C) Now if only these wayfinders could make our planes take off on time!
    D) "Do this, don't do that": can't you read the sign?

21. A) NO CHANGE
    B) us, even so, the
    C) us still the
    D) us. Still, the

22. Which of the following gives the best contrast with the information given in the first part of the sentence?

    A) NO CHANGE   → 前强用后
    B) and it's unlikely that it will ever be a major field of study.
    C) though obviously it's a pretty important field.
    D) since it's too complex for most people to understand.   因果

Questions 23-33. Read the following passage carefully before you choose your answers.

The South, but New or Silent?

In 1865, the Southern states, formerly the Confederacy, were at a major crossroads. They lost the war, and the union of American states **㉓** remain intact. **㉔**

By the 1880s, some prominent cultural figures in the South had begun to predict the fate of the "New South." **㉕** The term, in fact, was popularized by Atlanta-based journalist Henry Grady, who toured the country promising that the South had learned from its mistakes and was ready to be a newer, better version of itself. Grady pushed for the New South to be an industrial powerhouse, a goal to which he said the South was already very much on its way, **㉖** though it would still grow natural resources like cotton and tobacco.

Grady did not speak for all **㉗** of them, however. In fact, there were some who were deeply skeptical of the "newness" of Grady's plan. Grady **㉘** paid basically no attention to the idea that the South still had a race problem. He assured his northern audiences that "we have found out that… the free Negro counts more than he did as a slave." Unfortunately, Grady's new plan preserved many of the old racial politics of slavery, and many skeptics insisted that Grady's "New South" was really just a mirror image of the Old South. **㉙** After all, Grady was insistent that the South had its "race problem" under control at exactly the moment that violence toward African-Americans was reaching its cruelest heights.

Grady's conception may have carried the day for much of the late-nineteenth and early-twentieth centuries, but the ideas of **㉚** others have been ultimately more influential in how we understand the South today. George Washington Cable, for example, argues not for the chest-thumping, white-supremacist "New South" but for a "Silent South" that is characterized by self-awareness and reflection and takes some actual responsibility for the atrocities **㉛** they committed both before and after Emancipation.

While we may have a relatively straightforward view of what the "South" meant during the Reconstruction period, the dialogue between authors like Grady and Cable shows that **㉜** these were more complicated times. Many of the tensions that erupted during the Civil Rights movement of the 1950s and 1960s had been percolating since the previous century. Although the loudest cultural and political figures may be the ones whose voices we most remember, it is in fact the "Silent South" figures like Cable **㉝** who have moved the region forward and continue to do so.

23. A) NO CHANGE
    B) remaining
    C) had remained
    D) remained

24. Which of the following questions best introduces the subject that is to be discussed throughout the remainder of this essay?

    A) What caused the Civil War in the first place?
    B) How did the South lose the war when it seemed to have so much more motivation than the North?
    C) What kind of role would the Southern states play in the new union?
    D) What would happen to figures who had been prominent in the former Confederacy?

25. A) NO CHANGE
    B) The fact of the term's popularity came from base journalist Henry Grady from Atlanta, touring the country and learning mistakes for a better of himself.
    C) Henry Grady was the one from Atlanta-based journalism who went around the country with the promise of learning mistakes from the South and ready to be a version of itself that was newer and better.
    D) Henry Grady himself, Atlanta journalist, was the popularizer of the term in fact and promised the country the South had learned from mistakes and would be newer and better.

26. Which of the following true statements best maintains the focus of this sentence?

    A) NO CHANGE
    B) as evidenced by Grady-promoted schools like Georgia Tech.
    C) and some high schools in the South today are named after Grady.
    D) a speech that Grady famously gave to a crowd of New Englanders.

27. A) NO CHANGE
    B) Southerners,
    C) of us,
    D) mankind,

28. A) NO CHANGE
    B) just said whatever to
    C) was dismissive of
    D) completely didn't pay attention to

29. The author is considering deleting the phrase "of the Old South" and placing a period after the word image. Should the phrase be kept or deleted?

    A) Kept, because it is the only mention of the Old South in the entire passage.
    B) Kept, because it clarifies the metaphor presented in this sentence.
    C) Deleted, because it presents information that appears elsewhere in the passage.
    D) Deleted, because creates an image that is offensive to supporters of Grady.

30. A) NO CHANGE
    B) those
    C) those others
    D) his detractors

31. A) NO CHANGE
    B) one
    C) it
    D) some

32. A) NO CHANGE
    B) times were more complicated than that.
    C) these times were troubled times.
    D) it was a more complicated time.

33. A) NO CHANGE
    B) who are continuing the region's move into the forward future.
    C) who forward the region's move and continue it.
    D) are moving the region forward and are continuing its movement.

Questions 34-44. Read the following passage carefully
before you choose your answers.

The History of Digestion—Difficult to Stomach

The great period of "Enlightenment" came in the mid-
1700s, when intellectuals ❸❹ (especially France) from all
over the world became interested in the workings of nature
and the body as observable phenomena. In this period, the
idea that we all hold as a basic truth, ❸❺ that science can
explain and control the world as we experience it, was
born.

This is not to say, however, that they had it all figured
out in the 1700s. ❸❻ Many, scientific discoveries, were
still decades away. One such discovery has to do with the
mechanism of human digestion. Until the 1820s, digestion
was not well understood, and irregularities in digestion
were treated with a variety of wild, often unhelpful, methods. Then, ❸❼ after a series of strange events led to a major
breakthrough in the science of digestion.

In the 1820s, ❸❽ William Beaumont was sent to
Michigan's Fort Mackinac, a U.S. Army Surgeon. There,
in 1922, he encountered a patient named Alexis St. Martin.
St. Martin had been accidentally shot at close range,
and Beaumont was called in to treat his wounds. While
Beaumont did restore St. Martin to health, he also noticed
a curious hole, or *fistula*, in St. Martin's ribs that had failed
to ❸❾ shut up. The fistula was close to St. Martin's stomach
and gave oddly direct access to his digestive tract.

Beaumont conducted a series of experiments wherein
he placed foodstuffs directly into St. Martin's stomach and
watched ❹⓿ it's machinations. Beaumont would remove
the food periodically to observe the course of digestion.
These experiments showed Beaumont that there was a *gastric fluid* (what we now call "stomach acid") breaking the
food particles down. Whereas before Beaumont, scientists
believed that digestion was a purely muscular process,
Beaumont showed that the process was in fact ❹❶ an
interesting one, propelled by this mysterious fluid. In fact,
Beaumont demonstrated that the stomach muscles were
relatively minor ❹❷ players: he isolated samples of gastric
fluid in cups and allowed food to "digest" in those cups.

Beaumont and St. Martin would be tied to one another
for the rest of their lives, and not just by the strings
Beaumont used to pull his food samples out of ❹❸ St.
Martin's fistula. Unfortunately, Beaumont would abuse his
power over St. Martin, essentially turning his test subject
into a servant and making him "perform" his digestion for
crowds of onlookers. Even so, their collaboration is one
of those great accidents that move science forward. While
we may imagine that scientific discoveries are made during controlled experiments in sanitary labs, the history of
digestion ❹❹ is hilarious and weird!

34. The best place for the underlined portion would
be:

    A) where it is now.
    B) after 1700s and before the comma.
    C) after the word world.
    D) after the word body.

35. Which of the following statements most agrees
with information presented in the previous
sentence?

    A) NO CHANGE
    B) that you should do unto others as you would
    have them do unto you,
    C) that book learning is less important than
    research in a laboratory,
    D) that the United States was founded on truly
    scientific principles,

36. A) NO CHANGE
    B) Many scientific discoveries, were still
    decades, away.
    C) Many, scientific discoveries, were still,
    decades away.
    D) Many scientific discoveries were still
    decades away.

37. A) NO CHANGE
    B) as a series
    C) really, a series,
    D) a series

38. A) NO CHANGE
    B) U.S. Army surgeon William Beaumont was
    sent to Michigan's Fort Mackinac.
    C) William Beaumont, a surgeon serving in
    the U.S. Army, was sent to Michigan's Fort
    Mackinac.
    D) surgeon William Beaumont was sent to
    Michigan's Fort Mackinac, of the U.S.
    Army.

39. A) NO CHANGE
    B) shut.
    C) close. all mean "close".
    D) end.

40. A) NO CHANGE
    B) its
    C) they're
    D) there

41. Which of the following choices best completes
the contrast set up in the first part of this
sentence?

    A) NO CHANGE
    B) digestively motivated,
    C) a chemical one,
    D) difficult to describe,

42. A) NO CHANGE
    B) players, he isolated
    C) players he isolated
    D) players, isolating

43. A) NO CHANGE
    B) St. Martins'
    C) St. Martins
    D) St. Martin'

44. A) NO CHANGE
    B) shows us otherwise.
    C) is not so difficult to digest!
    D) puts science in perspective.

Writing & Language Drill 2

For each question in this section, circle the letter of the best answer from among the choices given.
Questions 1-11. Read the following passage carefully before you choose your answers.

A Change of Direction

Try to picture a film director: what do you see? Is it the old-Hollywood man with his monocle and riding crop? ❶ Or the brooding bearded guy guiding a series of confused actors through the secret finished project in his mind? Whoever you see, you almost certainly see a man. Film direction has often been criticized for being a boys' club, but things may be slowly changing with the stunning ❷ rise of director, Kathryn Bigelow.

In the long history of the Academy Awards, only four female directors have ever been nominated for Best Director. ❸ Bigelow was the first to win, for 2008's *The Hurt Locker*. Since 1982, Bigelow has been producing films of astounding quality, and the public has responded. ❹ Catherine Breillat and Chantal Akerman are critically admired, few people know *Fat Girl* or *Je Tu Il Elle*. A much broader public knows about *The Hurt Locker* and Bigelow's most recent film *Zero Dark Thirty*, detailing the lead-up to the capture of Osama Bin Laden. Bigelow has certainly made a name for herself, and ❺ bit by bit, she may be changing the landscape of Hollywood incrementally.

Bigelow was born in San Carlos, CA, in 1951, and after high school, she ❻ rolled in the San Francisco Art Institute, where she learned ❼ the ins and outs of the art world. It was this interest in visual media that led her on to the graduate program in film at Columbia University, where she made many prominent contacts in film and film criticism. A few years after finishing at Columbia, Bigelow directed her first full-length feature, *The Loveless* (1982). The film was the first in a series ❽ with strong female protagonists, so in addition to breaking down gender barriers in the profession, Bigelow has also torn down the arbitrary notion of what a "women's film" might be expected to look like. ❾ After all, her most famous work is in the military drama, and what could be more stereotypically masculine than that?

Bigelow's most important lesson to Hollywood has been to show that great film ❿ was neither masculine nor feminine. "I can't change my gender," she has famously insisted, "and I refuse to stop making movies." Bigelow hopes now that more women will get in to directing and that the industry will catch up with a set of gender standards that ⓫ are way different. With Bigelow as inspiration, we can only hope that film can reach its real potential without being shackled by old and meaningless demographic categories.

1. Which of the following sentences would be most in keeping with the tone and theme of this paragraph?

   A) Or the nerdy guy with his round spectacles whining instructions to the actors?
   B) Or do you not know how important the role of the director actually is?
   C) This image comes from many of the German émigré directors of the 1920s and 1930s.
   D) Hollywood has long been filled with many eccentric directors.

2. A) NO CHANGE
   B) rise of director Kathryn Bigelow.
   C) rise, of director, Kathryn Bigelow.
   D) rise, of director Kathryn Bigelow.

3. The writer is considering adding the phrase "while all the other awards went to male directors" after the word Director and before the period. Should the writer add this phrase here?

   A) Yes, because it adds an essential piece of information not given elsewhere in the passage.
   B) Yes, because the reader will not understand Kathryn Bigelow's achievements without it.
   C) No, because it is already implied in the sentence as it is written.
   D) No, because it suggests that female directors are not capable of winning the award.

4. A) NO CHANGE
   B) And Catherine
   C) Because Catherine
   D) While Catherine

5. A) NO CHANGE
   B) one day at a time,
   C) ever so slightly,
   D) OMIT the underlined portion.

   与 "bit by bit"
   相同在此多余 (redundant)
   删除.

6. A) NO CHANGE
   B) enrolled
   C) unrolled
   D) rickrolled

7. A) NO CHANGE
   B) art.
   C) about art.
   D) some of the arts.

   压了 vague or general

8. Which of the following best completes the idea expressed in this sentence?

   A) NO CHANGE
   B) that were produced by a variety of studios,
   C) interested in the structure of violence,
   D) OMIT the underlined portion.

   下一句提到 "military drama",
   + female protg.
   no evidence showed.

9. A) NO CHANGE
   B) However,
   C) Come on,
   D) Even so,

   ⇒ Continuation of the claim

10. A) NO CHANGE
    B) had been
    C) were
    D) is

11. A) NO CHANGE
    B) changed long ago.
    C) couldn't have been predicted.
    D) are sure to be outdated to anyone who thinks about it.

    → 语意相同 选最短, 最简洁.

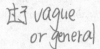

Questions 12-22. Read the following passage carefully before you choose your answers.

Research With a Brain... and Another Brain

As technology makes ⑫ <u>it's</u> way into every facet of our lives, more jobs reward expertise in a number of fields. Bioinformatics, at the intersection of computer science and biology, is one such field that has already had a ⑬ <u>tremendous and large</u> impact on the way we live today. Because it requires technical proficiency in a number of fields, bioinformatics can seem ⑭ <u>intimidating, but the</u> field is always growing and can lead practitioners down a number of fascinating paths.

Bioinformatics made news early this century with what is arguably one of the most remarkable scientific achievements of our age: ⑮ <u>people have been talking about it ever since.</u> A process over twenty years in the making, the Human Genome Project was completed in 2003. This work would not have been possible with traditional pen-and-paper laboratory methods. Even with the many scientists who worked on the project, the project required the science of ⑯ <u>bioinformatics—biological</u> research that uses computers to track, store, and read the data. This project has enabled scientists to begin to understand the basic blueprint of a human being, and this understanding has already led to huge gains in disease control.

While the Human Genome Project may grab the headlines, bioinformatics has a much more direct impact on our lives for the advances it has enabled in the field of agriculture. ⑰ Genetically-modified agricultural products are more or less the norm today, and the achievements in genetically-modified agriculture ⑱ <u>are</u> all the work of bioinformatics. Just as the Human Genome Project did with humans, daily experiments work to map the genomes of agricultural crops in order to understand how they grow. This genomic information has been used, for example, to increase some plants' nutritional value or to enable them to grow in poor soil. The effects on the crop yields of ⑲ <u>soybeans, cotton, and, maize</u> over the last twenty years have been undeniable. The percentage of cultivated land devoted to these genetically-modified soybeans, for instance, has ⑳ <u>shrunk to record lows</u> in some cases.

There has been significant debate as to the ethical value of bioinformatics and of genetically-modified crops and meats. There is no question, however, that ㉑ <u>it</u> will continue to grow, and this may well be because the potential benefits so far outweigh the potential risks. The food we eat may not be as nature intended it, but we are at least more protected from many of the famines that decimated historical populations. And beyond its influence in agriculture, ㉒ <u>bioinformatics, neither discounted nor denied with humans, records success.</u>

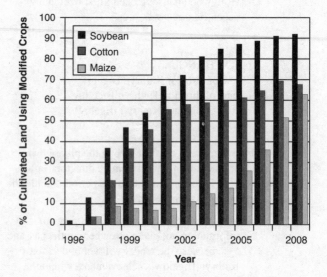

12. A) NO CHANGE
    B) its
    C) its'
    D) one's

13. A) NO CHANGE
    B) tremendous and not at all small
    C) tremendous, which is to say large,
    D) tremendous

14. A) NO CHANGE
    B) intimidating but the
    C) intimidating, but, the
    D) intimidating, the

15. Which of the following gives the most specific information regarding the achievement mentioned in this sentence?

    A) NO CHANGE
    B) all of them worked really hard.
    C) mapping the human genome.
    D) it's still not entirely complete.

16. A) NO CHANGE
    B) bioinformatics biological
    C) bioinformatics; biological
    D) bioinformatics. Biological

17. The writer is considering deleting the phrase "in the field of agriculture," ending the sentence with a period after the word enabled. Should the phrase be kept or deleted?

    A) Kept, because the remainder of the paragraph does not clarify which field is being discussed.
    B) Kept, because the sentence is vague without this information and does not adequately introduce the topic of the paragraph.
    C) Deleted, because it limits the scope of the achievements of bioinformatics.
    D) Deleted, because it distracts from the paragraph's main focus on the Human Genome Project.

18. A) NO CHANGE
    B) is
    C) can be
    D) would have been

19. A) NO CHANGE
    B) soybeans cotton, and maize
    C) soybeans, cotton, and maize
    D) soybeans, cotton and maize,

20. Which of the following contains accurate data based on the graph?

    A) NO CHANGE
    B) been entirely replaced
    C) been limited to three crops
    D) grown by over 900%

21. A) NO CHANGE
    B) bioinformatics
    C) they
    D) plants

22. A) NO CHANGE
    B) humans successfully deny and discount the record of bioinformatics and its science.
    C) neither discounted nor denied, bioinformatics of humans has been a recorded success.
    D) bioinformatics has a record of success with humans that cannot be discounted or denied.

Questions 23-31. *Read the following passage carefully before you choose your answers.*

The Study of Man and a Whole Lot Else

[1]

Anthropology is built from roots that mean "the study of man." That may seem like a pretty grandiose title for such a minor science. Most people are not even sure what anthropology is, let alone would consider it one of the central disciplines in how we understand human life. Nevertheless, upon closer inspection, we see that anthropology is at the core of ㉓ both the social sciences and the humanities as we understand those fields today.

[2]

Anthropology, unfortunately, was built, and it was at its most popular exactly when it was at its most controversial ㉔ on shaky foundations. That image of a European dressed in ㉕ their finery going out to gaze upon "the natives" of Africa was the norm at the birth of anthropology. [A] One of anthropology's earliest contributions to the public imagination, in fact, was the *stadial* theory of development—in other words, that European culture was at the highest "stage" of development and the natives of Africa or the aboriginals of the United States were many stages behind. Moreover, these anthropologists believed that we could essentially see our historical selves in ㉖ these. How they live now was a version of how we ourselves must have lived when we were less civilized.

[3]

㉗ After an inauspicious beginning, even so, the effects on the world and its people were tremendous. [B] This anthropological understanding influenced everything from how European countries colonized "less civilized" parts of the world to the wealthy classes treating the poor like animals.

[4]

Today, the effects of this empathy can be seen everywhere. Literary critics analyze texts and authors not according to one golden standard but according to the particular circumstances and contexts of each work. [C] Public-policymakers advise not according to what should work according to its success in their hometowns or countries but to what should work in a particular place given that ㉘ places need and population.

[5]

Anthropology has shown us how to live, and like the best ㉙ anthropologists, it has done so quietly, not insisting on its own superiority but by showing us how ㉚ its work is a lot more interesting than the work of other disciplines.

[6]

Anthropology still has a central place in the way we think, but anthropology shifted in the twentieth century. With the idea of "cultural relativism," German anthropologist Franz Boas explained that other cultures were not "less" anything; ㉛ they were simply different. A single standard of judgment was inappropriate for such a widely varying field of cultures. [D] The early twentieth century ushered in a new empathy, to the extent that we no longer understood, say, African culture as a lesser culture but as a different one, characterized by a cultural richness totally separate from our own.

23. A) NO CHANGE
    B) both the social sciences and the humanities, as we understand those fields today.
    C) both the social sciences, and the humanities, as we understand those fields, today.
    D) both the social sciences and the humanities as we understand those fields, today.

24. Assuming the punctuation were to be adjusted accordingly, the best placement for the underlined portion would be:
    A) where it is now.
    B) after the word unfortunately.
    C) after the word built.
    D) after the word popular.

25. A) NO CHANGE
    B) they're
    C) his
    D) the

26. A) NO CHANGE
    B) this.
    C) them.
    D) these native populations.

27. A) NO CHANGE
    B) This beginning was inauspicious, but even then, it had tremendous effects on how people saw the world.
    C) Inauspicious it may have been, but tremendous also was the effect of this beginning on the world.
    D) The beginnings of this world were inauspicious, but the effects of them were tremendous.

28. A) NO CHANGE
    B) place'
    C) places'
    D) place's

29. A) NO CHANGE
    B) anthropologists. It has
    C) anthropologists it has
    D) anthropologists have

30. Which of the following best concludes this paragraph and agrees with the main idea of the passage?
    A) NO CHANGE
    B) it can work in our particular moment, location, and frame of mind.
    C) it has finally overcome its controversial beginnings.
    D) it should really get more credit for how important it is.

31. Which of the following most effectively completes the idea presented in the first part of this sentence?
    A) NO CHANGE
    B) they were beyond our comprehension entirely.
    C) they were "more" civilized than anyone else.
    D) they were studying us the whole time.

Questions 32 and 33 ask about the preceding passage as a whole.

32. The best placement for Paragraph 6 would be:
    A) where it is now.
    B) after Paragraph 2.
    C) after Paragraph 3.
    D) after Paragraph 4.

33. Upon rereading the essay, the author concludes that the following information has been left out:

    Public-health officials figure out not how a disease could be contained in the abstract but within what the local conditions of the disease outbreak will allow.

    The sentence should be added at point:
    A) A.
    B) B.
    C) C.
    D) D.

Questions 34-44. Read the following passage carefully before you choose your answers.

A Chicken in Every Pot

[1] The American Dream has taken many forms: the big lawn, the white picket ❸❹ fence, including also the 2.6 children. [2] That man was Arthur Goldhaft, the unsung hero of twentieth-century poultry farming. [3] One of these American Dreams, "a chicken in every pot," has very clear origins. [4] The scene is Vineland, New Jersey, where a recent graduate of the veterinary school University of Pennsylvania has moved with his wife and children for a more countrified lifestyle than ❸❺ Philadelphia in the 1910s. ❸❻

Goldhaft was born in Philadelphia in 1886. He went to the Jewish Agricultural School in Woodbine, NJ. ❸❼ Suspecting that the school was one of the many reform schools the troubled Goldhaft was forced to attend as a child, he ❸❽ prayed to run away if necessary. In the end, he did no such thing: the school taught Goldhaft and many others the techniques of scientific farming, and it mapped the course of the rest of Goldhaft's life.

In the 1920s, President Herbert Hoover promised a "chicken in every pot," but agricultural science had trouble keeping the chickens alive long enough to be edible. ❸❾ A chicken typically needs to be about 6-10 months to get to an edible size. Goldhaft came to the rescue. His Vineland Poultry Laboratories developed a fowl pox chicken vaccine, which saved billions of chickens from death. Then, Goldhaft developed a reliable means for shipping the vaccine to all parts of the world, thus ensuring that everyone, not just those in Vineland, could have a "chicken in ❹❶ their pot." Since 1909, chicken consumption in the United States ❹❶ peaked in the 1960s and 1970s, as pork consumption has remained relatively constant.

Goldhaft would also aid in the disbursement of the laryngo-virus vaccine developed by Rutgers scientist Frank Beaudette. The two of them collaborated on a freeze-drying technique that would enable Beaudette to ship the vaccine to whoever needed it.

❹❷ Goldhaft's story is inspiring for any number of reasons. First, it shows that humble origins do not need to limit one's potential successes. Second, it shows that education can truly make a difference in one's life. And third, it shows that hugely influential events can begin in the most ❹❸ remote place. A "chicken in every pot" may have eventually been the promise of the Vineland Poultry Laboratories, but it was only really made possible by a small-city veterinarian trying to feed his family. The history of science is full of such ❹❹ stuff, and it can be comforting to think that many of the difficulties of contemporary life are just one chance discovery away.

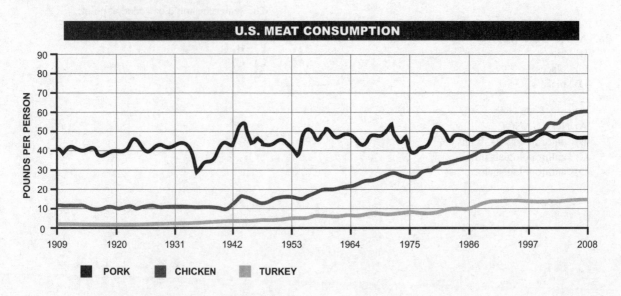

U.S. MEAT CONSUMPTION

POUNDS PER PERSON

90 80 70 60 50 40 30 20 10 0

1909 1920 1931 1942 1953 1964 1975 1986 1997 2008

■ PORK ■ CHICKEN ■ TURKEY

34. A) NO CHANGE
    B) fence, and the
    C) fence, too, also the
    D) fence, and some people thought of

35. A) NO CHANGE
    B) Philadelphia would be
    C) Philadelphia was
    D) Philadelphia could provide

36. The best placement for Sentence 2 would be:

    A) where it is now.
    B) before Sentence 1.
    C) after Sentence 3.
    D) after Sentence 4.

37. The writer wants to add the phrase "when he was
    15" to the sentence, adjusting the punctuation and
    capitalization as necessary. Where should the writer
    make this addition?

    A) At the beginning of the sentence
    B) After the word He
    C) After the word School
    D) After the word in

38. A) NO CHANGE
    B) cursed
    C) vowed
    D) swore

39. Which of the following sentences best agrees with
    the ideas in the previous sentence and leads most
    effectively to the next?

    A) NO CHANGE
    B) Vegetarian consciousness had not yet gained a
       foothold in the United States.
    C) Pigs and cows were doing just fine.
    D) A mysterious pox was killing chickens in droves.

40. A) NO CHANGE
    B) his
    C) my
    D) they're

41. Which of the following contains accurate data based
    on the graph?

    A) NO CHANGE
    B) has decreased slightly,
    C) has grown by nearly 500%,
    D) dropped precipitately in the 1980s,

42. Which of the following best introduces the conclud-
    ing paragraph of this essay?

    A) NO CHANGE
    B) What do you say we grab some chicken wings
       after this?
    C) If only Goldhaft could have lived to see the
       organic and free-range chicken movement.
    D) Chicken has overtaken beef as the most
       consumed meat in the United States.

43. A) NO CHANGE
    B) remote places.
    C) remote of all places.
    D) remote place in the world.

44. A) NO CHANGE
    B) paraphernalia,
    C) people and events,
    D) like,

Writing & Language Drill 3

For each question in this section, circle the letter of the best answer from among the choices given.
Questions 1-11. Read the following passage carefully before you choose your answers.

A Norwegian Struggle

Where is the line between fact and fiction? As an author, if you write about your own experiences but give them to a fictional character, are the experiences truly ❶ <u>made up out of thin air?</u> And what about those close to you? If the mother of your main character bears a resemblance to your own mother, where does ❷ <u>her</u> responsibility lie?

Contemporary Norwegian ❸ <u>writer, Karl Ove Knausgård, has built</u> a literary phenomenon out of exactly these questions. Knausgård's mammoth autobiographical work, *My Struggle*, contains over 3000 pages of detailed autobiography, ❹ <u>with names and identities the same as those from his own life.</u> His father's struggles with (and eventual death from) alcoholism, the difficulty of his first marriage, all of this and more feature in full, vivid detail in the pages of Knausgård's work. If Knausgård's books cannot be referred to as actual libel, they are nonetheless more revealing than many of the book's subjects, especially Knausgård's uncle Gunnar and ex-wife Tonje, deem ❺ <u>appropriate.</u>

My Struggle has a clear precedent in the early twentieth-century masterpiece *In Search of Lost Time*, the multi-volume novel by French author Marcel Proust. The difference there, however, was that while Proust's main character and narrator was named "Marcel," everyone else in the book had been given fictionalized names. Proust's great novel is considered one of the masterpieces of twentieth-century literature and the ❻ <u>definition</u> statement on how memory conditions human experience.

❼ <u>The similarities are many between Knausgård's and Proust's work. In contrast to the similarities, however, the differences are telling as well.</u> Knausgård's title comes from, of all places, Adolf Hitler, whose famous and troubling work *Mein Kampf* is quoted in the Norwegian *Min Kamp*, or *My Struggle*. Knausgård's critics wonder ❽ <u>with its title</u> why a book that already has the potential to anger and offend many people with its contents should also do so.

But Knausgård's success seems to be built on exactly these objections. The fact that he is known as the "Norwegian Proust" and not the "Norwegian Hitler" shows that his borrowing of Hitler's title has already done a good deal to take away the power of *Mein Kampf*. ❾ <u>Moreover,</u> literature has always been rooted in reality, and readers are free to interpret things as they wish. Isn't it possible, for example, that Proust's work seems less scandalous to us today because all of the people ❿ <u>on which</u> it is based are long dead? And come to think of it, nearly all of Knausgård's readers don't know the flesh-and-blood Gunnar, or Tonje, or Karl Ove any more than they would fictional characters. Knausgård's book has raised vital questions as a result, the most important of which may be, ⓫ <u>why would he name his book after a horrible dictator's autobiography?</u>

1. Which of the following choices fits most effectively with the style and tone of the first paragraph?

   A) NO CHANGE
   B) straight off the dome?
   C) fiction?
   D) coming from out of nowhere?

2. A) NO CHANGE
   B) your
   C) you're
   D) an author's

3. A) NO CHANGE
   B) writer Karl Ove Knausgård, has built
   C) writer, Karl Ove Knausgård has built
   D) writer Karl Ove Knausgård has built

4. Which of the choices is best aligned with the ideas presented in the first paragraph?

   A) NO CHANGE
   B) the six volumes of which are being released in the United States in 2015 and 2016.
   C) which has been translated into many languages beyond the original Norwegian.
   D) which is a special and remarkable work by a great writer.

5. A) NO CHANGE
   B) appropriated.
   C) appropriately.
   D) appropriations.

6. A) NO CHANGE
   B) definitional
   C) definitive
   D) definingly

7. How would these two sentences best be combined?

   A) NO CHANGE
   B) Both the similarities and differences between Knausgård's and Proust's work are telling; however, the differences are that much more so.
   C) The similarities are many between Knausgård's and Proust's work; nevertheless, the similarities and differences are equally many and just as telling.
   D) The similarities are many between Knausgård's and Proust's work, but the differences are telling as well.

8. The best placement for the underlined portion would be:

   A) where it is now.
   B) after the word book.
   C) after the word offend.
   D) after the word so (and before the period).

9. The author is considering deleting the phrase "and not the 'Norwegian Hitler'" from the preceding sentence. Should the phrase be kept or deleted?

   A) Kept, because it clarifies information presented in the latter part of the sentence.
   B) Kept, because the sentence is not grammatically complete otherwise.
   C) Deleted, because it repeats information stated explicitly elsewhere in the sentence.
   D) Deleted, because the mention of Adolf Hitler could be offensive to some readers.

10. A) NO CHANGE
    B) on whom
    C) on who
    D) whom

11. Which of the following choices provides the best conclusion to the essay by echoing themes presented in the first paragraph?

    A) NO CHANGE
    B) where does life end and fiction begin?
    C) how a man in his 40s write such a long book?
    D) can his family and friends ever forgive him?

Whose Look Is It Anyway?

Most moviegoers love the actors. Film buffs love the directors. So who is left to love the production designers? Production design (PD) has been an essential component of film ever since Hollywood came into ⑫ existence but cite the names of most PDs or Art Directors, and you'll get a blank stare. ⑬ Still, film is a visual medium, and it's impossible to maximize that visual aspect without the work of an accomplished Production Designer.

When we praise the "look" of a film, we usually think that we're tipping our hats to the director. In fact, ⑭ we admire equally the work of the PD, who guides the work of the costume designer, make-up stylists, special-effects ⑮ director, locations manager. The colorful pallet of a movie like *Finding Nemo* (2003) would've been impossible without the art direction of Ralph Eggleston, ⑯ who made it happen, and the rich period authenticity of a movie like *12 Years a Slave* (2013) is the great achievement of both Adam Stockhausen and ⑰ director Steve McQueen. In fact, from that crucial period from 1960-1975, ⑱ the Oscar for Best Actress was awarded to remarkably few Best Picture actresses. This makes sense—if a film doesn't have a distinctive "look," what does it actually have?

A production designer essentially "directs" all of those working on ⑲ the aspects of the film. ⑳ They're accountable for the work of set designers, make-up artists, computer designers, storyboard illustrators, and numerous others. He or she is involved in the set construction, in finding or constructing the furniture, structures, or buildings necessary for the look of a film. In the many period dramas that have become popular in recent years, from *Downton Abbey* on TV to *American Hustle* in film, the production designer consults with historians to ensure accuracy and authenticity so that viewers can have a more powerful visual experience. Producing that vision is impossible without the work of a good Production Designer. ㉑

As with many other aspects of film, Production Design can be a fine-art major, and for those who go into the profession, there is the Art Directors Guild of the International Alliance of Theatrical Stage Employees. Although production designers may not get all the accolades they deserve, there is no question that the look of what's in front of the camera would be impossible without those working so meticulously behind it. ㉒

Year/Film	Best Picture	Best Director	Best Production Design	Best Actor	Best Actress
1960 The Apartment					
1961 West Side Story					
1962 Lawrence of Arabia					
1963 Tom Jones					
1964 My Fair Lady					
1965 The Sound of Music					
1966 A Man For All Seasons					
1967 In the Heat of the Night					
1968 Oliver!					
1969 Midnight Cowboy					
1970 Patton					
1971 The French Connection					
1972 The Godfather					
1973 The Sting					
1974 The Godfather Part II					
1975 One Flew Over the Cuckoo's Nest					

12. A) NO CHANGE
    B) existence, but, cite
    C) existence, cite
    D) existence, but cite

13. All of the following alternatives to the underlined portion would be acceptable EXCEPT:

    A) Nevertheless,
    B) However,
    C) Moreover,
    D) Even so,

14. A) NO CHANGE
    B) equally we admire
    C) we're equally admiring
    D) we have also admired

15. A) NO CHANGE
    B) director and, the
    C) director and the
    D) director, and the

16. A) NO CHANGE
    B) who made the impossible into the possible,
    C) an accomplished production designer,
    D) DELETE the underlined portion.

17. A) NO CHANGE
    B) those of director
    C) that of director
    D) the director's

18. Which of the following pieces of information from the graph best supports the ideas presented in this passage?

    A) NO CHANGE
    B) nearly half of all Best Picture winners have also been Best Production Design winners.
    C) the award for Best Director exists in almost a 1:1 ratio with the award for Best Picture.
    D) there is an obvious disparity between the number of Best Actor winners in Best Picture films and Best Actress winners in Best Picture films.

19. A) NO CHANGE
    B) those in
    C) the visual aspects of
    D) DELETE the underlined portion.

20. A) NO CHANGE
    B) He or she is
    C) Their
    D) One's

21. The writers wants to add an introductory clause to this sentence that shows that the Production Designer's job is often underappreciated. Assuming that capitalization and punctuation are adjusted accordingly, which of the following would fit most appropriately here?

    A) Although many consider a film to be the result of a director's "vision,"
    B) While actors and actresses typically make all the money from a film,
    C) Like the producer him- or herself, who typically finances the film,
    D) While the counterpart in the theater is the art director and set designer,

22. The writer is considering ending the sentence at the word impossible and ending the sentence with a period. Should the writer keep the sentence as it is or make the change?

    A) Keep the sentence as is, because the production designer receives no credit without the phrase.
    B) Keep the sentence as is, because the sentence changes meaning without this phrase.
    C) Make the change, because the information presented is presented earlier in the paragraph.
    D) Make the change, because a sentence should always be made more concise if it is grammatically correct.

Questions 23-33. Read the following passage carefully before you choose your answers.

British Columbia's Pre- and Future History

Vancouver, British Columbia, is Canada's eighth most populous city, and it is known as one of the hotbeds of contemporary Canadian culture, alongside eastern cities Toronto and Montreal. Still, while nearly everyone knows about **㉓** them, few know about the importance of Native American culture within the coastal region of British Columbia. A **㉔** small community, of the Kwakwaka'wakw people, in the Pacific Northwest, links the area to its pre-European roots. Although the language, a collection of dialects known as Kwak'wala, is spoken by only about 250 people, the Kwakwaka'wakw continue to be a relevant force in the region and an inspiring reminder of an era that was cruelly uprooted in the early nineteenth century. **㉕**

㉖ According to this mythological narrative, the original settlers came to the area in animal form and became human when they arrived at the places they would settle. One of the major figures in this origin story, the Thunderbird, can still be seen in the many totems and carvings that remain, particularly from the late nineteenth century.

Much of what we know about the nineteenth-century Kwakwaka'wakw tribes **㉗** come from German-American anthropologist Franz Boas. In Boas's analysis, we can see the importance of weaving and woodwork, particularly as displays of wealth and power within the community. In fact, the most heavily studied aspect of Kwakwaka'wakw culture remains the *potlatch*, **㉘** which scholars devote much attention to, a gift-giving ceremony in which the wealthy demonstrate their extreme affluence by the vast quantities they are able to give away.

The survival of the potlatch and **㉙** the more general Kwakwaka'wakw is a minor miracle. Between 1830 and 1880, 75% of the tribe's population was killed by violence and disease. Canada outlawed the practice of potlatch in 1884, citing its wastefulness and expenditure as running contrary to the "civilized" values of white Canada. Policies like the potlatch ban **㉚** were instituted as part of a broader project of assimilation, designed to turn native populations into Canadians, not only by banning native practices but also by sending native children to harsh assimilationist schools.

The population of Kwakwaka'wakw today is just over 5,000. **㉛** However, the small community of Kwakwaka'wakw peoples remains committed to its traditions, and in the late twentieth century, a move away from assimilationist policies meant that the Canadian government was more willing to recognize and encourage cultivation of its native heritage. Things today may be as good as they've been at any time in history: the population growth of Aboriginal peoples in Canada from 2001-2006 **㉜** has declined 20.1%, with growth in British Columbia peaking at 42%. The Winter Olympics in Vancouver in 2010 showed that Canada has finally begun to see the influence of the Kwakwaka'wakw and others as integral to **㉝** its national character.

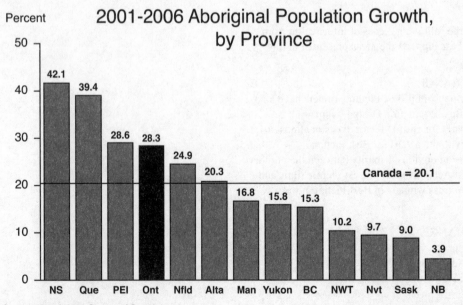

Percent

2001-2006 Aboriginal Population Growth, by Province

Canada = 20.1

NS	Que	PEI	Ont	Nfld	Alta	Man	Yukon	BC	NWT	Nvt	Sask	NB
42.1	39.4	28.6	28.3	24.9	20.3	16.8	15.8	15.3	10.2	9.7	9.0	3.9

Source: 2001 & 2006 Census of Canada

23. A) NO CHANGE
    B) it
    C) one
    D) Vancouver

24. A) NO CHANGE
    B) small community, of the Kwakwaka'wakw people, in the Pacific Northwest
    C) small community of the Kwakwaka'wakw people in the Pacific Northwest
    D) small community of the Kwakwaka'wakw people, in the Pacific Northwest,

25. At this point, the writer is considering adding the following true statement:

    The Cree, who live further to the east, have fared much better, with a contemporary population of over 200,000.

    Should the writer make this addition here?

    A) Yes, because it shows that the Kwakwaka'wakw should have moved further east.
    B) Yes, because it suggests that Canada's history is not as checkered as the rest of the passage states.
    C) No, because it adds an unnecessary detail to the passage's discussion of the Kwakwaka'wakw.
    D) No, because it minimizes the difficulties that the Kwakwakwa'wakw have faced throughout history.

26. Which of the following would best introduce the subject matter of this paragraph?

    A) There is little documented history of the Kwakwaka'wakw before the eighteenth century, but a rich oral history exists.
    B) Most Native American documented history comes from archaeologists and living oral historians.
    C) Like English settlers in the United States, English settlers in Canada killed off Native Americans in tragically high numbers.
    D) Using animals to explain prehistoric human behaviors has been a common practice throughout history.

27. A) NO CHANGE
    B) comes
    C) are coming
    D) came

28. A) NO CHANGE
    B) that scholars devote much attention to,
    C) much scholarly attention being devoted to it,
    D) DELETE the underlined portion.

29. A) NO CHANGE
    B) the, more generally, Kwakwaka'wakw
    C) the Kwakwaka'wakw, more generally
    D) the Kwakwaka'wakw in general

30. A) NO CHANGE
    B) have been instituted
    C) are instituted
    D) had been instituted

31. A) NO CHANGE
    B) Therefore,
    C) On the other hand,
    D) Next,

32. Which of the following gives accurate information based on the graph?

    A) NO CHANGE
    B) was just over 20%, with growth in some provinces reaching as much as 42%.
    C) has declined 20.1%, with growth in Alberta keeping pace with the national average.
    D) was just over 20%, with growth in Ontario seeing the most significant increase.

33. A) NO CHANGE
    B) its
    C) their
    D) they're

*Questions 34-44. Read the following passage carefully
before you choose your answers.*

A Sweet Invention in the Big Easy

㉞ Born in New Orleans, LA, on March 17, 1806, was
a man named Norbert Rillieux. Rillieux was the son of
Vincent Rillieux and Constance Vivant. Because Vivant
was a free woman of color and marriages between the
races were outlawed at the time, Vivant became Rillieux's
placée, or common-law wife. Race relations were slightly
less restrictive in Creole Louisiana **㉟** than in other parts
of the American South. **㊱** Norbert might have been born
into constricting circumstances elsewhere in the South,
Creole Louisiana afforded him recognition as his father's
son and access to education not available to other free
blacks or slaves.

The young Norbert attended Catholic schools in
Louisiana, and in the early 1820s, he went to Paris to study
at the École **㊲** Centrale, there he learned physics, mechanics, and engineering, and **㊳** became a noted expert in
steam engines. This remarkable education led to Rillieux's
eventual achievements in sugar refining and cemented his
place as one of the first African-American inventors in the
United States.

While studying at the École Centrale, **㊴** sugar refining emerged as an urgent concern for Rillieux. At that
time, Louisiana was a central hub in the sugar trade, but
the process of refining that sugar was **㊵** little understood.
Until then, sugarcane juice would be pressed from the cane,
and the juice would be heated until the water boiled, leaving a **㊶** gunky residue. This residue was then poured into
smaller and smaller pots until it achieved its maximum
thickness. The problem with such a method was that sugar
was lost at every step, and much of the sugar would burn
away because the heat was difficult to monitor.

After a failed attempt to start a sugar refinery with his
brother Edmond, Norbert patented his new sugar-refining
machine in 1843. The new machine addressed both major
issues with the old method of sugar **㊷** refining. All the
while making the process significantly safer for those men,
mainly slaves, who worked the machines. The machine
used vacuum pressure to lower the boiling point of the
relevant liquids. Heat could be easily controlled because
it comes from only one source—most of the **㊸** systemic
heat was recycled steam. That steam cycled through
stacked pans, where the sugarcane could essentially refine
itself, rather than require the workers to transfer the scald-
ing hot liquids by hand. By 1849, Merrick and Towne, the
Philadelphia manufacturers who sold Rillieux's new invention, could guarantee purchasers previously unheard-of
yields: **㊹** up to 18,000 pounds of sugar a day.

As historians of science learn more about the eighteenth and nineteenth centuries, they uncover more and
more odds-defying work from men and women who
were not given proper rights and recognitions in that era.
There's much more to this period, it seems, than George
Washington Carver.

34. A) NO CHANGE
    B) Norbert Rillieux was born March 17, 1806, in New Orleans, LA.
    C) On March 17th in 1806, Norbert Rillieux was born in Louisiana in New Orleans.
    D) Born in New Orleans, March 17th was the birthday of Norbert Rillieux in 1806.

35. A) NO CHANGE
    B) then were relations in
    C) than the race relations were in
    D) than those of blacks and whites in

36. A) NO CHANGE
    B) However, Norbert
    C) Because Norbert
    D) While Norbert

37. A) NO CHANGE
    B) Centrale there
    C) Centrale. There
    D) Centrale, there,

38. Which of the following best maintains the focus established in this sentence and paragraph?

    A) NO CHANGE
    B) lived a traditionally French lifestyle.
    C) did not have to contest with racial prejudice.
    D) became a teacher at the young age of 24.

39. A) NO CHANGE
    B) Rillieux's concentration led him to the process of refining sugar.
    C) his background in chemistry led him to a new way of refining sugar.
    D) Rillieux began to work on the chemical process of refining sugar.

40. Which of the following would best maintain the focus on the problems with refining sugar in the early eighteenth century?

    A) NO CHANGE
    B) a popular process.
    C) costly and inefficient.
    D) the "sweetest" job in town.

41. A) NO CHANGE
    B) gross
    C) syrupy
    D) bituminous

42. A) NO CHANGE
    B) refining; all
    C) refining all
    D) refining, all

43. A) NO CHANGE
    B) system's
    C) systems'
    D) systems

44. Which of the following would be support the statement made in the first part of this sentence?

    A) NO CHANGE
    B) and they could be on the cutting edge of technology, too.
    C) hiding the identity of the inventor all the while.
    D) how could anyone afford not to buy this machine?

Chapter 4
Writing and
Language Answers
and Explanations

ANSWER KEY

Writing & Language
Drill 1
1. C
2. D
3. A
4. A
5. B
6. D
7. D
8. C
9. B
10. D
11. A

12. B
13. B
14. A
15. C
16. D
17. A
18. C
19. C
20. B
21. D
22. A

23. D
24. C
25. A
26. B
27. B
28. C
29. B
30. D
31. C
32. D
33. A

34. C
35. A
36. D
37. D
38. B
39. C
40. B
41. C
42. A
43. A
44. B

Writing & Language
Drill 2
1. A
2. B
3. C
4. D
5. D
6. B
7. A
8. C
9. A
10. D
11. B

12. B
13. D
14. A
15. C
16. A
17. B
18. A
19. C
20. D
21. B
22. D

23. A
24. C
25. C
26. D
27. B
28. D
29. A
30. B
31. A
32. C
33. C

34. B
35. D
36. D
37. A
38. C
39. D
40. B
41. C
42. A
43. B
44. C

Writing & Language
Drill 3
1. C
2. B
3. D
4. A
5. A
6. C
7. D
8. D
9. A
10. B
11. B

12. D
13. C
14. C
15. D
16. D
17. A
18. B
19. C
20. B
21. A
22. B

23. D
24. C
25. C
26. A
27. B
28. D
29. D
30. A
31. A
32. B
33. B

34. B
35. A
36. D
37. C
38. A
39. D
40. C
41. C
42. D
43. B
44. A

ANSWERS AND EXPLANATIONS FOR WRITING & LANGUAGE DRILL 1

Passage I

1. **C**   The idea before the punctuation, *Even among those who know twentieth-century literature well*, is incomplete, so it cannot end with either a period or semicolon, eliminating (A) and (B). Choice (D) can also be eliminated because it introduces a contrast where none exists. Only (C) is correct.

2. **D**   If the phrase *Kenzaburo Oe or Yasunari Kawabata* were removed, the meaning and completeness of the sentence would not change. The phrase is therefore not essential to the meaning of the sentence and should be set off with commas, as (D) indicates.

3. **A**   Read the question carefully. It asks for a choice that *addresses the uncertainty expressed in the last sentence of the previous paragraph*. Only (A) notes this uncertainty, with the others either dismissing or ignoring the uncertainty mentioned in the previous sentence.

4. **A**   There should be a comma after every item in a list—in this case, *political extremist, actor, and body-builder*. This eliminates (B). Then, because the list is part of an introductory idea, there should also be a comma after the word bodybuilder, making (A) the correct answer.

5. **B**   The previous sentence indicates that Mishima was *pulled in many different directions*. The first part of this sentence refers to *contemporary French and German poets*, so the second part of the sentence should emphasize another influence that came from somewhere else. Choice (B) provides the best emphasis, explaining that Tachihara was a Japanese poet who worked in a classical form.

6. **D**   The verb in the underlined portion should agree with the other verb in this part of the sentence, *find*. Only (D) does so, with the other three choices using the form *tearing*.

7. **D**   The following sentence refers to a *disappointing error*. The most precise word in the underlined portion is therefore *misdiagnosing*, or (D).

8. **C**   Use POE by comparing the answer choices to the information presented in the timeline. Choice (A) can be eliminated because *Thieves* was published when Mishima was 23, and he had been rejected from military service at 18. Choice (B) can also be eliminated because *Thieves* was published in 1948 and Kawabata won the Nobel Prize in 1968. Choice (C) is correct about the publication date of *Thieves*. Choice (D) can be eliminated because Mishima graduated in 1947, and his first novel was published in 1948.

9. **B**   Keep the items in the list parallel! This list refers to a series of actions: *wrote… starred… became*. There's no need to add anything else, making (B) the correct answer.

10. **D** All four answers mean essentially the same thing, so choose the shortest that makes sense in the context. In this case, that is (D), *to overthrow*.

11. **A** Look at the direction of each of the transitions. Choices (B), (C), and (D) each establish a contrast in the sentence. Choice (A) does not and must therefore be the one that is NOT acceptable in the given context.

Passage II

12. **B** The idea presented at the beginning of the paragraph is that air travel can be frustrating, but in an airport, *you seem to know exactly where to go*. Choice (B) best paraphrases this idea.

13. **B** The portion of the sentence before the underlined portion ends with *by design*, so the underlined portion must refer back to this somehow. Choices (A) and (D) do not correctly modify the word *design*, and (C) implies a plural noun where there is none. Choice (B) is the only acceptable choice, suggesting that the *design is that of an environmental graphic designer*.

14. **A** This sentence refers to how environmental graphic designers *guide us* through, so the word *we* is appropriate in the underlined portion, unlike the pronouns given in (C) and (D). Then, (B) makes the sentence incomplete. The sentence is therefore correct as written.

15. **C** The conventional phrase is *speaks volumes*. Although some of the other words may have similar-seeming meanings, they do not work in this conventional phrase. Only (C) works in this context.

16. **D** All four answers mean essentially the same thing, so choose the shortest that makes sense in this context. In this case, that is (D), *enter*.

17. **A** This paragraph describes Atlanta's airport as a classic example of environmental graphic design. Choice (A) is therefore the best choice to introduce the paragraph; the others do not refer to Atlanta's airport at all.

18. **C** The first part of this sentence says that airports are typically *full of signs*. Atlanta's airport, by contrast, has few signs, as (C) suggests. Choice (D) changes the meaning, and (A) and (B) use *less*, which is typically for non-countable objects.

19. **C** This paragraph is mainly in the present tense, so the verb in the underlined portion must be in the present tense as well, eliminating (B) and (D). Then, (A) can be eliminated because the subject of the verb, *the subtle design of the lights and floors*, is singular. Only (C) remains as the correct answer.

20. **B** The paragraph as a whole describes the ways that the environmental graphic design of Atlanta's airport makes for easy navigation. Choice (B) summarizes this description, where the others are off-topic.

21. **D** The sentence as written contains a comma splice. The first idea in this sentence (*The work of graphic designers is all around us*) and the second idea (*still, the profession is working toward more significant recognition*) are both complete. They should therefore be separated by a period or semi-colon, as in (D).

22. **A** The first part of the sentence mentions that *there are no degree programs in environmental graphic design yet*, and (A) shows that this is changing. Choices (B) and (D) contain no contrast at all, and (C) contains a contrast but a meaningless one.

Passage III

23. **D** Keep the verbs consistent. The other verbs in this paragraph are *were* and *lost*. This one should be keep consistent with those, so it should be *remained*, (D).

24. **C** The remainder of the paragraph discusses certain intellectuals' plans for the "New South." The question here should be something along the lines of, *What would the new South look like?* Or *What was the South going to do now?* Choice (C) best encapsulates these questions. Choice (D) may seem plausible, but it places the emphasis on the wrong time period.

25. **A** Use POE! Choice (A) is the only one that communicates an actual idea. Choice (B) refers to the *base journalist Henry Grady*, which nothing in the passage supports. Choice (C) refers to *learning mistakes*, which doesn't make sense. Choice (D) is close, but *Henry Grady himself* is awkward, and (A) is clearer.

26. **B** The first part of this sentence suggests that the South was *already very much on its way* to becoming an *industrial powerhouse*. The underlined portion should agree with this idea, as only (B) does. Choices (C) and (D) are off-topic, and (A) disagrees with the earlier part of the sentence.

27. **B** In the sentence as it is written, the word *them* is ambiguous. Only (B) clarifies the referent for *them*: *southerners*.

28. **C** The sentence as written breaks with the formal tone of the rest of the essay. Choices (B) and (C) make similar mistakes. Therefore, only (C) can work in the context.

29. **B** Without the phrase "of the Old South," the idea of the *mirror image* is unclear. The sentence states that the New South is *the mirror image of* the Old South. If the phrase is removed, the sentence changes its meaning. The phrase should therefore be kept for the reason stated in (B).

30. **D** This sentence sets up a contrast between the ideas of *Grady* and the ideas of *others*. Choice (D), however, provides the clearest sense of who those *others* were and is therefore the correct answer.

31. **C**   The pronoun *they* is currently ambiguous because it doesn't seem to refer to anything in this sentence. Instead, this sentence is discussing "the South" and the things that *it* did. The best answer is therefore (C), which creates a pronoun referent that works.

32. **D**   The time referred to here is *the Reconstruction period*, which is singular. Therefore, the correct answer must refer to this as a time in the singular, as only (D) does.

33. **A**   If all four answers say essentially the same thing, choose the shortest that preserves the meaning. In this case, the best answer is (A), which lays the ideas out clearly and is free of awkward constructions, as in (B), (C), and (D).

Passage IV

34. **C**   *France* is a country, so the underlined portion should be placed somewhere in a discussion of places. In this case, the only place that could work is after the sentence's mention of *intellectuals from all over the world*, or (C).

35. **A**   The idea presented in the previous sentence has to do with *nature and the body as observable phenomena*. The underlined portion should relate to this idea somehow, as only (A) does, even if the other choices are true or plausible.

36. **D**   If you cannot cite a reason to use a comma, don't use one! No commas are required for any reason in this sentence, so the correct answer is (D).

37. **D**   As written, this sentence is incomplete because of the conjunction *after*. Choice (B) contains the same mistake. Then, (C) adds an unnecessary word in *really*, leaving only (D) as the correct answer.

38. **B**   As written, the sentence is awkwardly phrased, and it's not clear what *U.S. Army surgeon* refers to. When you are asked to shuffle through a bunch of nonsense sentences, start with the shortest. In this case, the shortest is (B), which is also the one that states its idea most directly.

39. **C**   A *wound* or *hole* on the body has to *close* in order to heal. Although *shut* and *end* may mean *close* in other circumstances, the only word that works idiomatically here is *close*, or (C).

40. **B**   This part of the sentence refers to the *stomach's machinations*. In other words, the sentence refers to *its machinations*, as in (B). Choice (A) is the contraction for the words *it is*, so it cannot apply here.

41. **C**   This is a contrast in this sentence between *a muscular process* and something else. Choices (A), (B), and (D) do not complete the contrast. Choice (C) accurately sets up the contrast between *a muscular process* and *a chemical one.*

42. **A**   The idea before the punctuation (*In fact, Beaumont demonstrated that the stomach muscles were relatively minor players*) and the one after it (*he isolated samples of gastric fluid in cups and allowed food to "digest" in those cups*) are both complete. A colon could therefore apply. The other choices either create comma splices or run-on sentences, however, and should therefore be eliminated.

43. **A**   In this sentence, the *fistula* belongs to *St. Martin*. It is therefore *St. Martin's fistula.* Choice (B) implies a plural noun where none exists, and (C) and (D) eliminate the necessary possession altogether.

44. **B**   Be sure the ideas are in keeping with the tone of the passage. Choices (A) and (C) change the tone, and (D) is essentially meaningless. Only (B) can work and completes the idea given earlier in the sentence.

ANSWERS AND EXPLANATIONS FOR WRITING & LANGUAGE DRILL 2

Passage I

1. **A** This sentence appears in a within a list of questions, so the sentence itself should be a question also, thus eliminating (C) and (D). Then, the paragraph is about *what you imagine* when you imagine a director, with which only (A) agrees.

2. **B** If you can't cite a reason to use a comma, don't use one. In this case, no commas are necessary, so (B) must be correct. There should not be a comma before *Kathryn Bigelow* because the sentence is no longer complete without these words.

3. **C** The words *only four female directors* suggest that all the rest of those nominated have been men. Therefore, it is not necessary to add the proposed information because it is already implied in the sentence.

4. **D** The sentence as written contains a comma splice. A word will need to be added to the beginning of the sentence to eliminate this error. Then, the ideas in this sentence (*critically admired...few people know*) are in contrast with one another, meaning that the sentence needs an opposite-direction transition, such as the one contained in (D).

5. **D** The underlined words *bit by bit* are redundant with the non-underlined word *incrementally*, so (A) should be eliminated. Choices (B) and (C) make the same mistake, so the best option is to eliminate the underlined portion altogether, as in (D).

6. **B** The correct word here is *enrolled*, particularly as it applies to a school or program. The best answer is therefore (B).

7. **A** Choose the most precise answer. In many cases, that will be the shortest answer, but in this case, the most precise answer is the longest, (A). Choices (B), (C), and (D) are too vague or too general.

8. **C** The next sentence discusses the *military drama*, which indicates an interest in the *structure of violence*, as in (C). While it may seem plausible that Bigelow's films would have strong female protagonists, there is no evidence for such a claim in the passage.

9. **A** The previous sentence states, *Bigelow has also torn down the arbitrary notion of what a "women's film" or "leading lady" might be expected to look like.* This sentence gives evidence of that claim, so the transition should signify some continuation of the idea. Choice (A) does this effectively, while the other choices are either irrelevant or contrasting.

10. **D** Bigelow is working today, so this sentence should be in the present tense. Also, in the terms of this sentence, her achievement *has been* to show that film *is* genderless. Choices (A), (B), and (C) are all in the past tense (in addition to their other faults), so (D) is the best answer.

11. **B** Since all four answers say similar things, choose the shortest that works in the given context. Choice (A) is the shortest, but it is not specific, and it is not in keeping with the tone of the rest of the best passage. The best option comes in (B), which is concise, specific, and tonally appropriate.

Passage II

12. **B** The antecedent for the underlined pronoun is *technology*, so *technology's way into every facet of our lives* should be rewritten with the pronoun *its*. Choice (A) gives the contraction *it is*, and (C) is grammatically incorrect.

13. **D** All four answer choices say essentially the same thing, so choose the shortest that works in the given context. In this case, that answer is (D), which contains all the necessary information but presents that information in the most concise way.

14. **A** The ideas before and after the punctuation are complete, so they should be separated with either a period, semi-colon, or comma-plus-coordinating-conjunction. In this case, that conjunction is *but*, making (A) the correct answer. Choice (C) cannot work because it adds an unnecessary comma after the word *but*.

15. **C** Only (C) presents a specific achievement. Choices (A) and (B) describe successes of a sort, but those are not as specific as (C).

16. **A** The idea before the punctuation is complete, but the idea after it is incomplete, thus eliminating (C) and (D). There must be something to separate the ideas, however, which also eliminates (B). All that remains is (A), which is appropriate because a long dash can be used after a complete idea, as it is here.

17. **B** If the writer were to delete this phrase, this sentence would contain no specific information, and it would not effectively introduce the idea of this paragraph. The part in question should therefore be kept, and for the reason stated in (B).

18. **A** The subject of this verb is *achievements*, thus requiring a verb agreeing with a plural noun. Choices (C) and (D) do so, but they change the meaning of the sentence. Choice (A) is therefore the best of the available answers.

19. **C**   These three items form a list of *soybeans, cotton, and maize*. A comma is required after every item in the list, thus eliminating (B) and (D). Then, because there should not be a comma after the word *and*, only (C) can work as the correct answer.

20. **D**   According to information presented in the figure, the percentage of cultivated land devoted to soybeans has grown from under 5% to over 90% since 1996. This is an increase of more than 900%, making (D) the correct answer.

21. **B**   In the sentence as written, the pronoun *it* is ambiguous because it could refer to a number of different things. The pronoun *they* in (C) is also ambiguous. Choice (D) clarifies the pronoun, but it does so incorrectly. *Bioinformatics* as a field *will continue to grow*, so the correct answer must be (B).

22. **D**   Find the clearest statement. Choice (A) cannot work because *records success* is meaningless. Choice (B) is ambiguous because the words *successfully deny and discount* does not have a clear meaning. Choice (C) does not make sense in the given context. Only (D) correctly clarifies the syntax of this sentence and puts ideas in their proper relation to one another.

Passage III

23. **A**   If you cannot cite a reason to use a comma, don't use one. There is no good reason to use a comma in the underlined portion, so the best answer is the one with no commas, (A).

24. **C**   The word *foundations* should go near the word *built* to complete the phrase *built on shaky foundations*. The modifier *on shaky foundations* does not make clear sense in any other part of the sentence.

25. **C**   The pronoun in the underlined portion refers back to *a European*, which is singular. The best answer is therefore (C), which contains a singular pronoun referring to this *European*.

26. **D**   The word *these* in the underlined portion is ambiguous, so (A) can be eliminated. Choices (B) and (C) do not fix the problem. Only (D) is adequately specific and is therefore the correct answer.

27. **B**   In the sentence as written, the words *even so* appear awkwardly in the middle of the sentence. Choice (A) can be eliminated. Choice (C) is a sentence fragment, and (D) inserts the ambiguous pronoun *them*. Only (B) contains a relatively clear meaning in which all words have a clear place.

28. **D**   This portion of the sentence could be rewritten to say *the need of that place*, or *that place's need*. Choices (A) and (B) do not indication this possession, so they can be eliminated. Choice (C) uses the plural *places*, which cannot work with the word *that*. Only (D) can work in the given context.

29. **A**   The first idea in this sentence (Anthropology has shown us how to live, and like the best anthropologists) is incomplete, so it cannot end with a period. Instead, the words like the best anthropologists serve as an introductory idea, which should be separated from the remainder of the sentence. Only (A) can work in the given context.

30. **B** An earlier part of this sentence as not insisting on its own superiority but… suggesting that the subsequent idea will need to be in contrast. Choice (A) gives no such contrast, nor does (D). Choice (C) can also be eliminated because the controversial beginnings are only a minor detail. Only (B) works in contrast with the first part of the sentence and agrees with the main idea.

31. **A** In order to clarify what will contrast with the idea that other cultures were not "less" anything, check the following sentence: A single standard of judgment was inappropriate for such a widely varying field of cultures. There should therefore be a word that signifies that other cultures are widely varying. Choice (A) would work in this context, and while (B), (C), and (D) might sound fine, there is no good reason to place them here in the passage.

32. **C** Paragraphs 2 and 3 discuss the nineteenth century, and Paragraph 6 shifts to discuss the twentieth century. Therefore, chronologically, Paragraph 6 should be placed after Paragraph 3, as (C) suggests.

33. **C** The sentence in question describes one of anthropology's influences in the present day. Paragraph 4 discusses how literary critics and public-policymakers use anthropology, so a discussion of economists use it would be appropriate here as well. Point C within Paragraph 4 is the best of the available options.

Passage IV

34. **B** The items in this sentence appear in a list, so it is essential to keep them parallel. Choices (A), (C), and (D) add unnecessary words, but (B) keeps the items in the list parallel.

35. **D** As written, the sentence compares the *countrified lifestyle* of Vineland with *Philadelphia*. A *lifestyle* cannot be compared with a city, so (A) gives a faulty comparison. Of the remaining choices, only (D) fixes the comparison.

36. **D** Sentence 2 begins with *That man*, so the sentence that precedes it should mention a man. Sentence 4 provides the referent with *a recent graduate*, so Sentence 2 should be placed after Sentence 4, as (D) suggests.

37. **A** The unit *the Jewish Agricultural School in Woodbine, NJ* must be kept intact, so Goldhaft's age cannot be inserted anywhere there, thus eliminating (C) and (D). Choice (B) creates an awkward phrase, *He when he was 15*, so the underlined portion can only be placed appropriately at the beginning of the sentence, as (A) suggests.

38. **C** The choices all contain words with similar meanings, but the sentence refers to some hypothetical future action. The best word in the context is therefore *vowed*, as in (C). Choice (D) holds the appropriate meaning, but the word *swore* does not work idiomatically with the word *to*.

39. **D** The sentence before the underlined portion refers to Herbert Hoover's promise of a "chicken in every pot." The sentence after the underlined portion says that Goldhaft came to the rescue. The intervening sentence should therefore discuss some complication to Hoover's promise, which Goldhaft will then resolve. Choice (D) provides that complication, suggesting that "a chicken in every pot" would not be possible as long as chickens were dying uncontrollably.

40. **B** The antecedent for the underlined pronoun is *everyone*, which is singular. Choices (A) and (D) refer to plural nouns, and (C) changes the meaning. Only choice (B), *his*, can work in the given context.

41. **C** According to the graph, chicken consumption has increased steadily since about 1935. Choices (B) and (D) are therefore untrue, and (A) describes a meat other than chicken. Only (C) accurately reflects the information in the graph.

42. **A** The final paragraph describes the significance of Goldhaft's achievement. Choice (B) is hilarious but does not introduce this topic. Choices (C) and (D) do not address Goldhaft's achievements at all. Only (A) effectively introduces the topic of this paragraph.

43. **B** This sentence discusses *influential events*, which must occur in *places*, rather than one particular *place*. Choices (A) and (D) are singular, so they can be eliminated. Choice (C) could work, but (B) is more concise, so (B) is the correct answer.

44. **C** As written, the sentence is not adequately specific, because the word *stuff* could refer to anything. Choice (B) makes the same mistake. Choice (D) does not work in the given context, so only (C) remains as the correct answer.

ANSWERS AND EXPLANATIONS FOR WRITING & LANGUAGE DRILL 3

Passage I

1. **C** Since all the answers communicate essentially the same thing, choose the shortest that fits with the tone. In this case, that is (C), *fiction*, as all the others are unnecessarily informal.

2. **B** This sentence is in the second person, about *your* responsibility as an author, so the pronoun in the underlined portion must match. The only choice that does so is (B). Choice (C) gives the contraction *you are*, and (D) changes to the third person.

3. **D** The author's name is essential to the completeness of the sentence. In order to see this clearly, take out the words *Karl Ove Knausgård*. You're left with *Contemporary Norwegian writer has built a literary phenomenon out of exactly these questions*. The sentence requires the words, so they should not be set off with commas. Choice (D) is the only one without commas, and is therefore correct.

4. **A** The first paragraph discusses the blurring of fact and fiction and how "fictional" real events and personages can be. Choices (B), (C), and (D) are all true, but they do not address this topic at all. Only (A) does, making it the correct answer.

5. **A** If *something* is *considered appropriate*, then *appropriate* describes *something*. If *something* is *considered appropriately*, then *appropriately* describes *considered*. In these case, the word *appropriate* describes how revealing *the books* are. Choice (A) is therefore correct.

6. **C** The underlined word describes the noun *statement*, so it must be an adjective, eliminating (A) and (D). Then, the word *definitional* is not frequently used and means "relating to a definition," where the word *definitive* means "done decisively and with authority," which is the more appropriate meaning here.

7. **D** When combining sentences, make things as concise as possible. There's no reason to combine sentences if you're not shortening them! Choice (D) is the best answer here because it does not repeat the words *similarities* and *differences* unnecessarily.

8. **D** The phrase *with its title* should act in parallel with the phrase *with its contents*. The best place for the underlined portion is therefore after the word *so*, (D), as to complete the comparison *to anger and offend many people with its contents should also do so with its title*.

9. **A**   The latter part of the sentence goes on to discuss Hitler, so the earlier part of the sentence can not only talk about Proust. In other words, the phrase under consideration should be kept because it clarifies what is being discussed at the end of this particular sentence, as (A) suggests.

10. **B**   *People* requires *who* or *whom*, which eliminates (A) immediately. The word *on* is necessary here with the verb *based*, which also eliminates (D). Then, (B) must be correct because *whom* is the object of the preposition *on*. In less grammar-jargon-ish terms, you'd say *on them* rather than *on they*, so use *whom* when you'd use *them*.

11. **B**   The first paragraph is all about the blurring between fact and fiction. Choices (A), (C), and (D) present some interesting questions, but the only one that deals with the subject matter of the first paragraph is (B).

Passage II

12. **D**   The first idea of the sentence (*Production design (PD) has been an essential component of film ever since Hollywood came into existence*) and the second (*cite the names of most PDs or Art Directors, and you'll get a blank stare*) are both complete. Therefore, a comma is required before the coordinating conjunction *but*, as in (D). Choice (B) has too many commas, and (C) creates a comma splice.

13. **C**   The word in the underlined portion, *Still*, when used in this way, is an opposite-direction transition. Therefore, other opposite-direction transitions would be acceptable, as in (A), (B), and (D). The only one that would NOT be acceptable is *Moreover*, (C), because that is a same-direction transition.

14. **C**   This verb should be parallel with the verb in the previous sentence, *are tipping*. The only combination that works among the answer choices comes in (C). The others might be correct in other contexts, but in this case, those verbs are not parallel with the surrounding verbs in this paragraph.

15. **D**   The underlined portion appears at the end of a list of *costume designer, make-up stylists, special-effects director,* and *locations manager*. The final comma should go before the word *and*, as in (D).

16. **D**   When the option to DELETE appears, give it special consideration. There must be a VERY good reason not to pick it. In this case, there is no such reason because the information presented in the underlined portion is implied earlier in the sentence. The best answer is therefore (D).

17. **A**   When the answer choices seem to say the same thing, find the shortest. In this case, the shortest is (A), which contains all the information that the others do in the fewest amount of words. The relative pronoun *that* is not necessary because of the word *both* that appears earlier in the sentence.

18. **B**   All the answer choices give true statements based on the graph, but this passage is about Production Designers, so only (B) can work in this passage.

19. **C**   When the option to DELETE appears, give it special consideration. There must be a VERY good reason not to pick it. In this case, there is such a reason: the sentence is not adequately specific without the underlined portion. Without the underlined portion, it sounds like the PD is directing the film itself, when in fact he directs those working on the *visual aspects* of the film, thus making (C) the best of the available answers.

20. **B**   This pronoun refers back to *A production designer* in the previous sentence. The pronoun should therefore be singular, eliminating (A). Choice (D) can also be eliminated because it is too impersonal for such a specific subject. Only (B) can work in the context.

21. **A**   The sentence as written contains the words *that vision*, so the first part of the sentence should given an indication of what *that vision* is, as only (A) does. In addition, (A) suggests that many people overestimate the role of the director and downplay that of the PD.

22. **B**   If the phrase were removed, the sentence would essentially state that no films are ever made because doing so is *impossible*. Therefore, keep the sentence as is, and for the reason stated in (B).

Passage III

23. **D**   It is unclear whether the word them refers to *Vancouver, Toronto, Montreal,* or some combination of those cities. The only choice that clarifies this ambiguity is (D), which states the exact city being discussed.

24. **C**   If you cannot cite a reason to use a comma, don't use one. In this case, no commas are necessary, so the best answer must be (C).

25. **C**   While the information given in this sentence is true and interesting, it does not have a place in this passage, which is about the Kwakwaka'wakw. The best answer is therefore (C), because the sentence should not be added.

26. **A**   This paragraph is about the "history" of the Kwakwaka'wakw before written history. It outlines some of the basic myths of the tribe. Choices (B), (C), and (D) do not address this mythology at all, but (A) does, with its mention of oral history.

27. **B**   The subject of the sentence is *Much*, which requires a singular verb, thus eliminating (A) and (C). Then, because the earlier part of this sentence and the next sentence's discussion of Boas are in the present tense, this verb should be as well. The best answer is therefore (B).

28. **D**   When the option to DELETE appears, give it special consideration. There must be a VERY good reason not to pick it. In this case, there is no such reason because none of the answers add anything that is not already implied in the words *most-heavily studied*. The best option is therefore to DELETE the underlined portion, as (D) suggests.

29. **D**   The meaning of the underlined portion is not clear. Choice (D) is the idiomatic pairing that works best in this sentence, which refers to the *potlatch* (one aspect of Kwakwaka'wakw culture) and *the Kwakwaka'wakw in general.*

30. **A**   This sentence is discussing a historical event, so it should be in the past tense. Only (A) and (D) are in the past tense, and (D) suggests that the bans were discontinued, when information in the passage makes it clear that they continue to this day. The best answer is therefore (A).

31. **A**   The sentence is correct as written. Choice (B) suggests that the remaining Kwakwaka'wakw remain true to their traditions because of their small population, which doesn't make sense. Choice (C) cannot work because it would need to follow *on the one hand*. Choice (D) cannot work because it implies a sequence where none is present. Only (A) works in the context by suggesting that *despite* the small population, that population continues to defend its traditions fiercely.

32. **B**   The line down the center of the graph gives the population growth among aboriginals in Canada as a whole, which was approximately 20.1%. The highest growth in a single province is that of Nova Scotia at 42%. While the second part of (C) is true, this graph shows population increases, so it cannot be said that the aboriginal population in Canada has *declined 20.1%*.

33. **B**   The referent for this pronoun is the word *Canada*, which is singular. The pronoun must therefore be singular as well, eliminating (C). Then, (A) and (D) because these are contractions, not possessive pronouns. Only (B) can work in the context.

Passage IV

34. **B**   Although the answers are technically grammatically correct, so choose the one that is clearest. Choice (B) is the most concise and puts all the terms in the sentence in the clearest relation to one another. Choices (C) and (D) each add some unnecessary word or piece of information.

35. **A**   All the choices give essentially the same information. Choice (A) would seem to be the least specific, but in fact it contains all the information that the others do. Therefore, since it is the most concise, (A) is the best answer.

36. **D**   As written, this sentence contains a comma splice—that is, two complete sentences separated by a comma. Choice (B) does not fix the problem. Choice (C) removes the obvious contrast between the two ideas. The best answer is therefore (D), which correctly subordinates the first idea in the sentence and shows that it contrasts with the second idea.

37. **C**   The ideas before and after the punctuation are both complete. Therefore, a comma is insufficient punctuation. Choice (B) is worse, and (D) adds an unnecessary comma. Only (C) separates the ideas appropriately with a period.

38. **A**   To this point, this paragraph is most concerned with Rillieux's education. Choices (B), (C), and (D) are all true, but only (A) maintains the focus of the paragraph.

39. **D**   Note the modifier at the beginning of this sentence: *While studying at the École Centrale.* This is clearly talking about Rillieux, so his name must follow the modifier. Only (D) fixes this error. Choice (B) suggests that his *concentration* was *studying at the École Centrale*, and (C) suggests that *his background* was doing so.

40. **C**   The paragraph goes on to describe how Rillieux's new sugar refining machine addressed the wastefulness and inefficiency of traditional sugar refining methods. Choice (C) is therefore best in keeping with the tone of the paragraph. Choices (A) and (B) are not adequately specific, and (D) is hilarious but is, alas, not in keeping with the tone of the paragraph.

41. **C**   Choices (A) and (B) are too informal for the context, and (D), even if you're not sure what it means, is far too technical. *Bituminous* typically refers to a kind of soft coal, so it actually doesn't have anything to do with what's being described here. Only (C) can work, as it actually gives a specific descriptor of what is happening in this process.

42. **D**   The idea before the punctuation (*The new machine addressed both major issues with the old method of sugar refining*) is complete, but the idea after it (*all the while making the process significantly safer for those men, mainly slaves, who worked the machines*) is not. Therefore, the punctuation in (A) and (B) cannot be used. There should be some pause here, however, which eliminates (C). Only (D) remains as the correct answer.

43. **B**   This sentence discusses *the heat* belonging to *the system.* Therefore, it should refer to *the system's heat*, as in (B). Choice (A) does not make sense, and (D) eliminates the possession required in the sentence. Choice (C) refers to multiple *systems*, where the sentence only indicates one.

44. **A**   There should be some mention of *previously unheard-of yields.* Only (A) gives any such mention in suggesting that the machines could yield *up to 18,000 pounds of sugar a day.* Choices (B), (C), and (D) may be grammatically correct, but they do not make sense in this particular context.

Part III
Math

   What Can You Expect to See on the Math Test?
5 Heart of Algebra Drills
6 Heart of Algebra Answers and Explanations
7 Problem Solving and Data Analysis
8 Problem Solving and Data Analysis Answers and
   Explanations
9 Passport to Advanced Math
10 Passport to Advanced Math Answers and
   Explanations
11 Additional Topics
12 Additional Topics Answers and Explanations

WHAT CAN YOU EXPECT TO SEE ON THE MATH TEST?

Some of the changes to the redesigned SAT are more obvious than others, especially if you've taken the previous version of the SAT, so here's a brief description of the differences to anticipate. To begin, there are now only two math sections (as opposed to three). This means that, in one section, you'll have to solve 37 questions in 55 minutes, so you'll want to practice working at this pace without interruption. In addition, as the second Math section must be completed without the use of a calculator, we have indicated questions in the upcoming drills that you should practice with nothing more than pencil and paper. To top off, there will now only be FOUR answer choices for multiple-choice problems as opposed to the traditional five choices!

The questions themselves have also gotten harder, both in subject matter—for example, trigonometry is now tested—and in presentation, where a single set of data might stretch across several problems, or where an extended-response grid-in question might have multiple parts. Because of these new aspects, mastering core concepts and understanding the theories behind fundamental mathematical principles – such as equation construction – will be critical. This book, then, will help to literally put your knowledge to the test. If practice makes perfect, then these questions, which have been expertly constructed to represent what you will see on the redesigned SAT, are the perfect practice.

Note that this book is not meant to serve as a library of test-taking techniques or content review—you can check out our upcoming *Cracking the New SAT* for that. However, we have included a few of our most successful strategies for tackling these new multiple-choice problems.

MULTIPLE-CHOICE STRATEGIES FOR THE MATH TEST

Plugging In

One of the most powerful techniques for the Math sections of the Redesigned SAT is what The Princeton Review calls Plugging In. This technique is great for turning complicated (or complicated-looking) problems into more straightforward questions.

Plugging In with Variables

You can Plug In on RSAT questions that use variables. To Plug In on these questions, you assign numerical values to the variables and solve the problem. The numerical answer to the question is the target. Then you Plug In the assigned value to the variables in the answer choices and eliminate each response that does not equal the target. If you have only one answer choice remaining, that's the correct response. If you have more than one answer remaining, change the numbers and Plug In again until only one choice remains. Given that the SAT is now four answer choices instead of five, this strategy takes even less time to apply and execute.

Let's see an example:

6. Xerxes is x years old and 4 years older than Zara. How old was Zara 7 years ago?

   A) $x - 3$
   B) $x - 4$
   C) $x - 7$
   D) $x - 11$

To Plug In on this problem, assign a value for the variable, x. Choose a value that will make the math straightforward. A good rule of thumb to remember when plugging in is to avoid using numbers that are also in the problem (either the question or answer choices), as well as the numbers 0 and 1. Make $x = 20$ by crossing off x in the problem and writing "20" in its place.

Now the problem looks like this:

6. Xerxes is 20 years old and 4 years older than Zara. How old was Zara 7 years ago?

This is now a comparatively straightforward arithmetic problem. If Xerxes is 20 and 4 years older than Zara, then Zara must be 16 years old. If Zara is 16 now, then 7 years ago she was 9. The answer to the question is 9, so this is the target. Circle your target value of 9.

Now, take your value for the variable, $x = 20$, and replace x with 20 in each answer choice. Eliminate any answer choice that doesn't equal your target, 9. Always check each answer choice with variables; sometimes you may pick a value for your variable that makes more than one choice work:

   A) $20 - 3 = 17$: eliminate
   B) $20 - 4 = 16$: eliminate
   C) $20 - 7 = 13$: eliminate
   D) $20 - 11 = 9$: keep

Because you're left with only one choice, you know that (D) must be the answer.

You can Plug In even if there's more than one variable in the problem. When there are multiple variables, you need to check for relationships between the variables, because that will affect how you Plug In.

For example:

15. Three times x is two more than half of y. What is the value of y?

    A) $6x + 4$

    B) $\dfrac{3x - 2}{4}$

    C) $6x - 2$

    D) $6x - 4$

Here, the two variables are in a relationship with each other. In other words, the value of one variable will change depending on what the other variable is, so Plug In for one variable and then solve. Make $x = 4$ in order to avoid any numbers already in the problem. Working the problem, "Three times x" becomes "Three times 4," or 12. Because 12 "is two more than half of y," then "half of y" must be 10. If half of y is 10, then y must be twice 10, or 20. The question is asking for the value of y, so 20 is your target; circle it.

Next, make $x = 4$ in each answer choice and eliminate those that do not equal 20:

    A) $6(4) + 4 = 28$: eliminate

    B) $\dfrac{3(4) - 2}{4} = 2.5$: eliminate

    C) $6(4) - 2 = 22$: eliminate

    D) $6(4) - 4 = 20$: keep

Choice (D) is the only choice which remains, so it must be your answer.

Hidden Plug Ins

The previous problem showed how you can Plug In with variables when the variables are in relationships with each other. You can also Plug In when there's a relationship even if there are no variables in the problem.

Let's see how this works:

33. The number of bacteria in petri dish A doubles every 10 minutes. The number of bacteria in petri dish B doubles every 6 minutes. If both petri dishes begin with the same number of bacteria, how many times greater will the number of bacteria in petri dish B be than the number of bacteria in petri dish A after one hour? (1 hour = 60 minutes)

This question is about the relative numbers of bacteria in each petri dish. This problem would be much easier if you knew the number of bacteria in each dish, so Plug In a number. Let's make the starting number of bacteria in each dish 4 (once again avoiding numbers in the problem).

Petri dish A doubles the number of bacteria every 10 minutes. Therefore, if it starts with 4 bacteria, there would be 8 bacteria after 10 minutes, 16 after 20 minutes, 32 after 30 minutes, 64 after 40 minutes, 128 after 50 minutes, and 256 bacteria after 60 minutes or 1 hour.

Petri dish B doubles the number of bacteria every 6 minutes. If it starts with 4 bacteria, there would be 8 bacteria after 6 minutes, 16 after 12 minutes, 32 after 18 minutes, 64 after 24 minutes, 128 after 30 minutes, 256 after 36 minutes, 512 after 42 minutes, 1024 after 48 minutes, 2048 after 54 minutes, and 4096 bacteria after 60 minutes or 1 hour.

Finally, to find how many times greater petri dish B is than petri dish A, you can divide B by A: 4096 ÷ 256 = 16, which is your answer.

Any time you have a relationship but no numbers provided, you can Plug In for the unknown values and work the problem using real numbers. Look for opportunities to do so, especially on questions involving percentages, ratios, or geometry.

Plugging In the Answers (PITA)

When the answer choices provided are values (not variables) and the question is asking something like "How much…," "How many…," or "What is the value of…," you can Plug In the Answers (PITA). You know that the answer to the question must be one of the four given responses. In many cases, it's easier to test the answer choices rather than work the question "the right way."

Let's look at an example:

28. If $\dfrac{(x+6)^2}{x+5} = \dfrac{1}{x+5}$, then $x =$

    A) −7
    B) −5
    C) 0
    D) 7

This question wants the value of x, so you can Plug In the Answers. Label the answers with what the question is asking; in this case, the answers are x. Next, try an answer in the problem. Start with a middle value; on many questions, if the answer doesn't work, you'll know whether you need a lesser or greater value. Start with choice (B); make $x = -5$:

$$\frac{(-5+6)^2}{-5+5} = \frac{1}{-5+5}$$

$$\frac{(1)^2}{0} = \frac{1}{0}$$

Well, this is interesting. You cannot divide by 0, so the answer cannot be (B); eliminate it. (If you see this before you Plug In, don't bother trying the answer: just eliminate it!) Furthermore, this doesn't help you decide whether you need a lesser or greater value for x, so try the other middle answer, (C):

$$\frac{(0+6)^2}{0+5} = \frac{1}{0+5}$$

$$\frac{36}{5} = \frac{1}{5}$$

This isn't true; eliminate (C). You need to make the left numerator less, so you need a lesser value for x: choose (A). If you aren't sure which direction to go, keep Plugging In!

Chapter 5
Heart of Algebra
Drills

Heart of Algebra Drill 1

For each question in this section, solve the problem and circle the letter of the answer that you think is the best of the choices given.

1. Each student at a high school throws away two pounds of garbage a day. If there are s students at the school and the non-students at the school throw away a total of 350 pounds of garbage a day, which of the following expressions represents how many pounds of garbage are thrown away at the school each day?

    A) $2(s + 175)$
    B) $2(s + 350)$
    C) $350(s + 2)$
    D) $350s$

2. If $2x - 2 = -1$, then $x =$

    A) 1
    B) 0.5
    C) −1.5
    D) −3

3. If $q = \dfrac{q+6}{3}$, then $q =$

    A) 2
    B) 3
    C) 5
    D) 6

4. What is the value of z if $2(z + 3) = 6$?

    A) −6
    B) −3
    C) −2
    D) 0

5. If $\dfrac{2x+1}{3} = \dfrac{4}{3}$, then $x =$

A) 1
B) 1.33
C) 1.5
D) 3

7. If $\dfrac{z+1}{3} = 0$, then $z + 1 =$

A) −1
B) $-\dfrac{1}{3}$
C) 0
D) 2

6. If $\dfrac{x+2}{3} = 2$, then $x =$

A) 2
B) 4
C) 6
D) 8

8. If $4(k+1) = k + 10$, then $3k =$

A) $\dfrac{3}{2}$
B) $\dfrac{5}{2}$
C) 2
D) 6

9. If $\dfrac{3a+2}{a} = 11$, then what is the value of $\dfrac{1}{a}$?

A) $\dfrac{1}{4}$

B) 4

C) 8

D) 11

10. What is the value of p if $\dfrac{5(p-1)}{4} - 1 = 0$?

A) 1

B) $\dfrac{5}{9}$

C) $\dfrac{5}{4}$

D) $\dfrac{9}{5}$

Heart of Algebra Drill 2

For each question in this section, solve the problem and circle the letter of the answer that you think is the best of the choices given.

1. If $3w < 27$, then which of the following describes all possible values of w ?

   A) $w > 9$
   B) $w > 7$
   C) $w < 8$
   D) $w < 9$

2. If $6t + 2 < 26$, then which of the following is a possible value for t ?

   A) 3.5
   B) 4
   C) 4.5
   D) 5

3. If $x > 6(x - 5)$, then which of the following must be true?

   A) $x > 6$
   B) $x > 5$
   C) $x < 6$
   D) $x < -6$

4. If $-13 \leq -2z - 3 \leq 1$, then which of the following describes all possible values of z ?

   A) $-5 \leq z \leq 2$
   B) $-2 \leq z \leq 5$
   C) $2 \leq z \leq 5$
   D) $-5 \leq z \leq -2$

5. If $7s - 14 \le 4 + 6s$, which of the following must be true?

    A) $s \ge 17$
    B) $s \le 18$
    C) $s < 19$
    D) $s < 18$

6. If $8 < -16 - 3c$, which of the following describes all possible values of c ?

    A) $c > 8$
    B) $c > 9$
    C) $c < -9$
    D) $c < -8$

7. If $\left(\dfrac{3d}{2}\right)\left(\dfrac{8d}{3}\right) \le 1$, which of the following inequalities must be true?

    A) $d \le \dfrac{1}{4}$

    B) $d \le \dfrac{1}{2}$

    C) $-\dfrac{1}{4} \le d \le \dfrac{1}{4}$

    D) $-\dfrac{1}{2} \le d \le \dfrac{1}{2}$

8. For all z such that $z > 0$, the square of one-half z is greater than 1 but less than 4. Which of the following inequalities gives all possible values of z ?

    A) $2 < z < 4$
    B) $\sqrt{2} < z < \sqrt{8}$
    C) $1 < z < 16$
    D) $2 < z < 32$

9. When selecting a scarf pattern to knit, Victoria will only choose a pattern that requires at least 480 rows and no more than 520 rows. If r represents a number of rows that she will <u>not</u> knit, an inequality that represents all possible values of r is

A) $|r - 20| > 20$
B) $|r - 500| > 20$
C) $|r - 500| < 20$
D) $|r + 100| > 20$

Heart of Algebra Drill 3

For each question in this section, solve the problem and circle the letter of the answer that you think is the best of the choices given.

1. Andy runs and eats breakfast every morning before work. When he runs, he burns 160 calories per mile for the first 3 miles. When he runs more than 3 miles, he burns 98 calories per additional mile. On Tuesday morning, Andy runs an additional x miles over 3 miles and then consumes y calories for breakfast. Which of the following functions, f, models the net number of calories Andy has lost after running and eating breakfast on Tuesday morning?

   A) $f(x, y) = 98x - y$
   B) $f(x, y) = 160x + 98x - y$
   C) $f(x, y) = 480 + 98x + y$
   D) $f(x,y) = 480 + 98x - y$

2. Sheila walks dogs on the weekend for extra income. For every dog she walks, she charges a flat rate of $20.00 for the first hour. For every additional minute of walking a dog, she charges an additional fee. If Sheila is asked to walk a dog an additional a minutes after the first hour, and she charges b dollars per additional minute, which of the following functions, d, models how much she will earn in terms of a and b ?

   A) $d(a, b) = 20 + a + b$
   B) $d(a, b) = 20ab$
   C) $d(a, b) = 20 + ab$
   D) $d(a, b) = 20 + 2(ab)$

3. Sam saved his money until he had $10,000 to invest. He invested x dollars into a certificate of deposit (CD) with an annual interest rate of 2.0%, and the remaining y dollars into a mutual fund with an annual interest rate of 1.5%. If his total interest earned from both accounts after one year was $193 dollars, which of the following is the value of y?

   A) $9,807
   B) $8,600
   C) $1,400
   D) $350

4. Hap is driving on the highway when his gasoline tank begins to leak. When he has one gallon left in his tank, he finds a gas station to pump more gas into the tank. As he pumps, he loses one-fourth of a gallon every ten minutes. If he pumps g gallons of gas over a period of m minutes, which of the following models the total amount of gas, in ounces, he has in his tank? (Note: 1 gallon = 128 ounces)

   A) $f(g, m) = 128(g) + g + m(g)$

   B) $f(g, m) = 128 + 128(g) - 32\left(\dfrac{m}{10}\right)$

   C) $f(g, m) = 128 + 128(g) - 128\left(\dfrac{m}{10}\right)$

   D) $f(g, m) = 1 + g - 32\left(\dfrac{m}{10}\right)$

5. An airplane flies at a constant altitude of 40,000 feet above sea level. As it starts to land, it descends at a constant rate of x feet per minute. At what altitude is the plane y minutes after it begins to descend?

A) $f(x, y) = 40,000 - xy$
B) $f(x, y) = 40,000 - 60xy$
C) $f(x, y) = 40,000 - x - y$
D) $f(x, y) = 40,000 - 60x - y$

6. Sara has a jar filled with 135 coins, which consist only of quarters and nickels. If Sara has a total of $22.75 in the jar, which of the following is the number of nickels Sara has in the jar?

A) 25
B) 55
C) 80
D) 130

Heart of Algebra Drill 4

For each question in this section, solve the problem and circle the letter of the answer that you think is the best of the choices given.

1. If $1 < r < 4$ and $0 < s < 5$, then what is the range of $r + s$?

   A) $-4 < r + s < 1$
   B) $1 < r + s < 9$
   C) $0 < r + s < 5$
   D) $0 < r + s < 10$

2. If $\dfrac{3x - 2}{4} = x$, then what is the value of x?

   A) -2
   B) 0
   C) $\dfrac{1}{3}$
   D) 2

$$-4 < x < 2$$
$$-1 < y < 3$$

3. Given the inequalities shown above, if x and y are integers, then which of the following expresses all the possible values of $\dfrac{x}{y}$, where $\dfrac{x}{y}$ is defined?

   A) $-12 \le \dfrac{x}{y} \le 6$
   B) $-\dfrac{4}{3} \le \dfrac{x}{y} \le \dfrac{2}{3}$
   C) $-2 \le \dfrac{x}{y} \le \dfrac{2}{3}$
   D) $-3 \le \dfrac{x}{y} \le 1$

4. What is the value of $x + 2$ if $\dfrac{5(x + 2)}{3} = 10$?

   A) 1
   B) 4
   C) 5
   D) 6

5. If $-7 < p < 8$ and $-3 < q < 9$, which of the following expresses all possible values of $p - q$?

A) $-4 < p - q < -1$
B) $-10 < p - q < -1$
C) $-10 < p - q < 11$
D) $-16 < p - q < 11$

6. If $\dfrac{4 - x}{x - 1} = -1$, then which of the following expresses all the possible values of x?

A) $x: x = -1$
B) $x: x = 0$
C) $x: x \neq 1$
D) $x:$ No real numbers

7. What is the value of $x - 1$ if $\dfrac{3(x - 1)}{4} = 9$?

A) 2
B) 8
C) 12
D) 13

8. What are all possible values of x if $\dfrac{3(x + 2)}{6} - \dfrac{x}{2} = 1$?

A) $x: x = 2$
B) $x: x = -2, 2$
C) $x: x = 1$
D) $x:$ All real numbers

Heart of Algebra Drill 5

This section contains two types of questions. For multiple-choice questions, solve each problem and circle the letter of the answer that you think is the best of the choices given. For Student-Response questions, denoted by the grid-in icon, write your answer in the blank space provided.

1. If $3x + y = 11$ and $2x + y = 7$, then $x =$

2. If $x + y = 9$, and $8(x + 3y) = 120$, what is the value of $x - y$?

   A) 0
   B) 3
   C) 7
   D) 9

3. The sum of a and 10 is twice as large as b, where both a and b are integers. If the sum of a and b is divisible by 4, which of the following CANNOT be the value of b?

   A) 6
   B) 8
   C) 10
   D) 14

4. Chloe is purchasing different types of yarn. She purchases a skeins of alpaca yarn for $3.49 each, and s skeins of silk yarn for $5.52 each, after taxes. If Chloe purchased a total of 14 skeins of yarn and spent a total of $73.22, which of the following sets of equations is true?

   A) $a + s = 14$
      $\$5.52a + \$3.49s = \$73.22$

   B) $2a + 12s = 14$
      $(\$3.49 + \$5.52)(a + s) = \$73.32$

   C) $a + s = 14$
      $\$3.49a + \$5.52s = \$73.22$

   D) $as = 14$
      $\$3.49a + \$5.52s = \$73.22$

5. If $4e - f = 9$ and $-2e + f = 5$, what is the value of e?

A) 7
B) 8
C) 11
D) 14

$$x + 3y = -7$$
$$2x - 3y = 13$$

7. Based on the system of equations above, what is the value of $\dfrac{x}{y}$?

A) -3
B) $-\dfrac{18}{13}$
C) $-\dfrac{2}{3}$
D) 2

6. If $7x + 12y = 10$ and $3x - 2y = 5$, what is value of $5x + 5y$?

A) 5
B) 7.5
C) 10.5
D) 15

$$\frac{7}{2}x + \frac{4}{3}y = 4$$
$$21x = 8(3 - y)$$

8. What is the solution set, if any, of the system of equations shown above?

A) $(2, \dfrac{9}{4})$
B) $(0, 3)$
C) No solutions
D) Infinitely many solutions

Heart of Algebra Drill 6

For each question in this section, solve the problem and circle the letter of the answer that you think is the best of the choices given.

1. If $2s + 10r = 2(2s - 5r) = 42$, then what is the value of r ?

   A) 0
   B) 1
   C) 1.4
   D) 14

2. Line m contains the points $(4, 16)$ and $(0, 8)$. At what point will line m intersect with line n if the equation of line n is $-8x + 4y = 24$?

   A) $(0,0)$
   B) $(-4, 0)$
   C) These lines do not intersect
   D) These lines intersect at infinite number of points

3. If $q = p - 3$, and $(4p + 4)/(2q) = 10$, what is the value of p ?

   A) 1
   B) 2
   C) 3
   D) 4

4. A yoga studio charges $8 dollars per student for its morning class and $16 dollars per student for its evening class. Three times as many students attended the evening class as attended the morning class. If the yoga studio earned $2,520 on Friday, how many people attended the morning class?

   A) 15
   B) 45
   C) 56
   D) 135

5. If $x - y = 4$ and $2x + 3y = 10$, what is the value of $3x + 2y$?

A) 4
B) 6
C) 10
D) 14

$$4x - 1y = 10$$
$$-4x + 1y = -10$$

6. Based on the system of equations above, which of the following must be true?

A) There is no solution to this system of equations.
B) (2, 10)
C) (20, –5)
D) There is an infinite number of solutions to this system.

$$2x - 3y = 17$$
$$-2x + 4y = -20$$

7. Based on the system of equations above, which of the following is a possible solution?

A) (–4, –3)
B) (–3, 4)
C) (3, 4)
D) (4, –3)

Heart of Algebra Drill 7

For each question in this section, solve the problem and circle the letter of the answer that you think is the best of the choices given.

1. At 7:00 A.M., a sewage treatment tank contains 3,000,000 gallons of water. Starting at 7:00 A.M., x gallons per minute flow into the tank, and y gallons per minute flow out of the tank. No water enters or leaves the tank otherwise. Which of the following functions, f, models the number of gallons of water in the sewage treatment plant at 8:00 A.M.? (Note: 1 hour = 60 minutes)

   A) $f(x, y) = 3,000,000 + 60xy$
   B) $f(x, y) = 3,000,000 - 60(x + y)$
   C) $f(x, y) = 3,000,000 + 60(x - y)$
   D) $f(x, y) = 3,000,000 + x - y$

2. When a solute is added to a solvent to create a solution, the change in freezing point can be determined by using the formula $\Delta T = K_f \times m \times i$, where ΔT = freezing point of pure solvent – freezing point of solution, in degrees Celsius; K_f is the freezing point depression constant for the solvent; m is the concentration of solute in molality, and i is the van 't Hoff factor. Pure water has a freezing point of 0 C. Solute NaCl (van 't Hoff factor = 2) is added to the solvent water to create a 0.1 molal solution with a freezing point of 0.372 C. Which of the following equations, if solved, would accurately determine the freezing point depression constant of water, given the provided information?

   A) $K_f = \dfrac{0 - (-0.372)}{(0.1)(2)}$

   B) $K_f = \dfrac{(0.1)(2)}{0 - (-0.372)}$

   C) $K_f = [0 - (-0.372)](0.1)(2)$

   D) $K_f = \dfrac{(0)(-0.372)}{2 - 0.1}$

3. Bombast Cable Company charges a flat monthly rate of $22.95 for its basic cable package. For every additional 10 channels added, a customer has an additional monthly charge of $1.25. Additional channels can only be purchased in groups of 10. For example, if a customer wants to add 12 channels, the customer would actually be charged for 20 channels or two groups of 10 channels. If a customer adds x channels to the package then, in terms of x, what is the charge after one year?

   A) $22.95 + 1.25\left(\dfrac{x}{10}\right)$

   B) $12(22.95) + 12(1.25)\left(\dfrac{x}{10}\right)$

   C) $12(22.95) - 12(1.25)\left(\dfrac{x}{10}\right)$

   D) $22.95 + \dfrac{12(1.25)}{\dfrac{x}{10}}$

4. Marguerite and Whitney are collecting canned goods for their neighborhood ThanksGiving-a-Can can drive. For each house they visit when collecting, they receive an average of 2 canned goods. If Whitney started with 4 cans from her own kitchen for the drive while Marguerite started with none, which of the following situations is correct at a given point during their can drive?

   A) When Marguerite has 4 cans, Whitney has 4 cans
   B) When Marguerite has 8 cans, Whitney has 12 cans
   C) When Marguerite has 12 cans, Whitney has 20 cans
   D) When Marguerite has 16 cans, Whitney has 24 cans

5. Chad and Julia run a life-coaching business, Go Get 'Em, that charges $150 per hour per client. They each have a weekly schedule of 20 clients who have 1-hour sessions each. Chad and Julia meet their students in an office for which they each pay $500 in monthly rental fees. If r represents the hourly rate that Go Get 'Em charges its clients, which of the following represents Go Get 'Em's profit, P, in one month? (Note: 1 month = 4 weeks)

A) $P = 80r - 500$
B) $P = 80r - 1,000$
C) $P = 160r - 500$
D) $P = 160r - 1,000$

Heart of Algebra Drill 8

For each question in this section, solve the problem and circle the letter of the answer that you think is the best of the choices given.

1. Which of the following lines is perpendicular to $3x - 7y = 28$?

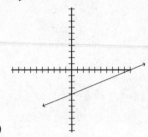

A)

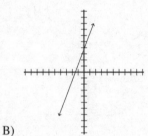

B)

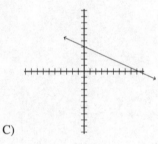

C)

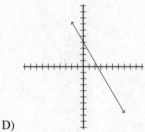

D)

2. Line p has a slope of zero and a y-intercept of 4. Line q has a slope that is undefined and an x-intercept of 3. What is the distance between the origin and the point of intersection between these two lines?

A) $3\sqrt{2}$
B) 4
C) $4\sqrt{2}$
D) 5

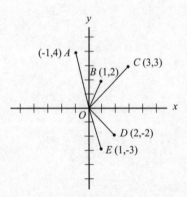

3. In the figure above, what is the average (arithmetic mean) of the slopes of OA, OB, OC, OD, and OE?

A) −5
B) −1
C) 0
D) 1

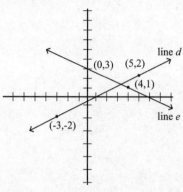

4. Which of the following systems of equations defines lines *d* and *e* in the *xy*-coordinate plane above?

   A) line *d*: $5x + 2y = 10$
      line *e*: $4x + y = 6$
   B) line *d*: $x + 5y = 15$
      line *e*: $3x - y = 6$
   C) line *d*: $-3x + 4y = 10$
      line *e*: $2x + 2y = 6$
   D) line *d*: $2x - 4y = 2$
      line *e*: $3x + 6y = 18$

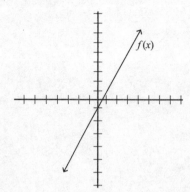

5. The graph of $f(x)$ is shown above. If the function *d* is defined by $d(x) = f(\frac{1}{2}x - 1)$, what is the value of $d(6)$?

   A) -1
   B) 1
   C) 3
   D) 5

6. Line *l* passes through points $(9, \frac{31}{7})$ and $(0, -\frac{4}{7})$.

   Line *m* is defined by the equation $y = -\frac{4}{7}x + \frac{5}{9}$.

   What is the point of intersection of line *l* and line *m* ?

   A) $(1, -\frac{1}{63})$
   B) $(0, \frac{5}{9})$
   C) $(-\frac{1}{63}, 1)$
   D) $(0, -\frac{4}{7})$

Chapter 6
Heart of Algebra
Answers and
Explanations

ANSWER KEY

Heart of Algebra Drill 1

1. A
2. B
3. B
4. D
5. C
6. B
7. C
8. D
9. B
10. D

Heart of Algebra Drill 2

1. D
2. A
3. C
4. B
5. B
6. D
7. D
8. A
9. B

Heart of Algebra Drill 3

1. D
2. C
3. C
4. B
5. A
6. B

Heart of Algebra Drill 4

1. B
2. A
3. D
4. D
5. D
6. D
7. C
8. D

Heart of Algebra Drill 5

1. 4
2. B
3. B
4. C
5. A
6. B
7. C
8. D

Heart of Algebra Drill 6

1. C
2. C
3. D
4. B
5. D
6. D
7. D

Heart of Algebra Drill 7

1. C
2. A
3. B
4. B
5. D

Heart of Algebra Drill 8

1. D
2. D
3. B
4. D
5. C
6. A

HEART OF ALGEBRA ANSWERS AND EXPLANATIONS

Heart of Algebra Drill 1

1. **A** Plug in! Make $s = 5$. If there are 5 students at the school, the students will throw away $5 \times 2 = 10$ pounds of garbage. The non-students throw away 350 pounds, so in total there will be $10 + 350 = 360$ pounds of garbage. This is your target. Plug In $s = 5$ and eliminate any choice which does not equal 360. The only choice which works is (A).

2. **B** Start by combining like terms. Add 2 to both sides: $\begin{array}{r} 2x - 2 = -1 \\ +2 \quad +2 \\ \hline 2x \quad = \quad 1 \end{array}$

   Then divide both sides by 2: $\dfrac{2x}{2} = \dfrac{1}{2} x = 0.5$, which is (B).

3. **B** Start by getting rid of the fraction. Multiply both sides by 3, which will cancel with the denominator of the fraction: $(3)q = (3)\dfrac{q+6}{3}$, $3q = q + 6$.

   Next, combine like terms by subtracting q from both sides, which leaves you with $2q = 6$. Finally, divide both sides by 2, and you find that $q = 3$, which is (B).

4. **D** Rather than distributing the 2 on the left side of the equation, you can divide both sides by 2 (which will cancel the 2 on the left side) and save yourself a couple of steps: $\dfrac{2(z+3)}{2} = \dfrac{6}{2}$, $z + 3 = 3$. Then subtract 3 from both sides, and you find that $z = 0$, which is (D).

5. **C** Start by multiplying both sides by 3 to cancel out the denominators. You are left with $2x + 1 = 4$. Then subtract 1 from both sides, so you have $2x = 3$. Finally, divide both sides by 2, and you find that $x = 1.5$, which is (C).

6. **B** Start by multiplying both sides by 3 to eliminate the denominator: $(3)\dfrac{x+2}{3} = 2(3)$ $x + 2 = 6$. Next, subtract 2 from both sides: $x = 4$. This is (B).

7. **C** Multiply both sides by 3: $(3)\dfrac{z+1}{3} = (3)0$, $z + 1 = 0$. Note that the question is asking for the value of $z + 1$, so you're done!

8. **D** Start by distributing the 4 on the left side of the equation: $4k + 4 = k + 10$. Next, combine like terms by subtracting k from both sides: $3k + 4 = 10$. Last, subtract 4 from both sides: $3k = 6$, which is (D).

9. **B**   Multiply both sides by the denominator, a: $(a)\dfrac{3a+2}{a} = (a)11$, $3a + 2 = 11a$

Combine like terms by subtracting $3a$ from both sides:
$$\begin{array}{r} 3a + 2 = 11a \\ -3a \qquad -3a \\ \hline 2 = 8a \end{array}$$

Divide both sides by 8, so $a = \dfrac{1}{4}$. However, the question asks for the value of $\dfrac{1}{a}$, so you need to take the reciprocal of both sides and find that $\dfrac{1}{a} = 4$, which is (B).

10. **D**   This problem can be solved by starting with adding 1 to both sides:
$$\begin{array}{r} \dfrac{5(p-1)}{4} - 1 = 0 \\ +1 \quad +1 \\ \hline \dfrac{5(p-1)}{4} = 1 \end{array}$$

Next, eliminate the denominator by multiplying both sides by 4:

$(4)\dfrac{5(p-1)}{4} = (4)1$, $5(p-1) = 4$

Next, divide both sides by 5:

$\dfrac{5(p-1)}{5} = \dfrac{4}{5}$, $p - 1 = \dfrac{4}{5}$

Finally, add 1 to both sides:

$p - 1 + 1 = \dfrac{4}{5} + 1$, $p = \dfrac{9}{5}$ That matches (D).

Drill 2

1. **D**   To solve, divide both sides of the inequality by 3. This results in $w < 9$, (D).

2. **A**   To solve, subtract 2 from both sides of the inequality to get $6t < 24$. Then divide both sides of the inequality by 6 to get $t < 4$. The only answer that is less than 4 is (A); the rest are too large for this inequality to be true.

3. **C**   To solve, distribute the 6 on the right side of the inequality to get $x > 6x - 30$. Then subtract $6x$ from both sides to get $-5x > -30$. Divide both sides by -5, making sure to flip the inequality sign since you are dividing by a negative number. This results in $x < 6$, (C).

4. **B**   Solve one half of the inequality at a time. Start with $-13 \le -2z - 3$. Add 3 to both sides of the inequality to get $-10 \le -2z$. Divide both sides by -2, making sure to flip the inequality sign since you are dividing by a negative number. This results in $5 \ge z$.

   Now solve $-2z - 3 \le 1$. Add 3 to both sides of the inequality to get $-2z \le 4$. Divide both sides by -2, making sure to flip the inequality sign since you are dividing by a negative number. This results in $z \ge -2$. Eliminate (A) and (C), leaving (B).

5. **B**   Start by combining like terms. Add 14 to both sides of the inequality to get $7s \le 18 + 6s$. Subtract $6s$ from both sides to get $s \le 18$. This makes (B) the correct answer.

6. **D**   Add 16 to both sides of the inequality to get $24 < -3c$. Divide both sides by -3, making sure to flip the inequality sign since you are dividing with a negative number. This results in $-8 > c$. Since c has to be less than -8, only (D) works as a correct answer choice.

7. **D**   Multiply the left side to get $\dfrac{24d^2}{6} \le 1$. Simplify the fraction: $4d^2 \le 1$. Divide by 4: $d^2 \le \dfrac{1}{4}$. Now take the square root of both sides, but be careful: Since d can be positive or negative, there will be two solutions, and for the negative solution, you will need to flip the sign. The two solutions are $d \le \dfrac{1}{2}$ and $d \ge -\dfrac{1}{2}$, so the correct answer is (D).

8. **A**   Translate the English into math: $1 < \left(\dfrac{z}{2}\right) < 4$. Square the fraction in the middle: $1 < \left(\dfrac{z}{2}\right)^2 < 4$. Multiply all parts of the equation by 4: $4 < z^2 < 16$. Finally, take the square root of all three parts of the equation: $2 < z < 4$. The correct answer is (A).

9. **B**   Plug In! The question wants to know which inequality represents the number of rows Victoria will not knit. Since the restrictions are 480 rows to 520 rows, select a number that is outside of that range and eliminate any answer choices that are not true. For example, if $r = 530$:

   A) $|530 - 20| > 20$ – NOT true
   B) $|530 - 500| > 20$ – True
   C) $|530 - 500| < 20$ – NOT true
   D) $|530 + 100| > 20$ – True

   Eliminate (A) and (D). Next, try plugging in with a number that shouldn't work. If we try $r = 500$, the inequalities should not work since that is a number of rows Victoria would knit:

   Answer B: $|500 - 500| > 20$ – NOT True
   Answer D: $|500 + 100| > 20$ – True
   Since (B) didn't work with $r = 500$ and did work with $r = 530$, this is the best answer choice.

Drill 3

1. **D** Plug In! Andy runs on Tuesday morning, so plug in an arbitrary value for x, such as $x = 2$. That means that Andy has run a total of 5 miles, after adding on the initial 3 miles. Therefore, Andy burns 160 calories per mile for the first 3 miles for a total of 480 calories, and he burns 98 calories per mile for the additional 2 miles for a total of 196 calories. Thus, the total number of calories he burns is 480 calories + 196 calories = 676 calories.

    However, don't forget to read the full question as it asks for the net number of calories Andy has lost. Similar to plugging in for the variable x, also plug in for y. If plugging in $y = 100$ calories, subtract that number from the calories burned as Andy is gaining calories instead of burning calories. Thus, $676 - 100 = 576$, which is the target number for the answer choices. Plugging in $x = 2$ and $y = 100$, (A) equals 96, (B) equals 416, and (C) equals 776. Thus, (D), which is equal to 576, is the correct answer.

2. **C** Plug In! Assign arbitrary values such as $a = 5$ for the additional minutes she walks a dog and $b = 2$ dollars for each of those additional minutes. Thus, for the 5 additional minutes, Sheila charges a total of \$10 (5 additional minutes × 2 dollars per minute). Since she charges \$20.00 for the first hour, she will then charge a total of \$20 + \$10 = \$30, which is your target number. Thus, (C) is the correct answer.

3. **C** While this problem seemingly needs equations to solve, plugging in the answers can be a more effective approach. Because the question asks for the value of y, label the answer choices with a column header of y and begin with either (B) or (C). If beginning with (B), Sam has invested \$8,600 in a mutual fund (y). The mutual fund earned an interest rate of 1.5%, so (0.015) × \$8,600 = \$129. Because Sam invested \$8,600 in the mutual fund, he invested \$1,400 in the CD since \$10,000 - \$8,600 = \$1,400. The interest rate earned on the CD was 2.0%, so (0.02) × \$1,400 = \$28. Since Sam's total amount of interest earned was \$193 and \$129 + \$28 = \$157, (B) is not the correct answer. Since we need a larger amount of total interest, the amount invested in the account with the lower interest rate must be smaller. Therefore, plug in \$1,400 in (C) for the amount invested in the mutual fund (y) and repeat the same steps as done for (B). With an interest rate of 1.5%, the \$1,400 in (C) would result in an interest amount of \$21. Then, \$8,600 would have been invested in a CD, and with a 2.0% interest rate, the CD would have earned an interest amount of \$172. Therefore, with the \$21 from the mutual fund and \$172 from the CD, Sam would earn a total interest amount of \$193 by investing \$1,400 in a mutual fund, making (C) the correct answer.

4. **B** Plug In, and choose numbers that will make the arithmetic as straightforward as possible. Since the question states that Hap loses ¼ of a gallon every ten minutes, plug in $g = 2$ and $m = 10$. If he pumps 2 gallons of gas in 10 minutes, he is losing ¼ a gallon of gas during that total time. Since 1 gallon = 128 ounces, Hap pumps in a total of 256 ounces of gas (2 gallons × 128 ounces), and he loses 32 ounces (1/4 × 128 ounces). 256 ounces pumped – 32 ounces lost = 224 ounces. Now, don't forget that Hap still has 1 gallon of gas in his tank. Therefore, his total amount of gas in ounces is the 224 ounces he retained while pumping, plus an additional 128 ounces for the gallon already in his tank. 224 + 128 = 352 ounces total, so 352 is your target number. Therefore, the correct choice is (B).

5. **A**   By plugging in $x = 5$ and $y = 10$, the plane descends 5 feet per minute over ten minutes, giving a total descent of 50 feet. Since the plane's previous altitude is 40,000 feet, its altitude after ten minutes is 40,000 feet – 50 feet, or 39,950 feet. Thus, the correct choice is (A).

6. **B**   We can effectively solve this problem by plugging in the answers. Label the answers as "# of nickels" and start with (B). If Sara has 55 nickels in the jar and she has a total of 135 coins, then she must have 80 quarters (# of quarters is the second column header) in the jar. Since 55(0.05) + 80(0.25) = $22.75, (B) is the correct answer.

Drill 4

1. **B**   When adding two inequalities, the inequalities can sometimes be stacked as follows:

$$
\begin{array}{r}
1 < r \quad\ < 4 \\
+0 < \quad s < 5 \\
\hline
1 < r + s < 9
\end{array}
$$

Thus, (B) is correct.

2. **A**   You want to start by getting rid of the fraction. To do so, you multiply both sides by the denominator of the fraction. Therefore, begin by multiplying both sides by 4:

$$(4)\frac{3x - 2}{4} = (4)x$$
$$3x - 2 = 4x$$

Next, you want to collect all the x terms on one side of the equation, so subtract $3x$ from both sides:

$$
\begin{array}{r}
3x - 2 = 4x \\
-3x \quad\ - 3x \\
\hline
-2 = x
\end{array}
$$

The answer is (A).

3. **D**   If x and y are integers, the possible values for x are –3, –2, –1, 0, and 1, and the possible values of y are 0, 1, and 2. However, you are looking for the range of values where $\frac{x}{y}$ is defined. An expression divided by 0 is undefined, so y can only equal 1 or 2. To find the range of $\frac{x}{y}$, make a chart testing the extremes of x with the possible values of y:

x	y	$\frac{x}{y}$
–3	1	–3
–3	2	$-\frac{3}{2}$
1	1	1
1	2	$\frac{1}{2}$

Therefore, the range of values is $-3 \le \frac{x}{y} \le 1$, (D).

4. **D**   Start by getting rid of the fraction. Multiply both sides by the denominator, 3:

$$(3)\frac{5(x+2)}{3} = (3)10$$

$$5(x + 2) = 30$$

You could distribute the 5 to the terms in the parentheses, but if you divide both sides by 5, the equation will be easier to deal with:

$$\frac{5(x+2)}{5} = \frac{30}{5}$$

$$x + 2 = 6$$

This is your answer. Be careful! The question is NOT asking for the value of x, so you're done!

5. **D**   Be careful here. If you simply stack and subtract the two equations, you'll get (A), which is incorrect. A better approach is to subtract both the upper and lower limits of q from both the upper and lower limits of p. This gives you four possibilities:

$$-7 - (-3) = -4$$
$$-7 - 9 = -16$$
$$8 - (-3) = 11$$
$$8 - 9 = -1$$

The range of $p - q$ will be defined by the smallest and largest of these four options, so $-16 < p - q < 11$, which is (D).

6. **D** Because the question is asking for the value of x, you can Plug In the Answers. Test (A) by making $x = -1$:

$$\frac{4-(-1)}{-1-1} = -1$$

$$\frac{5}{-2} = -1$$

This is not true, so you can eliminate (A). You can also eliminate (C), because (C) would let x equal any number that isn't 1. Next, try $x = 0$:

$$\frac{4-0}{0-1} = -1$$

$$\frac{4}{-1} = -1$$

This is also incorrect, so eliminate (B) and choose (D).

You can also approach this problem algebraically. Start by multiplying both sides of the equation by the denominator $x - 1$:

$$(x-1)\frac{4-x}{x-1} = (x-1)(-1)$$

$$4 - x = 1 - x$$

Add x to both sides, and you're left with $4 = 1$. This is obviously incorrect in all possible cases, which means that no values of x solve the equation. Choose (D).

7. **C** Start by eliminating the fraction. Multiply both sides by the denominator, 4:

$$(4)\frac{3(x-1)}{4} = (4)9$$

$$3(x-1) = 36$$

You could distribute the 3 to the terms in the parentheses, but if you divide both sides by 3, the equation will be easier to deal with:

$$\frac{3(x-1)}{3} = \frac{36}{3}$$

$$x - 1 = 12$$

This is your answer, (C). Be careful! The question is NOT asking for the value of x, so you're done!

8. **D**   Plug In the Answers! Test $x = 2$, as it shows up in three answer choices (2 is a real number, so it would be included in (D)):

$$\frac{3(2+2)}{6} - \frac{2}{2} = 1$$

$$\frac{3(4)}{6} - 1 = 1$$

$$2 - 1 = 1$$

$$1 = 1$$

This works, so 2 needs to be part of the answer; eliminate (C). Next, try –2:

$$\frac{3(-2+2)}{6} - \frac{-2}{2} = 1$$

$$\frac{3(0)}{6} - (-1) = 1$$

$$1 = 1$$

This also works; eliminate (A). Finally, try any other real number. Make $x = 0$:

$$\frac{3(0+2)}{6} - \frac{0}{2} = 1$$

$$\frac{3(2)}{6} = 1$$

$$1 = 1$$

This also works; choose (D).

If you want to approach this question algebraically, start by getting rid of the fractions. If you multiply both sides by 6, the fractions will clear:

$$6\left[\frac{3(x+2)}{6} - \frac{x}{2}\right] = 6(1)$$

$$3(x+2) - 3x = 6$$

Next, distribute the 3 on the left side of the equation: $3x + 6 - 3x = 6$

Finally, combine like terms: $6 = 6$

The x terms cancelled each other out; therefore, any value of x will work in the equation.

Drill 5

1. **4**   You want to isolate x. If you stack the equations and subtract, the y terms will cancel and you will be left with x:

$$3x + y = 11$$
$$-[2x + y = 7]$$
$$\overline{x= 4}$$

2. **B**   In order to solve this system of linear equations, one of the equations must be re-arranged so that it can be plugged in to the other equation. Therefore, start with the first equation, solving for x results in $x = 9 - y$. Now, plug this expression of x into the second equation and solve for y:

$$8(9 - y + 3y) = 120$$

Divide both sides by 8:

$$9 - y + 3y = 15$$

Subtract 9 from both sides:

$$-y + 3y = 6$$

$$2y = 6$$

$$y = 3$$

Thus, if $y = 3$, then $x = 6$. Finally, since the question asks to solve for the expression $x - y$, we can plug in the values for x and y, respectively, to get $6 - 3 = 3$. Therefore, (B) is the correct answer.

3. **B**   First, start by translating the problem from English into Math. The first equation can be written as $a + 10 = 2b$. We can use this information to now potentially eliminate some answer choices before proceeding in the problem.

For (A), if $b = 6$, then $a = 2$. The sum of a and b, or 8, IS divisible by 4, so eliminate this answer choice. For (B), if $b = 8$, then $a = 6$. The sum of a and b, or 14, is NOT divisible by 4, so this is the correct answer choice. For (C), if $b = 10$, then $a = 10$. The sum of a and b, or 20, IS divisible by 4, so (C) is eliminated. For (D), if $b = 14$, then $a = 18$. The sum of a and b, or 32, IS divisible by 4, so (D) is also eliminated.

4. **C**   This is a great question to illustrate process of elimination (POE). Since the question states that a total of 14 skeins of yarn are purchased, some of alpaca and some of s, then $a + s = 14$. Thus, eliminate (B) and (D). The problem then states that each skein of alpaca was purchased for \$3.49, and each skein of silk was purchased for \$5.52. This leaves (C) as this information is reflected in the second equation of that answer choice. Choice (A) has the values corresponding to the incorrect type of yarn.

5. **A** To most effectively solve this problem, employ the Stack-and-Solve method by stacking the equations. Once stacked, the equations can either be added or subtracted. We see that, by stacking, the variable f can be eliminated if we add the two equations together as follows:

$$\begin{array}{r} 4e - f = 9 \\ + \underline{-2e + f = 5} \\ 2e \quad\; = 14 \end{array}$$

Dividing both sides of the resulting equation $2e = 14$ gives us $e = 7$. Thus, (A) is correct.

6. **B** Again, stacking and adding these questions will result in the following solution:

$$\begin{array}{r} 7x + 12y = 10 \\ + \underline{3x - 2y = 5} \\ 10x + 10y = 15 \end{array}$$

Since the question asks for the value of $5x + 5y$, divide both sides by 2 to get $5x + 5y = 7.5$. Thus, (B) is correct.

7. **C** Start by isolating one of the variables. If you add the two equations together, the y terms will cancel and you can solve for x:

$$\begin{array}{r} x + 3y = -7 \\ + \underline{[2x - 3y = 13]} \\ 3x \quad\;\; = 6 \end{array}$$

You can divide both sides by 3, and you find that $x = 2$. Next, to determine the value of y, substitute $x = 2$ in the first equation and solve:

$$\begin{array}{r} 2 + 3y = -7 \\ \underline{-2 \qquad -2} \\ 3y = -9 \\ y = -3 \end{array}$$

If $x = 2$ and $y = -3$, then $\dfrac{x}{y} = -\dfrac{2}{3} =$, (C).

$$\dfrac{7}{2}x + \dfrac{4}{3}y = 4$$

$$21x = 8(3 - y)$$

8. **D** In the first equation, we have denominators of 2 and 3, so cancel the fractions by multiplying everything by the product of 2 and 3, which is 6:

$$6\left(\dfrac{7}{2}x + \dfrac{4}{3}y\right) = 6(4)$$

$$21x + 8y = 24$$

For the second equation, distribute the right side:

$21x = 24 - 8y$

Add $8y$ to both sides, so that the two equations will be in the same form:

$21x + 8y = 24$

As you can see, the two equations are identical. If two equations are the same, there will be an infinite number of solutions, which is (D).

Drill 6

1. **C**   To solve for r, separate the two equations:

    $2s + 10r = 42$ and $2(2s - 5r) = 42$. Distribute the second equation: $4s - 10r = 42$.

    Now stack and add the equations:

    $$\begin{aligned} 2s + 10r &= 42 \\ + \ 4s - 10r &= 42 \\ \hline 6s &= 84 \end{aligned}$$

    Divide both sides by 6 and solve: $s = 14$. Plug that value back into one of the equations for s and solve for r: $2(14) + 10r = 42$. Therefore, $r = 1.4$, and the correct answer is (C).

2. **C**   In order to solve this problem, first put line n into slope-intercept form by adding $8x$ to both sides and then dividing both sides by 4. This will result in $y = 2x + 6$. You now know that the slope of line n is 2 and the y-intercept is 6. Since you also know the y-intercept of line m as it is given in point $(0, 8)$, you know these are not the same lines. Eliminate (D).

    To determine whether or not (C) will be the answer, find the slope of line m by using the slope formula:

    $$\frac{8 - 16}{0 - 4} \quad \text{slope} = 2$$

    Since both lines m and n have a slope of positive 2, they are parallel and will never intersect. Thus, (C) is correct.

3. **D**   The question tells you that $q = p - 3$, so substitute $p - 3$ for the variable q in the second equation:

    $(4p + 4)/(2(p - 3)) = 10$
    Distribute the 2 in the denominator:
    $(4p + 4)/(2p - 6) = 10$
    Multiply both sides by $2p - 6$:
    $4p + 4 = 20p - 60$
    Combine like terms:
    $64 = 16p$
    Divide by 16 to get $p = 4$. The correct answer is (D).

4. **B**   You can solve this problem either by plugging in the answers or by writing out equations and substituting.

    To solve by plugging in the answers, start by labeling your answers as the morning class, and begin to work the problem with (B) or (C). If you use (B), then it is assumed there are 45 students in the morning class. The question states that there are 3 times as many attendees of the evening class than the morning class, so the evening class would have 135 attendees. The question says that the studio charges $16 for the evening class, $8 for the morning class, and earned a total of $2,520 total. So we need to multiply the 135 evening attendees by $16 and the 45 morning attendees by $8. This equals a total of $2,520, so you can select (B) and stop.

5. **D**   All you have to do here is stack and add the equations.

$$x - y = 4$$
$$+ \ \underline{2x + 3y = 10}$$
$$3x + 2y = 14$$

Since the question asks for $3x + 2y$, the answer is (D).

6. **D**   Stack and add the system of equations as follows:

$$4x - 1y = 10$$
$$+ \ \underline{-4x + 1y = -10}$$
$$0x + 0y = 0$$

Since these equations cancel each other out, they are the same lines. Thus, this system of equations has an infinite number of solutions, making (D) the correct answer.

7. **D**   Stack and add these equations:

$$2x - 3y = 17$$
$$+ \ \underline{-2x + 4y = -20}$$
$$y = -3$$

Since $y = -3$, eliminate (B) and (C). Now plug in $y = -3$ to the other equation to solve for x.

$$2x - 3(-3) = 17$$
$$2x + 9 = 17$$
$$2x = 8$$
$$x = 4$$

Thus, (D) is the correct answer.

Drill 7

1. **C**   Plug In! Make $x = 5$ and $y = 2$. If 4 gallons per minute flow into the plant, then over an hour (60 minutes), there will be $5 \times 60 = 300$ gallons added to the plant. If 2 gallons per minute flow out of the plant, then over an hour there will be $2 \times 60 = 120$ gallons removed from the plant. Therefore, after an hour there will be $3{,}000{,}000 + 300 - 120 = 3{,}000{,}180$ gallons in the plant. This is your target. Plug $x = 5$ and $y = 2$ into each answer and eliminate any choice which doesn't equal 3,000,180. The only choice that works is (C).

2. **A**   The freezing point depression constant is represented in the formula by K_f, so start by taking the formula $\Delta T = K_f \times m \times i$ and solving it for K_f. Divide both sides by $m \times i$ and you'll get $K_f = \dfrac{\Delta T}{m \times i}$. Now you can start filling in what you know about those variables. ΔT = freezing point of pure solvent – freezing point of solution; here the freezing point of pure water is 0, and the freezing point of the solution is –0.372, so $\Delta T = 0 - (-0.372)$. That should be in the numerator of your answer; that alone gets you to choice (A). As for the rest of the variables, m is the molality of the solution, here given as 0.1, and i is the van 't Hoff factor, here given as 2. Therefore, the denominator of your answer should have $(0.1)(2)$, which is also true only of (A).

3. **B**   Plug in numbers to see which equation works. If the customer wants 37 channels to be added, he would actually be billed for 40 channels, as per the company's policy, so $x = 40$. Thus, the customer has four additional monthly charges of $1.25, or a total additional monthly charge of $5.00. This surcharge will be added to the monthly rate of $22.95. Finally, the question asks for the yearly cost, so multiply the monthly charges by 12 for the yearly cost: 12($22.95) + 12($5.00) = $335.40, which is your target answer. Therefore, (B) is the correct answer.

4. **B**   These scenarios can be re-written so that the numbers of cans that Marguerite and Whitney have, respectively, can be represented as an ordered pair. Therefore, at the beginning of the can drive, when they have yet to visit any homes, (0, 4) correctly illustrates that Marguerite has zero cans and Whitney has four cans. In a graphical sense, this point would represent the y-intercept. Because they receive an average of 2 cans per house, the equation $y = 2x + 4$ models the described scenario in the question. Therefore, after plugging in all of the answer choices for which Marguerite's number of cans represents x and Whitney's number of cans represents y, (B) is the correct answer.

5. **D**   Because of the many nuances, it is best to solve this problem using bite-sized pieces. Let's take Chad's weekly clientele. He will meet with 80 clients in one month if he has a weekly schedule of 20 clients. To account for Julia's clientele as well, multiply 80 by 2 to get 160. Therefore, (A) and (B) can be eliminated as they have a coefficient of only 80 in front of the hourly rate r. Then, the total rent for the month of $1,000 ("…each pay $500…") must be deducted from the overall revenue, so (C) is eliminated. Thus, (D) is the correct answer.

Drill 8

1   **D**   In order to solve this problem, re-write the equation in slope-intercept form:

$$3x - 7y = 28 \rightarrow y = \frac{3}{(7)}x - 4$$

Therefore, the slope of this line is $\frac{3}{7}$. In order for a line to be perpendicular, it must have a slope that is the negative reciprocal of the slope of the given line. For (A), the line is $3x - 7y = 28$, so it is eliminated. Choice (B) has a positive slope, so it cannot be correct. Eliminate it as well.

Choice (C) has a slope that is the opposite sign of the equation in the problem, but it is not the reciprocal. Eliminate it. Choice (D) has a slope that is $-\frac{7}{3}$, which is the negative reciprocal of the original line, making (D) the correct answer.

2. **D**   Draw both lines on an x, y-coordinate plane and solve. If line p has a slope of 0 and a y-intercept of 4, then it is a horizontal line that lies on $y = 4$. If line q has a slope that is undefined and an x-intercept of 4, then it is a vertical line that lies on $x = 3$. These lines, therefore, intersect at point (3, 4).

Now draw a line from point (3, 4) to (0, 0) to form a right triangle with sides of 3 and 4. Therefore, the length of the hypotenuse is 5, making (D) correct.

3. **B**   This question is straightforward, but takes a bit of work, as to find the average, you'll first have to find the slope for each of the lines. Since you are given both end points of each line, the origin and the end point written on the graph, apply each set of points to your slope formula, $m = \frac{y_2 - y_1}{x_2 - x_1}$. Line OA's slope = −4, line OB's slope = 2, line OC's slope = 1, line OD's slope = −1, and line OE's slope = −3. Now find the average of the slopes: $\frac{(-4 + 1 + 2 + -1 + -3)}{5} = -1$. Thus, (B) is the correct answer.

4 **D**   Two strategies could be used to solve this problem: Plug in values for x and y, or re-write the equations in the answer choices in slope-intercept format and use process of elimination.

To plug in, use point (5,2) for line d and (0,3) for line e to find the following:

A) line d: 5(5) + 2(2) = 10 → NOT true
    line e: 4(0) + (3) = 6 → NOT true
B) line d: 5 + 5(2) = 15 → True
    line e: 3(0) - 3 = 6 → NOT true (careful! Make sure to check all five answer choices)
C) line d: -3(5) + 4(2) = 10 → NOT true
    line e: 2(0) + 2(3) = 6 → True (careful! Make sure to check all five answer choices)
D) line d: 2(5) − 4(2) = 2 → True
    line e: 3(0) + 6(3) = 18 → True

Thus, the correct answer is (D).

5. **C**   First, plug in 6 into the expression for f: $d(6) = f(\frac{1}{2}(6) - 1) = f(2)$. Then find 2 on the x-axis in the graph provided. Draw a line up until you hit the $f(x)$ line. Draw another line horizontally to the y-axis. The y value for $f(2)$ is 3, so (C) is correct.

6.   **A**   Use the slope formula to find the equation of line l: $m = \dfrac{y_2 - y_1}{x_2 - x_1}$,   so $m = \dfrac{\dfrac{31}{7} - \left(-\dfrac{4}{7}\right)}{9 - 0} = \dfrac{5}{9}$.

You already know the y-intercept of line l from the point $(0, -\frac{4}{7})$, so the equation of line l is

$y = \dfrac{5}{9}x - \dfrac{4}{7}$. To find the point of intersection, put the non-y sides of the equations equal to each other and solve:

$$\frac{5}{9}x - \frac{4}{7} = -\frac{4}{7}x + \frac{5}{9}$$

$$\frac{71}{63}x = \frac{71}{63}$$

$$x = 1$$

Only choice (A) has an x value of 1, but if needed, you can then plug $x = 1$ into the equation for either line and solve for y.

Another way to find the point of intersection is to graph both lines on your calculator. You'll be able to see that the lines intersect right at $x = 1$, which eliminates all answers other than (A).

You can also use Process of Elimination to Ballpark a few answers away. The y-intercept of line l is $(0, -\frac{4}{7})$, so $(0, \frac{5}{9})$ won't be on line l; eliminate choice (B). The y-intercept of line m is given by the b term: $(0, \frac{5}{9})$. $(0, -\frac{4}{7})$ will therefore not be on line m; eliminate choice (D). Finally, use the given equation of line m and Plug In the Answers. Making $x = 1$ will be much easier than making $x = -\frac{1}{63}$, so test choice (A). When $x = 1$, $y = -\frac{1}{63}$ on line m, so choose (A).

Chapter 7
Problem Solving
and Data Analysis

Problem Solving and Data Analysis Drill 1

This section contains two types of questions. For multiple-choice questions, solve each problem and circle the letter of the answer that you think is the best of the choices given. For Student-Response questions, denoted by the grid-in icon, write your answer in the blank space provided.

DIFFERENT TYPES OF LIGHT BULBS

Type of Bulb	Cost	Life Span
Incandescent	$0.50	Approximately 1,000 hours
Compact Florescent Lamp (CFL)	$1.50	Approximately 10,000 hours
Light Emitting Diode (LED)	$10	Approximately 25,000 hours

1. The table above shows the cost of the life span of several different types of light bulb. What is the ratio of the cost, in cents per hour of life span, of a compact florescent lamp to that of a light emitting diode?

   A) 1.5 to 5
   B) 3 to 8
   C) 3 to 10
   D) 4 to 5

2. A graphic designer creates an image for a t-shirt that measures 8 inches tall and 10 inches wide. She can use this image for small and medium t-shirts, but she must increase the size for a large t-shirt. She wants her final image for the large t-shirts to measure 9 inches tall and 11.25 inches wide. At what percent must she print out the image to obtain these measurements?

   A) 88.89%
   B) 107.5%
   C) 112.5%
   D) 125%

3. Target heart rates for various health benefits are calculated by taking different percents of a person's maximum heart rate, defined as the difference between 220 and the person's age. A heart rate in the aerobic zone is about 75% of the maximum heart rate and a heart rate in the fat-burning zone is about 55% of the maximum heart rate. What is the difference between the fat-burning heart rate and the aerobic heart rate of a person who is 35 years old?

   A) 37
   B) 44
   C) 51
   D) 55

ORIGINAL THRIFT STORE PRICES

Cost of items purchased on Monday	Cost of items purchased on Wednesday
$1.50	$0.98
$2.99	$1.99
$2.99	$2.55
$3.49	$4.98
$3.99	

4. Anya shops at a thrift store only on sale days. On Mondays, members with a savings card receive a 25% discount on all items. On select Wednesdays, members receive a 30% discount on all items. The chart above shows the original costs of the items Anya bought one week that included the special Wednesday discount. A tax of 6.25% of the total purchase is applied to the total after all discounts. What is the total amount Anya spent at the thrift store this week, including tax?

   A) $17.41
   B) $18.57
   C) $19.49
   D) $19.73

DENSITY OF SUBSTANCES

Substance	Density (g/cm³)
Aluminum	1.71
Copper	9.0
Iron	7.87
Lead	11.4
Osmium	?
Silver	10.5

5. The densities of various substances are listed in the table above. The ratio of the density of aluminum to the density of lead is 3 to x. The ratio of the density of osmium to the density of copper is x to 8. What is the density of osmium in grams per cubic centimeter?

Problem Solving and Data Analysis Drill 2

This section contains two types of questions. For multiple-choice questions, solve each problem and circle the letter of the answer that you think is the best of the choices given. For Student-Response questions, denoted by the grid-in icon, write your answer in the blank space provided.

1. The density of silver is 10.5 grams per cubic centimeter. If a nugget of silver weighs 2,100 grams, what is the volume of the nugget, in cubic centimeters?

2. One liter of water has a mass of 1000 grams. If there are 1000 milliliters in a liter, and 1 milliliter is equal to 1 cubic centimeter, what is the density of water, in grams per cubic centimeter?

    A) 1
    B) 1.1
    C) 10
    D) 11

3. A block of copper weighs 2,230 grams and measures 10 cm by 5 cm by 5 cm. Given that density is mass divided by volume, what is the density of copper in grams per cubic centimeter?

    A) 0.11
    B) 8.92
    C) 44.6
    D) 89.2

4. One match releases approximately 1,100 joules of heat energy when it is lit. If 1 joule equals 0.239 calories, how many of these matches must be lit to produce 2,100 calories of heat energy?

    A) 2
    B) 3
    C) 8
    D) 62

5. A certain 3D printer creates objects by building layers on top of each other. The average layer thickness is 102 μm (micrometers). There are 1,000,000 micrometers in a meter, and 1 inch equals 0.0254 meters. Approximately how many layers are needed to print an object one inch thick?

A) 250
B) 630
C) 2,540
D) 4,015

6. A certain 3D printer has a maximum build volume of 230 mm × 170 mm × 200 mm. If 1 inch equals 25.4 millimeters, which of the following is the best approximation of the printer's maximum build volume in cubic inches?

A) 782
B) 477
C) 308
D) 148

7. A typical race car is travelling at its maximum speed along a straight section of track. The distance it covers in 1 second is equal to the length of a football field, which is 120 yards or 360 feet. Given that there are 5,280 feet in a mile, what is the race car's maximum speed, in miles per hour?

A) 27
B) 82
C) 245
D) 528

8. During the typical Indy 500, the average pit stop is 15 seconds long and involves 6 crew members. Each of the 33 cars that race makes an average of 5 stops per race. If all cars finish the race, using full crews and making the expected number of pit stops, what is the total number of active work hours put in by the crews during pit stops?

A) 4.125
B) 41.25
C) 206.25
D) 247.5

9. Superman can run so fast that he can run on water as
    well as land, and he never gets tired. His average run-
    ning speed is Mach 4, or 4 times the speed of sound.
    For fun, he decides to run around the Earth's equator, a
    distance of 40,075 kilometers. If the speed of sound is
    340.29 meters per second, and there are 1,000 meters in
    a kilometer, approximately how many hours will it take
    for Superman to complete his run?

    A) 1.5
    B) 8
    C) 29
    D) 118

Problem Solving and Data Analysis Drill 3

This section contains two types of questions. For multiple-choice questions, solve each problem and circle the letter of the answer that you think is the best of the choices given. For Student-Response questions, denoted by the grid-in icon, write your answer in the blank space provided.

Questions 1 through 5 refer to the following graph.

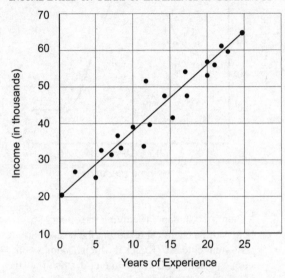

INCOME BASED ON YEARS OF EXPERIENCE AT COMPANY X

1. The scatterplot above shows the income, in thousands, of all the employees of Company X, based on years of experience in the industry. Based on the line of best fit to the data represented, what is the minimum starting salary, in thousands of dollars, at Company X?

2. The scatterplot above shows the income, in thousands, of all the employees of Company X, based on years of experience in the industry. Based on the line of best fit to the data represented, which of the following is the closest to the expected number of years of experience of an employee whose income is $30,000?

   A) 5
   B) 5.55
   C) 37
   D) 74

3. The scatterplot to the left shows the income, in thousands, of all the employees of Company X, based on years of experience in the industry. Based on the line of best fit to the data represented, which of the following is the expected income of an employee with 35 years of experience?

   A) $61,800
   B) $65,000
   C) $83,000
   D) $96,000

4. The scatterplot to the left shows the income, in thousands, of all the employees of Company X, based on years of experience in the industry. Based on the line of best fit to the data represented, which of the following is the closest to the average increase in income per additional year of experience?

   A) $900
   B) $1,800
   C) $4,500
   D) $9,000

5. The scatterplot on the previous page shows the income, in thousands, of all the employees of Company X, based on years of experience in the industry. Which of the following could be the equation of the line of best fit to the data represented, as shown on the graph?

    A) $y = 1.8x + 20$
    B) $y = 2x + 20,000$
    C) $y = 70x + 25$
    D) $y = 1,800x + 20,000$

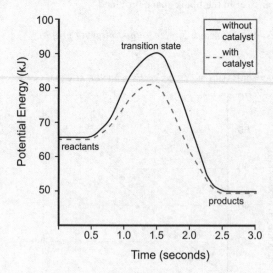

6. A chemistry student is studying the effect of a catalyst on a chemical reaction. She heats solid potassium chlorate ($KClO_3$), which becomes potassium chloride (KCl) and oxygen (O_2). She runs the reaction again, adding solid manganese dioxide (MnO_2) as a catalyst. She graphs the potential energy, in kilojoules, as a function of time. Which of the following statements is true of the graph above?

    A) The potential energy of the reactants was less than that of the products.
    B) The potential energy of the reaction was lowest during the transition state.
    C) The addition of the catalyst lowered the potential energy of the reaction during the transition state.
    D) The addition of the catalyst had no effect on the potential energy of the reaction.

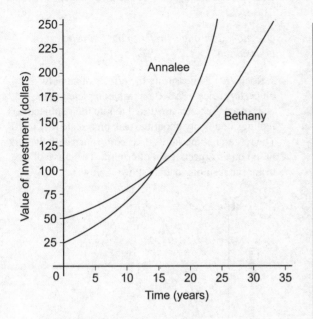

7. Annalee and Bethany start investing at the same time in accounts that will earn interest compounded annually. Both women intend to leave their investments in place until the total value reaches $250. After the initial deposit ($t = 0$), Annalee and Bethany check and record the value of their investments once every year. The value of the two investments was graphed and fitted with a smooth curve, as shown above, where each curve represents the value of one investment, in dollars, as a function of time, in years. Which of the following is a true statement regarding the investment values shown above?

A) For the first 15 years, Bethany's investment is growing at a higher average rate than Annalee's investment.

B) At $t = 0$, both investments are worth $100.

C) At $t = 0$, the value of Annalee's investment is 200% that of Bethany's investment.

D) At $t = 0$, Annalee has reached 10% of her goal and Bethany has reached 20% of hers.

Problem Solving and Data Analysis Drill 4

This section contains two types of questions. For multiple-choice questions, solve each problem and circle the letter of the answer that you think is the best of the choices given. For Student-Response questions, denoted by the grid-in icon, write your answer in the blank space provided.

1. When the vapor pressure of water at various temperatures is graphed, the values for the pressure increase slowly at lower temperatures. As the temperatures increase, the vapor pressure grows more rapidly. As the water reaches the boiling point of 100°C, the vapor pressure reaches 1 atm, or one standard atmosphere. If 760 mmHg is equivalent to one standard atmosphere, which of the following could be the graph of the vapor pressure of water?

A)

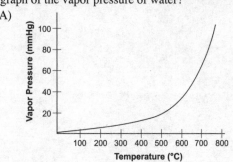

B)

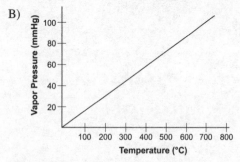

C)

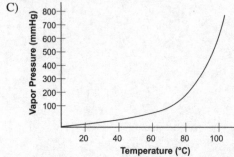

D)

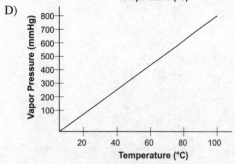

Questions 2 through 4 refer to the following information.

A researcher is measuring the effects of anxiety on performance of a certain task completed in the workplace. Subjects are asked to rate their subjective feelings of anxiety about the task on a scale of 1 to 10. The researcher measures their performance on the task based on an objective set of criteria. The curve of best fit for the resulting data is shown below.

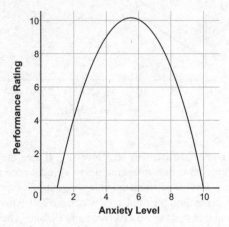

2. What level of anxiety could result in a performance score of 4?

3. What would be considered the optimal level of anxiety an employee should feel to perform at her best on this task?

A) 0
B) 5
C) 5.5
D) 10

4. More than one level of anxiety can result in a given performance score. Which of the following pairs of numbers indicating anxiety levels would result in the same performance score?

A) 2.5 and 8.5
B) 3.5 and 8
C) 4 and 6
D) 4.5 and 7.5

Questions 5 through 7 refer to the following information.

Two softball players are standing in a field facing each other. One player throws the ball up into the air and the other player catches it. A third player videotapes the throw and catch, and the three players analyze the film. They make the following graph of the ball's height above the ground as a function of time.

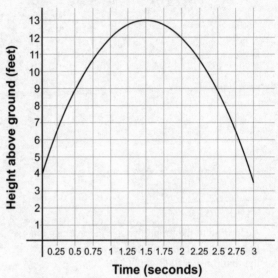

5. According to the graph, what is the height above the ground of the ball as it left the first player's hand?

A) 0
B) 3
C) 4
D) 13

6. If a point on the graph is to be defined as (x, y), where the x-coordinate is the time in seconds and the y-coordinate is the height of the ball in feet, which of the following shows the coordinates of the maximum height attained by the ball during its flight?

A) $(1.5, 13)$
B) $(4, 3)$
C) $(8, 1)$
D) $(13, 1.5)$

7. According to the graph, what is the average change in the height of the ball, in feet per second, during the first third of its flight?

A) 4
B) 8
C) 9
D) 12

8. A hot new product, the Dadget, comes on the market at the beginning of the year. Sales quickly take off, until it is discovered that the Dadget tends to catch fire easily. Sales plummet as the word spreads, while engineers scramble to correct the problem. They finally fix the issue, and sales increase once more, but lack of confidence in the Dadget prevents the company from reaching previous sales levels. Which of the following could be the graph of sales of the Dadget for the year?

A)

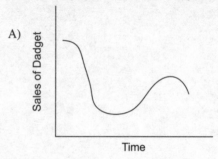

B)

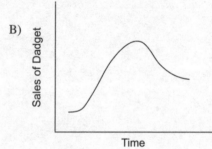

C)

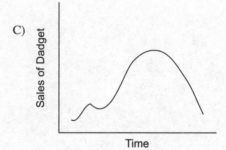

D)

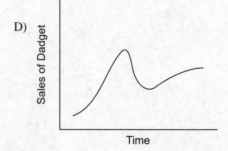

9. A student is graphing the potential energy, in kilojoules, of a certain chemical reaction. At the start of the reaction, the reactants have a constant level of potential energy. As the reactants reach their transition state, the potential energy increases and then drops off as the reaction nears completion. The resulting products have less potential energy than the reactants did. Which of the following could be the graph of the potential energy of this chemical reaction?

A)
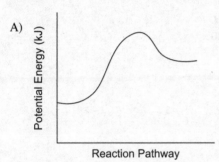

B)
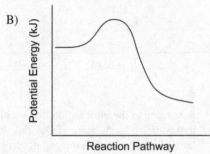

C)
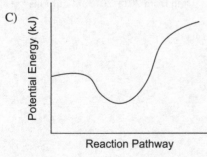

D)
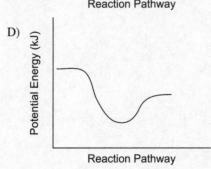

10. A chemistry teacher is giving a lesson on the kinetic molecular theory of gases. She explains to her students that they will be making graphs of the distribution of different speeds of molecules of an unknown gas at varying temperatures. At a given temperature, the graph peaks at the speed at which most molecules are moving. As the temperature is increased, the most probable speed increases, but the curve becomes broader as the spread of speeds increases. Given this information, which of the following graphs could represent the distribution of the molecular speeds of the unknown gas at various temperatures?

A)
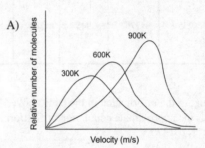

B)
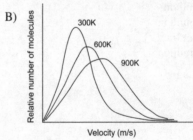

C)
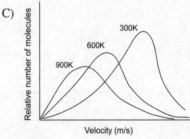

D)
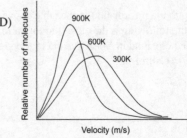

Problem Solving and Data Analysis Drill 5

This section contains two types of questions. For multiple-choice questions, solve each problem and circle the letter of the answer that you think is the best of the choices given. For Student-Response questions, denoted by the grid-in icon, write your answer in the blank space provided.

Questions 1 through 5 refer to the following information.

TOP FIVE STATES FOR NEW JOB GROWTH PER CAPITA, 2011-2013

	California	Colorado	North Dakota	Texas	Utah
Total Jobs Added in State	904,500	146,325	65,450	794,250	98,600
New Jobs per 10,000 Residents	235	275	945	300	330

1. According to the information in the table above, what was the approximate population of California from 2011-2013?

   A) 3.8 million
   B) 21.2 million
   C) 38.5 million
   D) 90.5 million

2. According to the information in the table above, which of the following is the closest to the ratio of job growth per capita in North Dakota to job growth per capita in California?

   A) 1 to 4
   B) 2 to 9
   C) 3 to 1
   D) 4 to 1

3. According to the information in the table to the left, approximately what fraction of the jobs added in the top five states for job growth were added in Utah?

   A) $\frac{1}{25}$

   B) $\frac{1}{20}$

   C) $\frac{1}{5}$

   D) $\frac{9}{20}$

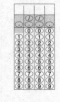

4. According to the information in the table to the left, the population of Colorado was how much greater than the population of Utah from 2011-2013, in millions?

Further data was gathered regarding the job growth in Texas by industry. The following chart shows the results.

New Jobs by Industry per 150,000 Jobs Added

Energy	25,000	Business Services	5,000
Construction	10,000	Finance/ Real Estate	5,000
Trade	15,000	Information Systems	30,000
Manufactuting	20,000	Other	40,000

5. According to the information on both tables, how many new jobs in Texas were added in the manufacturing industry from 2011 to 2013?

A) 19,500
B) 52,950
C) 105,900
D) 120,600

Questions 6 and 7 refer to the following information.

A media market research company surveyed 200,000 randomly selected people in each of 6 age groups regarding the ways in which they receive their news. Participants were asked if they received their news on the preceding day through traditional media (newspapers, television, and radio), through digital media (Internet, E-mail, social media, or podcasts), through both traditional and digital media, or if they did not get news from any of these sources. The results are shown in the table below.

How Americans Get Their News by Age Group
(in thousands)

	Traditional Media Only	Digital Media Only	Both Traditional and Digital	No News Source
18- to 24- year olds	40	32	66	62
25- to 29- year olds	60	30	68	42
30- to 39- year olds	50	24	90	36
40- to 49- year olds	78	16	82	24
50- to 64- year olds	88	12	78	22
65 years and older	124	2	42	32

6. Based on the information in the table, people in which of the following groups are most likely to receive news from both digital and traditional sources and which are most likely to have no news source at all?

	No News Source	Both Traditional and Digital Sources
A)	50- to 64-year-olds	65 years and older
B)	30- to 39-year-olds	18- to 24-year-olds
C)	25- to 29-year-olds	40- to 49-year-olds
D)	18- to 24-year-olds	30- to 39-year-olds

7. Based on the information in the table, which type of news source is inversely associated with age?

   A) Traditional only
   B) Digital only
   C) Both traditional and digital
   D) No news source

Problem Solving and Data Analysis Drill 6

For each question in this section, solve the problem and circle the letter of the answer that you think is the best of the choices given.

Questions 1 through 3 refer to the following information.

A media market research company surveyed 200,000 randomly selected people in each of 6 age groups regarding the ways in which they receive their news. Participants were asked if they received their news on the preceding day through traditional media (newspapers, television, and radio), through digital media (Internet, E-mail, social media, or podcasts), through both traditional and digital media, or if they did not get news from any of these sources. The results are shown in the table below.

HOW AMERICANS GET THEIR NEWS BY AGE GROUP
(in thousands)

	Traditional Media Only	Digital Media Only	Both Traditional and Digital	No News Source
18- to 24-year olds	40	32	66	62
25- to 29-year olds	60	30	68	42
30- to 39-year olds	50	24	90	36
40- to 49-year olds	78	16	82	24
50- to 64-year olds	88	12	78	22
65 years and older	124	2	42	32

1. If the United States population at the time of this survey included approximately 21 million people ages 25 to 29, approximately how many people ages 25 to 29 got news from digital media on a typical day at that time?

   A) 10.3 million
   B) 7.14 million
   C) 6.3 million
   D) 3.15 million

2. An additional 1,500 people in the 40- to 49-year-old age group were surveyed. Which of the following is most likely the number of people from the follow-up survey that reported they received their news exclusively from traditional media?

   A) 375
   B) 585
   C) 615
   D) 660

3. Of the 50- to 64-year-olds whose only source of news was traditional media, 1,000 were selected at random to do an additional survey in which they were asked what traditional media they preferred. There were 375 people in this follow-up survey who said they preferred print media, and the other 625 preferred a different traditional media. Using the data from both surveys, which of the following is most likely to be an accurate statement?

   A) About 16,500 people 50 to 64 years old would report preferring print media for their news source.
   B) About 24,250 people 50 to 64 years old would report preferring print media for their news source.
   C) About 33,000 people 50 to 64 years old would report preferring print media for their news source.
   D) About 55,000 people 50 to 64 years old would report preferring print media for their news source.

Top Five States for New Job Growth per Capita, 2011-2013

	California	Colorado	North Dakota	Texas	Utah
Total Jobs Added in State	904,500	146,325	65,450	794,250	98,600
New Jobs per 10,000 Residents	235	275	945	300	330

4. According to the information given in the table above, which of the following conclusions can be drawn about per capita job growth in the top five states?

A) Job growth was greatest in North Dakota because it had the greatest number of jobs added per 10,000 residents.

B) Job growth was greatest in Texas because it had the greatest number of total jobs added.

C) Job growth was lowest in North Dakota because it had the fewest number of total jobs added.

D) Job growth was lowest in Colorado because it had the fewest number of jobs added per 10,000 residents.

Problem Solving and Data Analysis Drill 7

This section contains two types of questions. For multiple-choice questions, solve each problem and circle the letter of the answer that you think is the best of the choices given. For Student-Response questions, denoted by the grid-in icon, write your answer in the blank space provided.

Questions 1 through 7 refer to the following information.

A dietician working in a pediatrician's office is examining the diets of the patients seen there. She has the parents of each patient record their child's consumption of fruits and vegetables each day for four weeks. She then averages the values for each child to find the grams of fruits and vegetables consumed daily by that child, rounded to the nearest quarter of a thousand. Each child's average consumption is marked as a dot on the graph below.

FRUITS AND VEGETABLES CONSUMED BY AGE

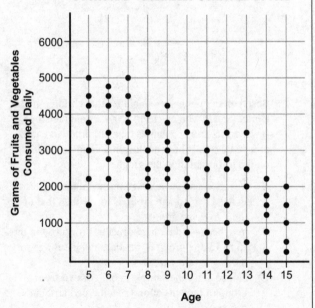

 1. What is the mode of the data gathered, in grams of fruits and vegetables, consumed daily?

2. Which of the following ages has the greatest range of values for fruits and vegetables consumed daily?

   A) Age 5
   B) Age 7
   C) Age 9
   D) Age 12

3. The median consumption value for 8-year-olds is how much greater than the median consumption value for 13-year-olds?

   A) 2,750
   B) 2,000
   C) 1,250
   D) 750

4. Which of the following children has an average daily consumption of fruits and vegetables, in grams, that is farthest away from the mean for his age group?

   A) The 7-year-old whose average consumption is 1,750 grams daily
   B) The 9-year-old whose average consumption is 1,000 grams daily
   C) The 12-year-old whose average consumption is 3,500 grams daily
   D) The 13-year-old whose average consumption is 3,500 grams daily

5. For which of the following age groups is the median value for daily consumption of fruits and vegetables, in grams, closest to the mean of that group?

   A) The 6-year-old group
   B) The 10-year-old group
   C) The 13-year-old group
   D) The 15-year-old group

6. Which of the following is the closest to the mean consumption of fruits and vegetables, in grams, of children over 11 years of age?

   A) 1,500
   B) 1,650
   C) 2,350
   D) 3,000

7. Based on her data, she concludes that children in the United States who are 13 to 15 years old consume fewer fruits and vegetables than children who are 7 to 9 years old. Is her conclusion a valid one, based on the information in the graph?

   A) Yes, because the average of the values for those in the 13 to 15 age group is lower than that of the 7 to 9 age group.
   B) Yes, because the range of values for those in the 13 to 15 age group is smaller than the range for those who are 7 to 9.
   C) No, because the sample is only drawn from a group of patients at one specific pediatrician's office.
   D) No, because the data was provided by the children's parents and not the children themselves.

Problem Solving and Data Analysis Drill 8

This section contains two types of questions. For multiple-choice questions, solve each problem and circle the letter of the answer that you think is the best of the choices given. For Student-Response questions, denoted by the grid-in icon, write your answer in the blank space provided.

Questions 1 and 2 refer to the following information.

An online payment system allows users to purchase a virtual currency called "Dabcoin" with any legal currency, such as U.S. dollars or Japanese yen. When the user purchases Dabcoins, the online payment system converts the user's home currency into Dabcoins at the daily exchange rate, and then charges a customer service fee that is 5% of the value of the customer's Dabcoins.

1. On Monday, the official exchange rate, in U.S. dollars per Dabcoin, is $34. If a customer can spend a maximum of $750 on Dabcoins and is charged the 5% fee, what is the greatest number of Dabcoins the customer can purchase, rounded to the nearest whole number?

2. On Tuesday, the customer service fee was increased to 11.6% of the value of the customer's Dabcoins. If the maximum number of Dabcoins that could be purchased for $750 on Tuesday is equal to the number of Dabcoins that could be purchased for $750 on Monday, what was the exchange rate, in U.S. dollars per Dabcoin, on Tuesday? (Round your answer to the nearest whole number.)

Questions 3 through 5 refer to the following information.

John is conducting an experiment for his Economics class. Each morning on eight consecutive days, he sells homemade waffles in front of the school cafeteria. On the first day, he charges $1 per waffle, and he raises the price by one dollar per day for the duration of the experiment. He records both the price and his net profits per day in the table below, but neglects to fill in his profits on days 2 and 7. To find the missing values for days 2 and 7, he writes a quadratic equation that accurately models the relationship between price and net profits.

Price per waffle (in dollars)	Net profits (in dollars)
1	7
2	
3	15
4	16
5	15
6	12
7	
8	0

3. What is the sum of the net profits, in dollars, that John earned on days 2 and 7? (Disregard the $ sign when gridding in your answer.)

4. John discovers that the quadratic equation that accurately models his results is of the form $N = -(p - a)^2 + c$, where p is the price, N is the net profits, and a and c are constants. What is the value of $a + c$?

5. Suppose that John added a ninth day to the experiment, and raised the price of waffles to $9 per waffle. If the quadratic equation he wrote is accurate, what would John's net loss be, in dollars, on day 9? (Disregard the $ sign when gridding in your answer.)

Chapter 8
Problem Solving and Data Analysis Answers and Explanations

ANSWER KEY

Problem Solving and Data Analysis Drill 1

1. B
2. C
3. A
4. D
5. 22.5

Problem Solving and Data Analysis Drill 2

1. 200
2. A
3. B
4. C
5. A
6. B
7. C
8. A
9. B

Problem Solving and Data Analysis Drill 3

1. 20
2. B
3. C
4. B
5. D
6. C
7. D

Problem Solving and Data Analysis Drill 4

1. C
2. 2 or 9
3. C
4. A
5. C
6. A
7. B
8. D
9. B
10. B

Problem Solving and Data Analysis Drill 5

1. C
2. D
3. B
4. 2.3 or 2.33
5. C
6. D
7. B

Problem Solving and Data Analysis Drill 6

1. A
2. B
3. C
4. A

Problem Solving and Data Analysis Drill 7

1. 2,250
2. A
3. D
4. B
5. B
6. A
7. C

Problem Solving and Data Analysis Drill 8

1. 21
2. 32
3. 19
4. 20
5. 9

PROBLEM SOLVING AND DATA ANALYSIS
ANSWERS AND EXPLANATIONS

Drill 1

1. **B**   Start by calculating the cost of the CFL in cents per hour by dividing the cost, $1.50 or 150 cents, by the life span, 10,000 hours. 150 cents ÷ 10,000 hours = 0.015. Do the same for the LED: 1,000 cents ÷ 25,000 hours = 0.04. Now make the ratio of CFL cost to LED cost: 0.015 to 0.04. This is not one of the choices, though, so you need to manipulate the ratio a bit. You can write ratios as fractions as well, so this one would be $\frac{0.015}{0.04}$, which equals 0.375. Check the answer choices to see which one also equals 0.375 when written as a fraction. Choice (B) does, so it is correct. Another approach could be to multiply the ratio of 0.015 to 0.04 by 1,000 to get rid of the decimal. The new ratio is 15 to 40, which is divisible by 5, simplifying to 3 to 8.

2. **C**   The large shirts need a larger image, so the correct answer must be greater than 100%. Eliminate (A). Now, Plug In the Answers, starting with (B). If the original height of 8 inches is printed out at 107.5%, the result will be 8 × 1.075 = 8.6. This is not the required height of 9, so eliminate (B) and try (C). Since 8 × 1.125 = 9, (C) has the correct height. There is no need to try the width, since it must work; (D) would make both dimensions too large.

3. **A**   Find the maximum heart rate first. The difference between 220 and 35 is 185. The aerobic rate is 75% of this number, so multiply $\frac{75}{100}$ by 185 to get 138.75. The fat-burning rate is 55% of 185, or $\frac{55}{100}$ (185) = 101.75. Now find the difference between these two heart rates: 138.75 – 101.75 = 37, which is (A).

4. **D**   Start by finding the total cost of the items purchased on Monday, then apply the discount to them all at once. Add all 5 items for a total of $14.96. The discount for these items was 25%, so Anya paid 75% of their total cost. $\frac{75}{100}$ ($14.96) = $11.22. Now do the same for Wednesday's items. The total is $10.50. The discount is 30%, so Anya pays 70%, and $\frac{70}{100}$($10.50) = $7.35. Add the totals for the two days and apply the tax all at once. $11.22 + $7.35 = $18.57. Multiply this by $\frac{6.25}{100}$ to get an additional $1.16 in tax (once you round down a bit), so the total bill is $18.57 + 1.16 = $19.73. This matches (D).

5. **22.5** Explanation: Ratios can be written as fractions, so start with the ratio of the densities of aluminum and lead. Find the numbers you need from the chart, 1.71 and 11.4 respectively, and write them as a fraction set equal to the given ratio of 3 over x, like this: $\dfrac{1.71}{11.4} = \dfrac{3}{x}$

Cross multiply to get $1.71x = 34.2$, then divide both sides by 1.71 to get $x = 20$. Now use this value in the second ratio: $\dfrac{osmium}{9.0} = \dfrac{20}{8}$

Cross multiply to get $8(osmium) = 180$, then divide both sides by 8 to get $osmium = 22.5$.

Drill 2

1. **200** The density of silver is given in "grams per cubic centimeter." Even if you don't remember that density = mass ÷ volume, you can figure out that you need to take the value in grams and divide it by the value in cubic centimeters. Plug In the values you know and solve for the volume.

$$10.5 = \dfrac{2{,}100 \text{ grams}}{\text{volume}}$$

Therefore, volume = 2,100 ÷ 10.5 = 200 cubic centimeters.

2. **A** The liter of water will be equivalent to 1,000 milliliters of water. Each of those milliliters is equivalent to one cubic centimeter, so the liter of water is equivalent to 1,000 cubic centimeters. Density is defined as the mass divided by the volume. Even if you forget that, you are asked for the density "in grams per cubic centimeter." This means that the 1,000 grams get divided by the 1,000 cubic centimeters, which equals 1.

3. **B** The question tells you that density is mass divided by volume, but you don't have the volume of the block. Volume = length × width × height, so the volume of the block is 10 × 5 × 5 or 250 cubic centimeters. Now Plug In what you know to find the density.

Density = $\dfrac{2{,}230 \text{ grams}}{250 \text{ cm}^3}$ = 8.92 grams per cubic centimeter.

4. **C** When asked for a specific amount, Plug In the Answers. Start with (B) and assume you have 3 matches. Together, the energy produced by the 3 matches equals 3 × 1,100 joules = 3,300 joules. Each joule equals 0.239 calories, so multiply 3,300 by 0.239 to get 788.7 calories for the 3 matches. This is not nearly enough, so eliminate (B) and the smaller answer in (A). Choice (B) produced an answer that was about a third of the required amount of 2,100 calories, so (C) is likely correct. Use the same steps to calculate that 8 matches would produce 8,800 joules or 2,103.2 calories, just slightly more than required. Therefore, (C) is the credited response.

5 **A** When asked for a specific amount, Plug In the Answers. Start with (B) and assume there are 630 layers. If each layer is 102 μm thick, then the total thickness is 630 × 102 = 64,260 μm. Since an inch equals 0.0254 meters, convert that to micrometers by multiplying by 1,000,000 to get 25,400 μm in one inch. The total thickness of 630 layers is much more than that, so (B) can be eliminated. Choices (C) and (D) are too big as well, so (A) is the credited response. 250 layers would have a thickness of about 25,500 μm, which is very close to the given value.

6. **B** Convert each of the dimensions given in millimeters to inches, using the conversion rate given, starting with 230 mm.

$$\frac{25.4 \text{ mm}}{1 \text{ inch}} = \frac{230 \text{ mm}}{x}$$

Cross-multiply and solve for x to find that 230 mm equals about 9 inches. Follow the same method to convert 170 mm to 6.7 inches and 200 mm to 7.9 inches. Since the question asks for an approximation and the answers are not too close, you don't have to get too specific with your decimals. Volume = length × width × height, so multiply the three dimensions in inches to get the volume in cubic inches. $9 \times 6.7 \times 7.9 = 476.37$, so (B) is the closest approximation.

7. **C** The question gives the distance travelled in 1 second in both yards and feet. Since the other information in the problem regards feet per mile, focus on the measurement in feet. There are 60 seconds in a minute, and in each the car travels 360 feet, so it travels 360 feet × 60 seconds = 21,600 feet in one minute. There are 60 minutes in an hour, so multiply by 60 again to find that it travels at 1,296,000 feet per hour. Now set up a proportion to find out how many miles that would be:

$$\frac{1 \text{ mile}}{5,280 \text{ feet}} = \frac{x}{1,296,000 \text{ feet}}$$

Cross multiply and solve for x to find that the car's speed is about 245 miles per hour.

8. **A** There are a few ways to solve this problem. You could calculate the time spent by one crew on one stop and multiply that by the number of stops and cars racing. If 6 men work for 15 seconds each on one pit stop, that stop totals 90 seconds of work time. Convert this to 1.5 minutes and multiply that by the 5 stops for that car to get 7.5 minutes. There are 33 cars, so 7.5 minutes × 33 cars = 247.5 minutes total time. The question asks for work *hours*, and there are 60 minutes in an hour, so divide 247.5 by 60 to get 4.125 hours of work time. You could also do the steps in a different order, converting 15 seconds to 0.25 minutes first, or finding the total number of crew members before calculating the time, but any method should end up at the same answer if you calculate carefully.

9. **B**   Start by calculating Superman's speed: Mach 4 = 4 × 340.29 = 1,361.16 meters per second. The distance he plans to run is in kilometers, so multiply 40,075 kilometers by 1,000 to get a total distance of 40,075,000 meters. Distance = rate × time, so 40,075,000 m = (1,361.16 m/s) × time. Solve this to get a time of 29,441.8 seconds. There are 60 seconds in a minute and 60 minutes in an hour, so one hour has 3,600 seconds. Set up a proportion to find out how many hours 29,441.8 seconds equals:

$$\frac{1\,\text{hour}}{3,600\,\text{seconds}} = \frac{x}{29,441.8\,\text{seconds}}$$

Cross multiply and solve for x to get 8.18 hours, which is closest to (B).

Drill 3

1. **20**   Even with 0 years of experience, an employee at Company X will make $20,000. No salaries are less than this, so it can be assumed that this is the minimum starting salary. Expressed in thousands of dollars, this will simply be 20, just as it's written on the graph.

2. **B**   Income is shown on the vertical axis of the graph, given in thousands of dollars. Look for the mark indicating 30, or $30,000, on this axis, then draw a horizontal line from the mark at 30 to the line of best fit. Once you hit it, draw a vertical line straight down to the horizontal axis. It should hit just to the right of the mark for 5 years of experience. Therefore, (B) must be correct, since it is just slightly more than 5. Draw your lines carefully, using your scantron sheet as a straightedge if necessary, to avoid trap answers like the close-but-not-quite (A).

3. **C**   The graph does not show employees with 35 years of experience. However, the line of best fit can be expected to continue to fit the data once it goes off the end of the chart. At the high end of the data shown, an employee is already making $65,000 with 25 years of experience. Therefore, with 10 more years of experience, that employee should be making more than $65,000. Eliminate (A) and (B). You can use some Ballparking now, if you continued the line of best fit off the right side of the graph, it would hit somewhere just above $80,000 at 35 years of experience. Choice (D) is much too large, so (C) must be the credited response. You can also solve for it more precisely by calculating the slope of the line of best fit. Since the starting salary is $20,000 and the salary for an employee with 10 years of experience is $38,000, we know that for every ten years of experience, the salary increases by $18,000. Add $18,000 to the $65,000 salary for an employee with 25 years of experience to get $83,000.

4 **B**   At 0 years of experience, an employee makes $20,000, and at 25 years of experience, an employee makes $65,000. That is an increase in income of $45,000 for an additional 25 years of experience. To find the increase in income *per year* of experience, divide $45,000 by 25 years to get $1,800 per year.

5. **D**   Pick a point on the line of best fit and Plug In the x- and y-values into the equation in each answer choice. The correct equation will be true with the given values. Avoid using the point at which x = 0, as the answer choices are usually written so that more than one will be true with those values. Try the point (25, $65,000) and check all 4 equations. Choice (D) is true, so it is the credited response. Be careful with (A) – Plugging In 25 for x gives you 65, but the graph shows incomes in the thousands, so you want 65,000, not 65.

6. **C** Check out each statement one at a time to see if it is supported by the graph. Choice (A) compares the potential energy, read on the vertical axis, of the "reactants" and "products." The section of the graph labeled "reactants" has a higher potential energy than the section labeled "products," so eliminate (A). Choice (B) refers to the "transition state," which is indicated as the rise in potential energy in the middle of the reaction. This means the reaction's potential energy is the highest in this state, not the lowest, so eliminate (B) as well. Choices (C) and (D) refer to the reaction with the catalyst, which the key indicates is the dashed line. This line definitely differs from the solid line graphing the potential energy without the catalyst, so (D) can be eliminated. Choice (C) is the credited response, as the potential energy is slightly lower during the transition state with the catalyst.

7. **D** Three of the four answer choices refer to $t = 0$, so look at that time on the graph. Time in years is on the horizontal axis, and $t = 0$ is all the way to the left of the graph. At this time, Annalee's investment was $25 and Bethany's investment was $50. Be sure to read the lines carefully, since they cross each other, to avoid mixing up the two amounts. Now check out the answers that refer to these values. Choice (B) can be eliminated, since it is not true. Choice (C) indicates that Annalee's investment has twice the value of Bethany's investment, but this is the opposite of what the graph shows, so eliminate (C). Choice (D) refers to goals, which were $250 for both women. Annalee's initial $25 investment is 10% of her $250 goal, and Bethany's initial $50 investment is 20% of her $250 goal. Therefore, (D) is the credited response. Choice (A) is false, since the curve of Annalee's investment goes up faster than that of Bethany's, increasing about $75 in the first 15 years while Bethany's only increases about $50.

Drill 4

1. **C** The description of vapor pressure in the question says that it starts increasing slowly at first, and it grows more rapidly as the temperature increases. This is describing an exponential relationship, not a linear one, so the graphs with straight lines can be eliminated. This means the correct answer must be (A) or (C). Now, look up the one specific value given in the question. At a temperature of 100° C, the vapor pressure should be about 760 mmHg. The graph in (A) shows a temperature of 760° C corresponding to a pressure of 100 mmHg. In other words, the numbers on the axes are reversed. Eliminate (A) and choose (C), which has the correct values where they belong.

2. **2 or 9** Find the performance scores on the vertical axis and look for the mark indicating a score of 4. Draw a horizontal line from this mark, using your scantron sheet as a straightedge if necessary, until you intersect the graph. If you draw the line all the way across, you will hit the graph twice. Pick either one of these points of intersection and drop a vertical line down from it to the horizontal axis, where anxiety levels are measured. One point of intersection gives an anxiety level of 2 and the other gives an anxiety level of 9. Either choice is correct.

3. **C** The highest level of performance is shown at the peak in the middle of the graph. This peak indicates a performance level of just over 10. Use your scantron sheet as a straightedge to see the corresponding anxiety level for a performance of just over 10. It should hit between the marks for 5 and 6, making (C) the credited response.

4. **A** Get out your scantron sheet for use as a straightedge and start drawing some lines. Start with (A) and an anxiety level of 2.5, read on the horizontal axis. Draw a vertical line up to the graph, then over to the vertical performance axis. You should hit this axis at about 5.5. Do the same for the anxiety level of 8.5, which should also hit at a performance score of 5.5. Since the two performance scores are the same, (A) is the credited response. Check out the other answer choices, just to be certain. None of them give the same performance score.

5. **C** It can be assumed that the ball left the player's hand at a time of 0. From there, it goes up and then comes back down. At a time of 0, the height of the ball is 4 feet above the ground.

6. **A** The maximum height of the ball on the graph is 13 feet. Height is the y-coordinate, so eliminate all answer choices except (A). Choice (D) is the trap – it switches the coordinates of the point in question.

7. **B** The ball is in the air for 3 seconds, so the time in question is the first third of that, or simply the first second. At a time of 0, the ball was at a height of 4 feet above the ground. After one second, the height had increased to 12 feet above the ground. This is a change in height of 8 feet. To find the average per second, you need to divide the distance in feet by the number of seconds. $8 \div 1 = 8$, so (B) is the credited response.

8. **D** The question describes an initial rapid increase in sales, so (A) can be eliminated. The increase in (C) is not steep enough initially, so it can be eliminated as well. Choice (B) shows a steep initial increase and the sharp drop in sales after the problem was discovered, but it doesn't show the sales numbers going back up. Therefore, (B) can also be eliminated, and (D) is the credited response.

9. **B** Following the description in the question, the reaction starts out with a constant level of potential energy before it increases. Therefore, (C) and (D) can be eliminated, as they feature a drop in potential energy, not an increase. The question also states that the "resulting products" have less potential energy than the "reactants" at the start of the reaction. This means that the end of the line should be lower than the start of the line, so (B) is the credited response.

10. **B** Use Process of Elimination and start with the easiest piece of information. In this case, the most straightforward information is that the curves get broader as the temperature increases. This means that the line for 900K should be wider than the one for 300K, which should have the skinniest peak. Eliminate (A) and (D). The question also states that as the temperature increases, the most probable speed increases. This means that the peak for 300K should be with the lower velocities on the left and the peak for 900K should be further to the right, where the higher velocities are. Eliminate (C) and choose (B).

Drill 5

1. **C** The chart shows the total number of jobs added in the state and the number added per 10,000 residents in that state. Use that information to set up a proportion that can be used to solve for the population of California. It should look like this:

    $$\frac{235}{10,000} = \frac{904,500}{population}$$

    Now, cross-multiply to get 235(*population*) = 10,000(904,500) = 9,045,000,000. Now divide both sides by 235 to get *population* = 38,489,361 or 38.5 million.

2. **D** Get the data you need from the chart, making sure to look at per capita numbers and not total jobs added. North Dakota's per capita growth was 945, and California's per capita growth was 235. The ratio is 945 to 235, or approximately 4 to 1, making (D) the correct answer.

3. **B** Add up all the values for the total jobs added in the five states. 65,450 + 98,600 + 794,250 + 146,325 + 904,500 = 2,009,125. Of this total, Utah accounts for 98,600 jobs, so the fraction is $\frac{98,600}{2,009,125}$. This doesn't simplify to any of the answers, but the decimal value is 0.049, which rounds to 0.05. Of the given fractions, (B) is the closest.

4. **2.3 or 2.33**
    The chart shows the number of jobs added in total and the number per 10,000 residents in that state. Use that information to set up a proportion that can be solved to find the population of Colorado. It should look like this:

    $$\frac{275}{10,000} = \frac{146,325}{population}$$

    Now, cross-multiply to get 275(*population*) = 10,000(146,325) = 1,463,250,000. Now divide both sides by 275 to get *population* = 5,320,909. Now do the same for Utah to get a population of 2,987,878. The difference between the two populations is 2,333,030, or 2.33 million. When rounding on grid-ins, make sure to do it at the last step to get an answer that is as accurate as possible.

5. **C** Use the data on the second table to figure out what portion of the new Texas jobs were in manufacturing jobs. The second chart tells you that 20,000 of every 150,000 new Texas jobs were in manufacturing. That part of the proportion would be $\frac{20,000}{150,000}$ or $\frac{2}{15}$. The total number of jobs created in Texas was 794,250, so $\frac{2}{15}$ of those are manufacturing jobs. Multiply $\frac{2}{15}$ by 794,250 to get 105,900 jobs.

6. **D** There are two parts to each correct answer, so there are two chances to use Process of Elimination. Start with the "No News Source" column in the answers. This corresponds to the column all the way to the right on the table. Since the number of people questioned in each group is the same, you just need to find the one with the largest number in this column. The 18- to 24-year-olds have the largest number and are therefore more likely to have no news source. From this, you can eliminate every choice but (D), which must be correct. Be careful not to mix up the two columns and choose (B) accidentally.

7. **B** To determine association of variables, you want to look for a pattern in the data. Look at the trends in each column to see if the numbers are increasing, decreasing, or show no patterns. For (A), the numbers in the Traditional Only column are kind of all over the place. There is no clear pattern and no association. For the Digital Only column, the numbers decrease with increasing age. This is a definite association, and an inverse one since the numbers go down as the age goes up. Check out (C) and (D), just to be sure. The No News Source numbers go down for the most part, but they increase slightly again with those 65 and over, so (B) is the best choice.

Drill 6

1. **A** Look at the row for 25- to 29-year-olds on the table. Those that got their news digitally are included in both the Digital Only column AND the Both Traditional and Digital column. Those numbers are 30 and 68, respectively, and those are in thousands, so 98,000 total people in this age group got their news digitally. That is about half of the total 200,000 surveyed, so about half of all 21 million 25- to 29-year-olds would get news digitally. Use Ballparking to see that (A) is the closest to half of 21 million. To calculate exactly, divide 98,000 by 200,000 to get the portion of the age group you want, then multiply that portion by the total 21 million people in the group. You get 10,290,000, which rounds to 10.3 million.

2. **B** In the initial survey, 78,000 out of 200,000 people in this age group reported getting their news from traditional media. If another 1,500 people were surveyed, the same portion is likely to also use only traditional media. Set up a proportion with the given numbers and solve it for the number of traditional-media-users in the new sample.

$$\frac{78,000}{200,000} = \frac{x}{1,500}$$

Cross-multiply to get $200,000x = 117,000,000$, then divide both sides to get $x = 585$.

3. **C** In the follow-up survey, 375 out of 1,000 people in this age group (37.5 percent) preferred print media for their news source. Since these people were selected randomly, their views should reflect the larger group of 50- to 64-year-olds in the initial survey. One could expect that the same percent of all the people in this age group would also prefer print media. Take 37.5 percent of that total, 88,000, to get 33,000 of the original group that prefer print media. Therefore, (C) is correct.

4. **A**   Start by eliminating any choice that is definitely contradicted by the data. Choice (B) is false, since California added the greatest total number of jobs. Choice (D) is false – California had the lowest per capita number. Between (A) and (C), (A) is a better conclusion since the question asks about per capita job growth, not the total number of new jobs. Eliminate (C) and choose (A).

Drill 7

1. **2,250**   The mode of a set of data is the number that appears on the list most frequently. To find the mode in grams of fruits and vegetables consumed, look along each horizontal line representing one value in grams and see which one has the most dots on it. For example, the line for 1,000 grams has 5 dots on it, one for each of the ages 9, 10, 12, 13, and 15. Use your scantron sheet as a straight-edge to check the values between thousands, as the ones off the gridlines are harder to see. For 2,250 grams, there are 6 dots, meaning 6 kids had that average consumption. No other value has more dots, so 2,250 is the mode.

2. **A**   For each of the given ages, look up the largest consumption value and the smallest one. The range will be the difference between the two values. For 5-year-olds, the largest value is 5,000 and the smallest is 1,500, so the range is 5,000 – 1,500 = 3,500. For 7-year-olds, the high value is the same as the one in (A), but the low value is greater, so the range will be smaller. Eliminate (B) and try (C): the values for 9-year-olds are 4,250 and 1,000, and the range is 3,250, so (A) is still the greatest. Eliminate (C) and move on to (D): for 12-year-olds the values are 3,500 and 250 for a range of 3,250. Eliminate (D) and choose (A).

3. **D**   Look up the values for 8-year-olds: they are 2,000, 2,250, 2,500, 3,000, 3,500, and 4,000. The median is the middle number in a set, but this set has an even number of data points. In this case, average the two middles ones (2,500 and 3,000) to get the median of 2,750 for the 8-year olds. The 13-year-olds are easier: the middle number of the 5 values is 2,000. Make sure you don't miss that outlier at the top. The difference between these two medians is 2,750 – 2,000 = 750, which is (D).

4. **B**   This is a question that might work for Ballparking, depending on the distribution of the data points. If any one of these age groups had a cluster of data points in the middle, with one outlier point far away from the rest, then that would be the likely answer. The 12-year-old group's values seem pretty evenly distributed and close together, so eliminate (C). The other three age groups have one outlier point, and these points are the ones listed in the answer choices. The high value for the 13-year-olds seems closer to the rest in that group than the lowest values in the 7- and 9-year-old groups, so that is not likely to be the answer. Eliminate (D) and try (A) and (B). Check out each answer choice by calculating the mean consumption for that group, then seeing how far away the given child is. For 7-year-olds, add up all 7 values (1,750, 2,750, 3,250, 3,750, 4,000, 4,500, and 5,000) to get a total of 25,000. Divide that by 7 to get an average of 3,571.4 grams daily for 7-year-olds. The child in (A) consumes 1,750 grams, so he is 1,821.4 away from his age group's average. Follow the same steps for 9-year-olds to find that their average is 2,857.1. The child in (B) consumes 1,000 grams, for a difference of 1,857.1. This is greater than the value for (A), so (B) is correct.

5. **B** This is a question that might work for Ballparking, depending on the distribution of the data points. If any one of these age groups has a symmetrical spread of data points, with one right near the middle, then that would be the likely answer. The 6-year-old group's values are not evenly distributed, and there is not one point right in the middle, so eliminate (A). The same is true of the 13-year-olds, so eliminate (C). The other two age groups are both symmetrically distributed about a central value. Check out each answer choice by calculating the mean consumption for that group, then seeing how close that is to the median value. For 10-year-olds, add up all 7 values (750, 1,000, 1,500, 2,000, 2,250, 2,750, and 3,500) to get a total of 13,750. Divide that by 7 to get an average of 1,964.3 grams daily for 10-year-olds. The median, or middle, value for 10-year-olds is 2,000, so the median and the mean differ by 35.7 grams. Follow the same steps for 15-year-olds to find that their average is 1,050 grams daily. The median value is 1,000, for a difference of 50 grams. The difference for the 15-year-olds is greater than the difference for the 10-year-olds. Therefore, (D) can be eliminated, and (B) is correct.

6. **A** Very carefully look up and add all the values for children over 11 years of age—that is, those 12-15 years old. There are 23 values on the list, so take your time and enter them slowly and carefully into your calculator. Once you get the sum, which is 34,500, you divide by the number of children, 23, to get the mean. 34,500 ÷ 23 = 1,500, which is (A). Another way to approach a tedious question like this would be to Ballpark. If you don't have time to add up all 23 numbers, look at what might be reasonable for the average or mean. All these values are between 250 and 3,500, and they are pretty evenly distributed in that range. Choices (C) and (D) seem much too high for the mean of the data for kids over 11, so guess (A) or (B) and keep moving.

7. **C** Start with Process of Elimination and get rid of answers that aren't true. Just by looking at the graph, choice (A) seems to be true, so hang on to it for now. Choice (B) is false, because the range for 8-year-olds (2,000) is equal to that of 13-year-olds. Eliminate (B). Choices (C) and (D) are both possible, but (D) is less likely to cause a problem with the conclusions. It is more likely that parents would accurately record fruit and vegetable intake than 5- and 6-year-olds would. Eliminate (D). Between (A) and (C), (C) is a better reflection of what one must do to draw conclusions about the general population. If the dietician truly wants to draw conclusions about children in the United States as a whole, she needs to study children from more than just one pediatrician's office. The best she can conclude with the information in (A) is that, at *this particular location*, children who are 13 to 15 eat fewer grams of fruits and vegetables than children who are 7 to 9 years old. Choice (C) is the best answer.

Drill 8

1. **21**   Let x equal the number of Dabcoins. Then write an inequality: $34x + \dfrac{5}{100}(34x) \leq 750$. Simplify to get $35.7x \leq 750$, and solve to get $x \leq 21.008$. Rounding to the nearest whole number, we get $x = 21$.

2. **32**   This question requires that the previous question be solved correctly. Since the number of Dabcoins is 21 on both days, we can write a new inequality: $21y + \dfrac{11.6}{100}(21y) \leq 750$. Simplify: $23.436y \leq 750$. Then solve: $y \leq 32.002$, so the nearest whole number is 32.

3. **19**   Since the data can be represented by a quadratic equation, the graph of the data will be a parabola. A parabola is symmetrical around its vertex, and day 4, the highest value, represents the vertex of this parabola. Therefore, the profits on day 3 will equal the profits on day 5, the profits on day 2 will equal the profits on day 6, and the profits on day 1 will equal the profits on day 7. The missing values are 7 and 12, so the sum is 19.

4. **20**   The part of the equation that is squared can never be negative; it must be 0 or positive. Therefore, at the vertex, which is day 4, $(p - a)$ will be 0, which means $c = 16$. Since $(p - a) = 0$ on day 4, $4 - a = 0$ and $a = 4$. Finally, $16 + 4 = 20$.

5. **9**   Plug the values generated from the previous question into the given equation: $N = -(9 - 4)^2 + 16$. $N = -9$, so the net loss is $9.

Chapter 9
Passport to
Advanced Math

Passport to Advanced Math Drill 1

For each question in this section, solve the problem and circle the letter of the answer that you think is the best of the choices given.

1. Polymerase chain reaction is a technique used to copy a portion of DNA. An enzyme is added to a sample of DNA. The resulting mixture is then subjected to a cycle of temperatures. During each cycle, each strand of DNA is copied, resulting in twice the number of strands in the mixture. Which of the following equations accurately represents the resulting number of strands in a sample with s initial strands after c temperature cycles?

   A) s^c
   B) $s(2^{c-1})$
   C) $s(2^c)$
   D) sc

2. What is the vertex of the parabola defined by the equation $y = x^2 + 4x - 12$?

   A) $(0, -12)$
   B) $(-6, 0)$
   C) $(-2, -16)$
   D) $(2, -12)$

3. At launch, a space shuttle achieves an acceleration of 3 g (where g = 9.8 m/s²). Which of the following functions, f, represents how far the space shuttle has traveled, in meters, after t seconds of accelerating at this rate?

   (Note: to find displacement, use the equation $s = \frac{1}{2}at^2$, where a is acceleration and t is time elapsed.)

   A) $f(t) = 3t$
   B) $f(t) = 29.4t^2$
   C) $f(t) = 14.7t^2$
   D) $f(t) = 9.8t^2$

4. The vertex form of a parabola's equation is $y = (x - h)^2 + k$, where point (h, k) is the vertex of the parabola. What is the vertex form of the parabola represented by the standard form equation $y = x^2 - 2x + 8$?

   A) $y = (x - 1)^2 + 7$
   B) $y = (x + 1)^2 + 11$
   C) $y = (x - 1)^2 + 8$
   D) $y = (x - 4)^2$

5. Bacteria grow asexually by a single bacterium dividing into two bacteria. These bacteria can themselves divide again and again. Assume a petri dish contains a single bacterium that divides exactly once per hour. Which of the following functions, $f(t)$, represents the number of bacteria in the petri dish after t hours?

A) $f(t) = 2t$

B) $f(t) = 2^t$

C) $f(t) = (t + 1)^2$

D) $f(t) = t^2$

6. Which of the following accurately expresses $3^{\frac{t}{2}+1} \cdot 5^{1-\frac{t}{2}}$ in the form $A \cdot B^t$?

A) $15 \cdot \left(\sqrt{\dfrac{3}{5}}\right)^t$

B) $15 \cdot \left(\dfrac{15}{4}\right)^t$

C) $\sqrt{\dfrac{3}{5}} \cdot 15^t$

D) $15 \cdot \left(\sqrt{15}\right)^t$

Passport to Advanced Math Drill 2

For each question in this section, solve the problem and circle the letter of the answer that you think is the best of the choices given.

1. Cube A has a volume of 3 ft³. Cube B has a volume of 9 ft³. Which of the following expresses the ratio of the side length of cube A to the side length of cube B?

   A) $3^{\frac{1}{2}} : 3^2$

   B) $3 : 3^{\frac{2}{3}}$

   C) $3^{\frac{1}{3}} : 3^{\frac{2}{3}}$

   D) $3^3 : 3^5$

2. $2x^3 + 4x^2 + 2x =$

   A) $2x(x-1)^2$
   B) $2(x+1)^3$
   C) $2x(x+1)^2$
   D) $x(x+2)^2$

3. $4x^2 + 12x + 14 =$

   A) $(2x+6)^2 - 18$
   B) $(2x+3)^2 + 5$
   C) $(4x+3)^2 + 5$
   D) $(2x-3)^2 + 5$

4. The standard form of the equation of a circle is $(x-h)^2 + (y-k)^2 = r^2$, where the center of the circle is at point (h, k) and the radius of the circle is r. What is the standard form of the equation of the circle defined by the equation $x^2 + y^2 - 6x + 8y = 0$?

   A) $(x-6)^2 + (y+8)^2 = 0$
   B) $(x+3)^2 + (y+4)^2 = 25$
   C) $(x-3)^2 + (y+4)^2 = 25$
   D) $(x-3)^2 + (y+4)^2 = 5$

5. $x^{\frac{2}{3}} + 8y^{\frac{5}{3}} =$

   A) $\sqrt[3]{x^2 + 8y^5}$

   B) $\sqrt[3]{x^2 + 512y^5}$

   C) $\sqrt[3]{x^2} + \sqrt[3]{512y^5}$

   D) $\sqrt[3]{x^2 + 2y^5}$

6. Which of the following expressions is NOT equal to $4x^2 - 32x + 64$?

   A) $4(x^2 - 8x + 16)$
   B) $(2x - 8)^2$
   C) $4(x + 4)(x - 4)$
   D) $4(x - 4)^2$

7. Which of the following is equivalent to $x^{24} - 18x^{12} + 82$?

   A) $(x^{12} - x^6\sqrt{18})^2 + 82$
   B) $x^{24} + 18x^{12} - 18x^{12} + 82$
   C) $(x^{12} - 9)^2 + 1$
   D) $(x^2 - 9)^{12} + 1$

8. Which of the following accurately rewrites the expression $\dfrac{5 \cdot 3^{2t-1}}{6 \cdot 2^{t+1}}$ in the form $A \cdot B^t$?

   A) $\dfrac{5}{6} \cdot \left(\dfrac{9}{2}\right)^t$

   B) $\dfrac{5}{4} \cdot \left(\dfrac{9}{2}\right)^t$

   C) $\dfrac{5}{36} \cdot \left(\dfrac{3}{2}\right)^t$

   D) $\dfrac{5}{36} \cdot \left(\dfrac{9}{2}\right)^t$

Passport to Advanced Math Drill 3

This section contains two types of questions. For multiple-choice questions, solve each problem and circle the letter of the answer that you think is the best of the choices given. For Student-Response questions, denoted by the grid-in icon, write your answer in the blank space provided.

 1. If $x^2 - 12x = -11$, and $x > 1$, then $x =$

3. $[x^3 - 2x + 3] + [2x^2 + 2x - 4] =$

A) $x^3 - 2x^2 - 4x + 7$
B) $x^3 + 2x^2 - 1$
C) $2x^5 + 2x^4 - 8x^3 + 10x^2 + 14x - 12$
D) $3x^2 - 1$

2. What is the positive difference between the roots of the equation $(x + 1)^2 = 16$?

A) 2
B) 5
C) 8
D) 16

4. For which value of c does the equation $2x^2 + c = 8x$ have exactly 1 value for x?

A) −8
B) 0
C) 2
D) 8

5. If $7x + 3 = -x^2$, then $x =$

A) $\dfrac{-7 \pm \sqrt{61}}{-2}$

B) $\dfrac{-7 \pm \sqrt{37}}{2}$

C) $\dfrac{-3 \pm \sqrt{-19}}{14}$

D) $\dfrac{3 \pm \sqrt{37}}{2}$

6. $(5z^8 - 2z^3 + z) - (-4z^4 + 2z^3 + z) =$

A) $5z^8 + 4z^4$

B) $5z^8 - 4z^4 + 2z$

C) $5z^8 - 4z^4 - 4z^3 + 2z$

D) $5z^8 + 4z^4 - 4z^3$

Passport to Advanced Math Drill 4

This section contains two types of questions. For multiple-choice questions, solve each problem and circle the letter of the answer that you think is the best of the choices given. For Student-Response questions, denoted by the grid-in icon, write your answer in the blank space provided.

1. If $\dfrac{x^2 + 3x - 10}{x - 2} = 3$, then $x =$

    A) -5

    B) -4

    C) -2

    D) 2

3. Which of the following is an actual solution to the equation $\sqrt{x + 7} - x = 1$?

    A) -3

    B) -2

    C) 2

    D) 3

2. If $\sqrt[3]{x + 3} = 2$, then $x =$

    A) 5

    B) 1

    C) -1

    D) -3

4. If $\dfrac{x^2 - x}{x + 4} = \dfrac{x + 24}{x + 4}$, then what is the value of x?

5. Which of the following most completely expresses the solution set of the equation $\dfrac{x+12}{x-3} = \dfrac{x^2}{x-3}$?

A) $x = -4$
B) $x = -4, 3$
C) $x = -3, 4$
D) $x = 4$

Passport to Advanced Math Drill 5

This section contains two types of questions. For multiple-choice questions, solve each problem and circle the letter of the answer that you think is the best of the choices given. For Student-Response questions, denoted by the grid-in icon, write your answer in the blank space provided.

1. If $x - y = 3$, then $x^2 - 2xy + y^2 =$

3. If $x^2 - y^2 = 18$, and $x + y = 3$, then $y - x =$
    A) -6
    B) -3
    C) 3
    D) 6

2. $(2x - 3)(x + 4) =$
    A) $2x^2 + 5x - 12$
    B) $2x^2 + x - 12$
    C) $2x^2 + 11x + 12$
    D) $3x + 1$

4. If $x + y = 7$ and $x^2 + y^2 = 42$, then $xy =$
    A) 49
    B) 7
    C) 3.5
    D) -7

5. Where defined, $\dfrac{36x^7 + 36x^4}{48x^6 + 24x^4} =$

A) $\dfrac{3x + 9}{10}$

B) $\dfrac{36x^{11}}{24\left(2 + x^{10}\right)}$

C) $\dfrac{3\left(x^3 + 1\right)}{2\left(2x^2 + 1\right)}$

D) $\dfrac{3\left(x^7 + x^4\right)}{2\left(2x^3 + x^2\right)^2}$

6. Which of the following graphs could be used to solve the system of equations $y = 2x + 3$ and $x^2 + y^2 = 9$?

A)

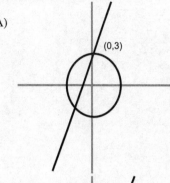

B)

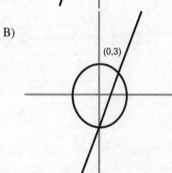

C)

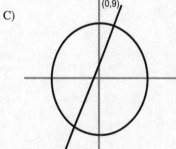

D)

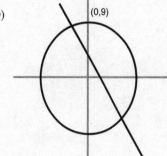

7. Where defined, $\dfrac{x^4 - 7x^3 + 21x^2 - 30x + 18}{x^2 - 4x + 6} =$

A) $x^2 - 3x + 3$
B) $x^2 - 11x + 17$
C) $x^4 - 7x^3 + 31.5$
D) $x^2 - 3x - 3$

8. When $x \neq -2$, $\dfrac{x^4 - 2x^3 - 8x^2 + 2x + 4}{x + 2} =$

A) $x^3 - 4x^2 + 2$
B) $x^3 - 8x + 5$
C) $x^3 - 2x^2 - 8x + 1$
D) $x^3 - 4x + 2$

9. If $x^2 - y^2 = 13$ and $x - y = 12$, then $x =$

A) $\dfrac{157}{24}$

B) $\dfrac{131}{12}$

C) $\dfrac{157}{12}$

D) $\dfrac{13}{12}$

Passport to Advanced Math Drill 6

For each question in this section, solve the problem and circle the letter of the answer that you think is the best of the choices given.

1. The standard form of a quadratic equation is $y = ax^2 + bx + c = 0$. Which of the following must be true of the graph of a quadratic equation when $a < 0$?

   A) The parabola graphed opens downwards.
   B) The parabola graphed opens upwards.
   C) There are two x-intercepts.
   D) The slope of the graph is undefined for all values of x.

2. The function $f(x)$ (not shown) has $(x + 2)$ as one of its factors. Which of the following must be true about the graph of $f(x)$?

   A) $f(x)$ includes the point $(2,0)$
   B) $f(x)$ includes the point $(0,2)$
   C) $f(x)$ includes the point $(2, 0)$
   D) $f(x)$ includes the point $(0, 2)$

3. The generic formula for determining the force, F, in pounds, exerted on an object by a wind can be found using the equation $F = A \ (0.00256 \ V^2) \ C_d$, where A is the area of the object, V is the windspeed in miles per hour, and C_d is the drag coefficient of the object. A boat has a square sail with a drag coefficient of 2. If the sides of the sail were halved, the velocity of the wind doubled, and the drag coefficient remained the same, then what would be the change in force on the sail?

   A) The resulting force would be one-quarter the original force.
   B) The resulting force would be one-half the original force.
   C) The resulting force would be equal to the original force.
   D) The resulting force would be double the original force.

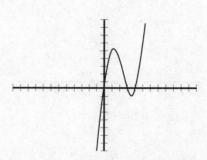

4. The graph of $f(x)$ is shown above. Which of the following accurately represents the function $f(x)$?

   A) $f(x) = x(x + 3)(x + 4)$
   B) $f(x) = (x - 3)(x - 4)$
   C) $f(x) = (x + 3)(x - 4)$
   D) $f(x) = x(x - 3)(x - 4)$

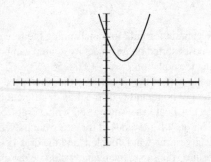

5. The equation $y = (x - 2)^2 + 3$ is shown in the graph above. Which of the following shows the graph of $y = 2(x - 2)^2 + 3$?

A)

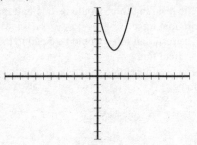

B)

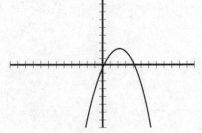

C)

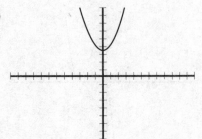

D)

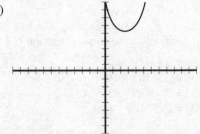

6. The graph of the function $f(x)$ contains the points $(-2, 0)$, $(\frac{5}{2}, 0)$, and $(3, 0)$. Which of the following could be f?

A) $f(x) = 2x^3 + 3x^2 - 17x + 30$
B) $f(x) = 2x^3 - 7x^2 - 7x + 30$
C) $f(x) = 2x^3 + 7x^2 - 7x - 30$
D) $f(x) = 2x^3 + 3x^2 - 17x - 30$

7. The value of the function f at every point x is the sum of the cube of x, x, and 3. Which of the following could be the graph of $f(x)$?

A)

B)

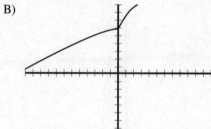

C)

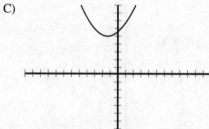

D)

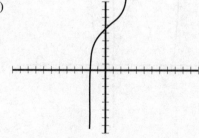

Passport to Advanced Math Drill 7

For each question in this section, solve the problem and circle the letter of the answer that you think is the best of the choices given.

1. If $f(x) = 0.5x^3 - 4x^2 + x - 2$, then $f(2) =$

    A) −12
    B) −8
    C) −4
    D) 16

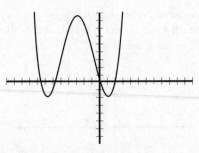

3. The graph of $f(x)$ is shown above. If $g(x) = -f(x) + 1$, then which of the following could be the graph of $g(x)$?

    A)
    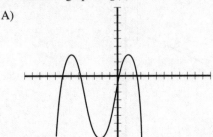

    B)
    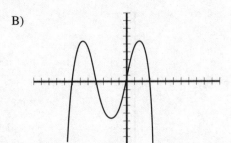

2. Jerry borrows x dollars against a line of credit and y dollars against his credit card. Jerry models his initial debt as follows:
    $x + y = 10{,}000$

    Jerry continues to use his line of credit and his credit card, paying back the debt when his finances allow. Six months later, Jerry's debt can be modeled as follows:
    $1.24x + 0.76y = 10{,}480$

    Which of the following must be true?

    A) The amount Jerry owes on his line of credit increased over the six month period.
    B) The amount Jerry owes on his credit card increased over the six month period.
    C) Initially, Jerry borrowed the same amount against his line of credit as he borrowed against his credit card.
    D) After six months Jerry owed more on his credit card than on his line of credit.

    C)
    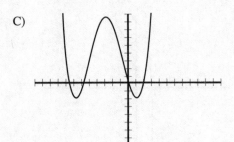

    D)
    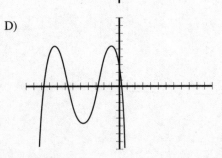

4. Kinetic energy, K, in Joules (J), can be found using the equation $K = \frac{1}{2}mv^2$, where m is the mass in kilograms (kg) and v is the velocity in meters per second (m/s). Which of the following equations represents the velocity of a 17 kg object with a kinetic energy of 19,763 J?

A) $v = \dfrac{2\sqrt{19{,}763}}{17}$

B) $v = \dfrac{\sqrt{2 \times 19{,}763}}{17}$

C) $v = \sqrt{\dfrac{2 \times 19{,}763}{17}}$

D) $v = \dfrac{\sqrt{17 \times 19{,}763}}{2}$

5. The value of $1 + \left(-\dfrac{3}{5}\right) + \left(-\dfrac{3}{5}\right)^2 + \left(-\dfrac{3}{5}\right)^3 + \left(-\dfrac{3}{5}\right)^4$ can be determined using the equation $s = \dfrac{1}{1 - \left(-\dfrac{3}{5}\right)}$, where s is the sum of the infinite geometric sequence with a common ratio less than 1. Which of the following equations could be used to determine the value of $1 + \dfrac{3}{4} + \dfrac{9}{16} + \dfrac{27}{64} + \dfrac{81}{256}$?

A) $s = \dfrac{1}{1 - \dfrac{1}{4}}$

B) $s = \dfrac{1}{1 - \dfrac{3}{4}}$

C) $s = \dfrac{1}{1 + \dfrac{3}{4}}$

D) $s = \dfrac{\dfrac{3}{4}}{1 - \dfrac{3}{4}}$

Chapter 10
Passport to Advanced Math
Answers and Explanations

ANSWER KEY

Passport to Advanced Math Drill 1

1. C
2. C
3. C
4. A
5. B
6. A

Passport to Advanced Math Drill 2

1. C
2. C
3. B
4. C
5. C
6. C
7. C
8. D

Passport to Advanced Math Drill 3

1. 11
2. C
3. B
4. D
5. B
6. D

Passport to Advanced Math Drill 4

1. C
2. A
3. C
4. 6
5. C

Passport to Advanced Math Drill 5

1. 9
2. A
3. A
4. C
5. C
6. A
7. A
8. A
9. A

Passport to Advanced Math Drill 6

1. A
2. C
3. C
4. D
5. A
6. B
7. D

Passport to Advanced Math Drill 7

1. A
2. A
3. B
4. C
5. B

PASSPORT TO ADVANCED MATH ANSWERS AND EXPLANATIONS

Drill 1

1. **C** Plug In! Because 2 is in a couple of the answer choices, avoid using that number. Instead, make $s = 4$ and $c = 3$. Each cycle doubles the number of strands in the mixture, so if the mixture starts with 4 strands, then after the first cycle there will be 8 strands. After the second cycle there will be 16 strands, and after the third 32. This is your target. Make $s = 4$ and $c = 3$ in each answer choice. Only (C) equals 32.

2. **C** There are a few ways to solve this problem. The easiest is to remember that, given a quadratic function in the form $y = a^2 + bx + c$, the x-value of the vertex is at $-\dfrac{b}{2a}$. In this case, $a = 1$ and $b = 4$, so the vertex will be at the point when $x = -2$. Only (C) fits.

   If you don't remember that formula, you can also find the vertex by remembering that a parabola is symmetrical. If you find the x-values for a given y-value, the midpoint between the x-values will be the same as the x-value at the vertex. The easiest point to find is when $y = 0$. You can factor $x^2 + 4x - 12 = 0$ as $(x + 6)(x - 2) = 0$. Therefore, $x = -6$ or 2; the midpoint is the average of the x-values: $\dfrac{-6+2}{2} = -2$. Only (C) has an x-coordinate of -2.

3. **C** An acceleration of 3 g is equal to $3 \times 9.8 = 29.4$ m/s^2. This is your "a" value for the displacement equation. The variable t represents time both in the function and the displacement equation. Therefore, the function should be $f(t) = \dfrac{1}{2}(29.4)(t^2)$, or $14.7t^2$. This matches (C).

4. **A** You are looking for an equation which is equivalent to the equation $y = x^2 - 2x + 8$, so if you Plug In a value for x into this equation, the answer will give you the same value for y. Make $x = 2$, and you find $y = 2^2 - 2(2) + 8 = 8$. That's your target. Make $x = 2$ and eliminate choices which do not equal 8. The only choice which works is (A).

   Algebraically, if a quadratic function is shown in the standard form $ax^2 + bx + c = 0$, then the vertex has an x value equal to $-\dfrac{b}{2a}$, so $x^2 - 2x + 8$ has a vertex of $-\dfrac{-2}{2(1)} = 1$. This means the vertex form of the equation should include $(x - 1)^2$ (note the vertex form is $(x - h)^2 + k$, so you need to *subtract* 1); eliminate (B) and (D). To find the y value of the vertex, plug $x = 1$ into the equation: $y = 1^2 - 2(1) + 8 = 7$, so the vertex form should be $y = (x - 1)^2 + 7$, (A).

5. **B** Plug In! In a case like this, where the growth is exponential, it's best to start at $t = 0$ and determine the first few values of $f(t)$ one at a time. When $t = 0$, you're at the start of the experiment, so there's only 1 bacterium in the petri dish. Choice (A) equals 0 when $t = 0$, so eliminate it. At $t = 1$, the bacterium has split into 2 bacteria, so $f(1) = 2$. Out of the remaining choices, only (B) equals 2 when $t = 1$.

6. **A** Remember your MADSPM exponent rules: you Add exponents when you're Multiplying, and you Subtract exponents when you're Dividing. In addition, when everything is multiplied together, you can gather the terms in one fraction. Therefore, you can rewrite the expression as follows:

$$3^{\frac{t}{2}+1} \cdot 5^{1-\frac{t}{2}} = 3^{\frac{t}{2}} \cdot 3 \cdot \frac{5}{5^{\frac{t}{2}}} = \frac{3^{\frac{t}{2}} \cdot 3 \cdot 5}{5^{\frac{t}{2}}}$$

To simplify the fractions in the exponents, rewrite using parentheses:

$$\frac{3^{\frac{t}{2}} \cdot 3 \cdot 5}{5^{\frac{t}{2}}} = \frac{\left(3^{\frac{1}{2}}\right)^{t} \cdot 3 \cdot 5}{\left(5^{\frac{1}{2}}\right)^{t}}$$

Rewrite the exponent of $\frac{1}{2}$ as a square root, and combine the terms with no exponent and the terms to the exponent of t:

$$\frac{\left(3^{\frac{1}{2}}\right)^{t} \cdot 3 \cdot 5}{\left(5^{\frac{1}{2}}\right)^{t}} = 3 \cdot 5 \cdot \frac{\left(\sqrt{3}\right)^{t}}{\left(\sqrt{5}\right)^{t}} = 15 \cdot \left(\sqrt{\frac{3}{5}}\right)^{t}$$

This is (A).

Drill 2

1. **C** The relationship between volume and side length in a cube is given by the equation $V = s^3$. If Cube A has a volume of 3, then $3 = s^3$. If you take the cube root of each side, then you find that the side of Cube A is $\sqrt[3]{3}$. Similarly, the side of cube B is $\sqrt[3]{9}$. The ratio of side lengths is therefore $\sqrt[3]{3} : \sqrt[3]{9}$. However, the answer choices have fractional exponents. The cube root of a number is the same as that number to the power of $\frac{1}{3}$. So, you can rewrite $\sqrt[3]{3} : \sqrt[3]{9}$ as $3^{\frac{1}{3}} : 9^{\frac{1}{3}}$. Closer, but you still need to get rid of that 9. 9 is equal to 3^2, so you can substitute that into your ratio to get $3^{\frac{1}{3}} : \left(3^2\right)^{\frac{1}{3}}$. The exponents rules tell you to multiply exponents when there are parentheses; doing so gives you a ratio of $3^{\frac{1}{3}} : 3^{\frac{2}{3}}$, which is (C).

2. **C** One approach is to Plug In! Make $x = 3$: $2(3^3) + 4(3^2) + 2(3) = 2(27) + 4(9) + 6 = 54 + 36 + 6 = 96$. This is your target. Make $x = 3$ in each answer choice and eliminate any choice which doesn't equal 96. The only choice which works is (C).

Another approach is to factor. All the terms are divisible by $2x$, so you can factor that out, and you get $2x(x^2 + 2x + 1)$. The quadratic expression in the parenthesis is the common quadratic $x^2 + 2xy + y^2 = (x + y)^2$, so you can factor the quadratic expression: $2x(x + 1)^2$.

3. **B** All of the answer choices are created by completing the square. You can tell because each answer choice has a binomial squared. In this case, because the coefficient with x^2 is not 1, completing the square will be a pain. Instead, Plug In. Make $x = 2$. This makes the original expression $4(2)^2 + 12(2) + 14 = 16 + 24 + 14 = 54$. This is your target. Make $x = 2$ in each answer choice and eliminate what doesn't equal 54. Only (B) works.

4. **C** Start by rewriting the equation with the x terms and y terms listed together:
$x^2 - 6x + y^2 + 8y = 0$
Next, to get the equation into standard form, you want to complete the square. Start with the x terms. Take half of the coefficient on the x (–6), square it, and add that to both sides. Half of –6 is 3, and 3^2 is 9, so add 9 to both sides of the equation:
$x^2 - 6x + 9 + y^2 + 8y = 9$
Now $x^2 - 6x + 9$ is a perfect square; it factors into $(x - 3)^2$, so you can rewrite the equation:
$(x - 3)^2 + y^2 + 8y = 9$
You can do the same to the y terms. Half of 8 is 4, and $4^2 = 16$, so add 16 to both sides of the equation:
$(x - 3)^2 + y^2 + 8y + 16 = 9 + 16$
Now $y^2 + 8y + 16$ is a perfect square; it factors into $(x + 4)^2$, so you can rewrite the equation again:
$(x - 3)^2 + (y + 4)^2 = 25$
That matches (D). Note you do not need to take the square root of 25; that would change the value of the equation. Instead, the radius is left squared.

5. **C** The easiest way to approach this problem is to Plug In. Exponents with a denominator of 3 are the same as cube roots, so pick numbers which are easy to take the cube root of. Make $x = 27$ and $y = 8$:
$$27^{\frac{2}{3}} + 8(8)^{\frac{5}{3}} = \left(\sqrt[3]{27}\right)^2 + 8\left(\sqrt[3]{8}\right)^5 = 3^2 + 8\left(2^5\right) = 9 + 256 = 265$$

265 is your target. Next. Make $x = 27$ and $y = 8$ in your answers. The only answer which works is (C). Alternatively, you may remember your rules with regards to radicals: you can combine with addition and subtraction only if the stuff within the radical is the same. In this case, the first term will have an x in the radical, the second term a y. The radicals aren't the same, so they can't be combined. The only choice which doesn't combine the radicals is (C).

6. **C** Plug in! Make $x = 2$. $4(2^2) - 32(2) + 64 = 16$. This is your target. Make $x = 2$ in each answer choice and look for the choice that does NOT equal 16. Choice (C) is your answer; it equals –48 when $x = 2$.

7. **C** One approach to this question is to Plug In. Make $x = 2$: $2^{24} - 18(2^{12}) + 82 = 16{,}703{,}570$. This is your target. Make $x = 2$ in each answer choice and eliminate what doesn't equal $16{,}703{,}570$:

A) $(2^{12} - (2)^6 \sqrt{18})^2 + 82 = 14{,}626{,}660.4$
B) $2^{24} + 18(2)^{12} - 18(2)^{12} + 82 = 16{,}777{,}134$
C) $(2^{12} - 9)^2 + 1 = 16{,}703{,}570$
D) $(2^2 - 9)^{12} + 1 = 244{,}140{,}626$

Only (C) works.

Another approach is to take each answer choice and expand it out. Choice (B) is the most easily eliminated, as $18x^{12} - 18x^{12} = 0$, leaving you with $x^{24} + 82$, which won't equal $x^{24} - 18x^{12} + 82$. Choices (A) and (C) are more easily evaluated if you remember the common quadratic $(x - y)^2 = x^2 - 2xy + y^2$. Choice (A) therefore expands to $x^{24} - 2x^{18} \sqrt{18} + 18x^{12} + 82$; not what you want. Choice (C) expands to $x^{24} - 18x^{12} + 81 + 1$, or $x^{24} - 18x^{12} + 82$. Choose (C).

Choice (D) is nasty: $(x^2 - 9)^{12}$ is the same as $(x^2 - 9)(x^2 - 9)(x^2 - 9)(x^2 - 9)(x^2 - 9)(x^2 - 9)(x^2 - 9)$ $(x^2 - 9)(x^2 - 9)(x^2 - 9)(x^2 - 9)(x^2 - 9)$, which expands out to 13 separate terms. Definitely not what we're looking for.

Finally, you can try factoring the original expression. The trick here is recognizing that $x^{24} - 18x^{12} + 82$ is almost $x^{24} - 18x^{12} + 81$, which, as discussed before, is $(x^{12} - 9)^2$. Therefore, you're looking for $(x^{12} - 9)^2 + 1$, which is (C).

8. **D** To put the expression in the form $A \cdot B^t$ you need to separate the t exponents from the rest of the expression. To do so, remember your MADSPM exponent rules. When you divide, you subtract exponents, so the expression 3^{2t-1} in the numerator is the equivalent of $\dfrac{3^{2t}}{3}$. You multiply exponents when you have parentheses, and you want to isolate the t as the only exponent in the expression to get to $A \cdot B^t$ form. Therefore, you can rewrite 3^{2t} as $(3^2)^t$, or 9^t. Therefore, $3^{2t-1} = \dfrac{9^t}{3}$. Similarly, in the denominator, $2^{t+1} = 2^t + 2$.

With these factors in mind, we can turn to the original expression. Use the above equations and substitute in to the expression:

$$\frac{5 \cdot 3^{2t-1}}{6 \cdot 2^{t+1}} = \frac{5 \cdot \dfrac{9^t}{3}}{6 \cdot 2^t \cdot 2}$$

Move the 3 in the denominator of $\dfrac{9^t}{3}$ to the denominator of the primary fraction and rearrange the terms so the terms to the power of t are to the right of the terms that are to no power:

$$\frac{5 \cdot \dfrac{9^t}{3}}{6 \cdot 2^t \cdot 2} = \frac{5 \cdot 9^t}{2 \cdot 3 \cdot 6 \cdot 2^t}$$

Finally, multiply terms to no power together and rewrite everything as the product of two fractions:

$$\frac{5 \cdot 9^t}{2 \cdot 3 \cdot 6 \cdot 2^t} = \frac{5 \cdot 9^t}{36 \cdot 2^t} = \frac{5}{36} \cdot \left(\frac{9}{2}\right)^t$$

This is (D).

Drill 3

1. **11** The given equation is a quadratic. Start by setting the quadratic equal to 0: $x^2 - 12x + 11 = 0$. Next, factor the quadratic. 11 is prime; it only has integer factors 1 and 11. Those equal to 12, so you can factor this quadratic to $(x - 11)(x - 1) = 0$. This means that $x = 11$ or $x = 1$. However, the question indicated that $x > 1$, so the only possible value of x is 11.

2. **C** There are a few ways to approach this question. One way is to manipulate the quadratic equation into the form $ax^2 + bx + c = 0$ then factor or use the quadratic formula to solve. However, an easier way is to begin by taking the square root of both sides:
$$\sqrt{(x+1)^2} = \sqrt{16}$$
$$x + 1 = \pm 4$$
That means the two roots are when $x + 1 = 4$ and $x + 1 = -4$. Solving these two equations, you find that the roots are at $x = 3, -5$. The difference between the roots is therefore $3 - (-5) = 8$, (C).

3. **B** One approach to this question is to Plug In. Make $x = 2$. The question then becomes $[2^3 - 2(2) + 3] + [2(2^2) + 2(2) - 4] = [8 - 4 + 3] + [8 + 4 - 4] = 7 + 8 = 15$. That is your target. Make $x = 2$ in each answer choice and look for the choice which equals 15.
You can also add the terms together. Addition can be done in any order, so it's best to start by rewriting the terms in order from greatest to least degree:
$x^3 + 2x^2 - 2x + 2x + 3 - 4$
Then combine like terms:
$x^3 + 2x^2 + 0x - 1$
Remove the $0x$ term, and you get $x^3 + 2x^2 - 1$, which is (B).

4. **D** The first step is to recognize that the equation is a quadratic function. As with all quadratic equations, set the equation equal to 0:
$$\begin{array}{r} 2x^2 + c = 8x \\ \underline{-8x \quad -8x} \\ 2x^2 - 8x + c = 0 \end{array}$$
Now, there are a few ways you can approach the problem at this point. First, you can Plug In the Answers. The question wants the value of c, so start by testing (C) and making $c = 2$:
$2x^2 - 8x + 2 = 0$
Now, solve the quadratic and determine whether there's only one value of x. If you try to factor, you'll find that the quadratic doesn't break into nice binomials; this is probably not the answer, so test another answer. Try (D), $c = 8$:
$2x^2 - 8x + 8 = 0$
Factor out a 2 then factor:
$2(x^2 - 4x + 4) = 0$
$2(x - 2)(x - 2) = 0$

$x - 2 = 0$, so $x = 2$

There's only one value for x, so (D) is the answer.

Alternatively, you can use the discriminant. In a quadratic function, the discriminant is $b^2 - 4ac$, when the quadratic is in the form $ax^2 + bx + c = 0$. A quadratic will have exactly one value of x when the discriminant is equal to 0.

Using the equation given, you can put in the values of a and b and solve for c:

$(-8)2 - 4(2)(c) = 0$

$64 - 8c = 0$

$-8c = -64$

$c = 8$

This is (D).

5. **B** To solve this quadratic equation, first set the equation equal to zero by adding x^2 to both sides; you get $x^2 + 7x + 3 = 0$. This won't factor nicely; 3 only has integer factors 1 and 3, which don't add up to 7. Furthermore, the answer choices give away that the result isn't pretty. In this case, use the quadratic formula: $x = \dfrac{-b \pm \sqrt{b^2 - 4ac}}{2a}$, when the equation is in the form $ax^2 + bx + c$. In this case, $a = 1$, $b = 7$, and $c = 3$. Plug in these values and solve:

$$x = \frac{-7 \pm \sqrt{7^2 - 4(1)(3)}}{2(1)}$$

$$x = \frac{-7 \pm \sqrt{49 - 12}}{2}$$

$$x = \frac{-7 \pm \sqrt{37}}{2}$$

This is (B).

6. **D** Start by distributing the negative in the second set of parentheses by switching all the "+" signs to "−" signs and vice versa:

$(5z^8 - 2z^3 + z) - (-4z^4 + 2z^3 + z) = (5z^8 - 2z^3 + z) + (+ 4z^4 - 2z^3 - z) =$

Next, list the terms in order of greatest to least degree:

$5z^8 + 4z^4 - 2z^3 - 2z^3 + z - z$

Combine like terms:

$5z^8 + 4z^4 - 4z^3$

This is (D).

Drill 4

1.　**C**　Factor the numerator of the fraction. You want two numbers which are factors of 10 and have a difference of 3. 2 and 5 work. Because the b term ($3x$) is positive, make the larger factor positive:

$$\frac{(x+5)(x-2)}{x-2} = 3$$

You can then cancel ($x-2$) in the numerator and denominator, so you're left with $x + 5 = 3$. Subtract 5 from both sides and you find that $x = -2$, which is (C).

Note that you can eliminate (D) immediately, as you cannot have a value of x which would cause the denominator of a fraction to equal 0.

2.　**A**　To clear a cube root, cube both sides of the equation:

$$\left(\sqrt[3]{x+3}\right)^3 = 2^3$$

$x + 3 = 8$

Subtract 3 from both sides:

$x = 5$

This is (A).

3.　**C**　Plug In the Answers! Negative numbers are tricky to work with, so start with (C). Make $x = 2$ in the equation:

$\sqrt{2+7} - 2 = 1$

$\sqrt{9} - 2 = 1$

$3 - 2 = 1$

$1 = 1$

This works, so choose (C).

If you want to use algebra, here's how to go about this question. Start by adding x to both sides to isolate the radical:

$\sqrt{x+7} = x+1$

Square both sides to clear the radical. Don't forget to FOIL the right side of the equation:

$x + 7 = x^2 + 2x + 1$

Because you're solving a quadratic equation, set the equation equal to 0:

$0 = x^2 + x - 6$

Factor to find the values of x:

$0 = (x + 3)(x - 2)$

$x = -3, 2$

Because your original equation contains a radical (and you're stuck between two answers), you need to check for extraneous solutions. You saw what happens when you plug $x = 2$ into the equation; see what happens when $x = -3$:

$\sqrt{-3+7} - (-3) = 1$

$2 + 3 = 1$

$5 = 1$ (?!?)

This obviously isn't true; $x = -3$ is an extraneous solution to this equation.

4. **6** Start by multiplying both sides by $x + 4$ to clear the fractions. You're left with $x^2 - x = x + 24$. This is a quadratic, so set it equal to 0. This results in the equation $x^2 - 2x - 24 = 0$. Factor this equation to solve. 24 has factors 4 and 6 that have a difference of 2, so you can factor this equation as $(x + 4)(x - 6) = 0$. This means that $x = -4, 6$. However, your original equation has $x + 4$ in the denominator of both fractions. If $x = -4$, then you are dividing by 0, which is not allowed. Therefore, the only actual solution to this equation is $x = 6$.

5. **C** Begin by multiplying both sides by $x - 3$ to clear the fraction:
$x + 12 = x^2$
Because this equation is a quadratic, set it equal to 0:
$x^2 - x - 12 = 0$
Factor. 12 has factors 3 and 4 which have a difference of 1, so the quadratic factors as follows:
$(x + 3)(x - 4) = 0$
This means that x equals -3 or 4. Because your initial equation had fractions with variables in the denominator, you need to check against the original. Neither -3 nor 4 make the denominators of the original fractions equal to 0, so both are actual values of x.

Drill 5

1. **9** There are a couple ways to approach this problem. One would be to Plug In. Use the first equation and make $x = 5$ and $y = 2$. Plug these values into the second equation and you get $5^2 - 2(5)(2) + 2^2 = 9$. Another approach is to recognize the common quadratic $(x - y)^2 = x^2 - 2xy + y^2$. Therefore, if $x - y = 3$, then $x^2 - 2xy + y^2 = (x - y)^2 = 3^2 = 9$.

2. **A** One approach is to use the FOIL technique: First, Outside, Inside, Last. In other words, you multiply the first terms, then the outside terms, then the inside terms, then the last terms, then add the products. Be careful with negatives:
$(2x)(x) = 2x^2$
$(2x)(4) = 8x$
$(-3)(x) = -3x$
$(-3)(4) = -12$
$2x^2 + 8x + (-3x) + (-12) = 2x^2 + 5x - 12$
This is (A).

Alternatively, you can Plug In. Make $x = 2$, so $(2(2) - 3)(2 + 4) = (1)(6) = 6$. This is your target. Make $x = 2$ in each answer choice. The only choice which equals 6 when $x = 2$ is (A).

3. **A**   The quadratic $x^2 - y^2$ factors into $(x + y)(x - y)$. You can substitute $x + y = 3$ in for the first factor, so you get $3(x - y) = 18$. Divide both sides by 3, and you find that $x - y = 6$. If you multiply both sides of this equation by –1, you find that $-x + y = -6$, which can be written as $y - x = -6$, which is (A).

4. **C**   This question is testing your knowledge of the common quadratic $(x + y)^2 = x^2 + 2xy + y^2$. The key to recognizing this is noticing that the question is asking for xy, which is half the middle term that results when you square the first equation. The xy term is also conveniently left out of the second equation; this is another clue that the common quadratic may be useful.

To solve this problem, square the first equation. You get $x^2 + 2xy + y^2 = 49$. Now you can stack this equation with the second equation and subtract to isolate the xy term:

$$\begin{array}{r} x^2 + 2xy + y^2 = 49 \\ - \left[x^2 + y^2 = 42 \right] \\ \hline 2xy = 7 \end{array}$$

To solve for xy, divide both sides of this equation by 2. You find that $xy = 3.5$, which is (C).

5. **C**   Start by factoring the numerator and denominator of the fraction. Look for the greatest factors of the terms; that way you determine the simplest form of the fraction. The greatest factor of $36x^7$ and $36x^4$ is $36x^4$, and the greatest factor of $48x^6$ and $24x^4$ is $24x^4$. You can use the Distributive Property to factor $36x^4$ from the numerator and $24x^4$ from the denominator:

$$\frac{36x^7 + 36x^4}{48x^6 + 24x^4} = \frac{36x^4 \left(x^3 + 1 \right)}{24x^4 \left(2x^2 + 1 \right)}$$

Now you can reduce the fraction. The parenthetical expressions cannot be reduced, but you can reduce the terms in front. $\dfrac{36x^4}{24x^4} = \dfrac{3}{2}$, so you can simplify $\dfrac{36x^4 \left(x^3 + 1 \right)}{24x^4 \left(2x^2 + 1 \right)}$ to $\dfrac{3 \left(x^3 + 1 \right)}{2 \left(2x^2 + 1 \right)}$, which is (C).

6. **A**   Start with the easiest piece of information first. You need the line $y = 2x + 3$ as part of your answer. This equation is already in $y = mx + b$ form, so you can look for the features of the line right from this equation. This line has a positive slope of 2, so the line should go from bottom-left to upper-right; eliminate (D). Next, the line has a y-intercept of 3, so it needs to cross the y-axis at $(0, 3)$; eliminate (B). The other equation, $x^2 + y^2 = 9$, describes a circle centered on the origin using the circle equation $x^2 + y^2 = r^2$, where r is the radius of the circle. In this case, $r^2 = 9$, so $r = 3$. Therefore, the point at the top of the circle should be 3 units from the origin; in other words, point $(0, 3)$, not $(0, 9)$. Eliminate (C) and choose (A). If you don't remember how this formula works, plug the given points into the equation and eliminate choices which are not true with those points.

7. **A** The easiest way to approach this problem is to Plug In. Make $x = 2$:

$$\frac{2^4 - 7(2)^3 + 21(2)^2 - 30(2) + 18}{2^2 - 4(2) + 6} = \frac{16 - 56 + 84 - 60 + 18}{4 - 8 + 6} = \frac{2}{2} = 1$$

1 is your target. Make $x = 2$ in your answers and eliminate choices which do not equal 1.

Only (A) works.

8. **A** Plug in! Make $x = 2$. The problem then becomes:

$$\frac{2^4 - 2(2)^3 - 8(2)^2 + 2(2) + 4}{2 + 2} = \frac{-24}{4} = -6$$

−6 is your target. Make x = 2 in each answer choice and eliminate any choice that doesn't equal −6. The only answer choice which equals −6 when x = 2 is (A).

9. **A** The first equation is the difference of squares. Factor the left side:

$(x + y)(x - y) = 13$

You can then substitute $x - y = 12$ for the right set of parentheses:

$(x + y)(12) = 13$

Divide both sides by 12:

$x + y = \dfrac{13}{12}$

You now have two linear equations. To isolate x, you can stack the two equations and add; the y terms will cancel:

$x - y = 12$

$+ \underline{x + y} = \dfrac{13}{12}$

$2x \quad = 12 + \dfrac{13}{12}$

To add 12 and $\dfrac{13}{12}$, make 12 into a fraction over 12; $12 = \dfrac{144}{12}$, so $12 + \dfrac{13}{12} = \dfrac{157}{12}$. Be careful! This is the value of $2x$; to find x, divide by 2. You find that $x = \dfrac{157}{24}$, (A).

Drill 6

1. **A**   Plug In! It's easiest to graph a quadratic if you make the equation as simple as possible. Make $a = -1$, $b = 0$, and $c = 0$, so the equation is simply $y = -x^2$. If you have a graphing calculator, you can graph it, or you can sketch out points on a rough xy coordinate plane. Either way, you end up with a graph like this:

    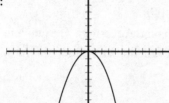

    This opens down, so keep (A) and eliminate (B). The parabola touches the x-axis only at point (0, 0), so (C) is also incorrect. Finally, an undefined slope is a vertical line; this graph isn't vertical at all points, so eliminate (D) and choose (A).

2. **C**   If $(x + 2)$ is one of the factors of $f(x)$, then $f(x) = 0$ when $(x + 2) = 0$. Solving $(x + 2) = 0$ for x shows you that $x = -2$. This means that, on the graph of $f(x)$, when $x = -2$, $y = 0$. Point $(-2, 0)$ therefore must be included in the graph of $f(x)$; this is (C).

3. **C**   Because you have a square sail and the sides of the square are changing, you can substitute s^2 for A in the original equation. Because everything in the equation is multiplied, you can rearrange the terms in the equation. Substituting $A = s^2$ and $C_d = 2$ into the equation and moving the variables to the front, the original force is as follows:

    $$F = s^2 \times V^2 \times 0.00256 \times 2$$

    The side of the sail is halved, so if the original side is s, the new side is $\dfrac{s}{2}$. Similarly, if the velocity is doubled and the original velocity was V, the new velocity is $2V$. The equation for the new force is as follows:

    $$F = \left(\frac{s}{2}\right)^2 \times (2V)^2 \times 0.00256 \times 2$$

    Square both terms:

    $$F = \frac{s^2}{4} \times 4V^2 \times 0.00256 \times 2$$

    The 4 coefficient on V cancels with the denominator of 4, so you're left with:

    $$F = s^2 \times V^2 \times 0.00256 \times 2$$

    This is what you started with, so the force on the sail hasn't changed.

4. **D** Every time the graph of $f(x)$ crosses the x-axis, there is a zero of the function at that point. The answer choices are in factored form, so you can simply look for the answer choices which have the zeroes you need. The function goes through the origin, point $(0,0)$. That means the function should include $(x + 0)$, or x, as a factor. Eliminate (B) and (C). The function also crosses the x-axis at $(3,0)$ and $(4,0)$. You would therefore have factors $(x - 3)$ and $(x - 4)$. The factors have a minus sign because when you plug in the values of x at the zeroes, the factor itself becomes zero. For instance, when $x = 3$, the factor $(x - 3)$ becomes $(3 - 3)$ or 0. Therefore, your answer is (D).

If you don't remember these rules, you can also Plug In on the question. The graph includes the points $(0,0)$, $(3,0)$, and $(4,0)$. Input those values for x in each function and eliminate the answer if the function does not equal 0 when x equals 0, 3, or 4.

5. **A** The given equation is in the vertex form of a quadratic: $y = a(x - h)^2 + k$. In this form, the vertex of the equation is at point (h, k). The graph you're looking for in the answers doesn't change the vertex of the original equation; eliminate (C) and (D), because they change the vertex. The variable a in the vertex form makes the graph become wider or narrower. If $a > 1$, the graph becomes narrow; choose (A). Choice (B) flipped the graph, which requires a negative value for a.

6. **B** Plug In the points given into the answers. Make $x = -2$ into each answer and eliminate the choices which do not equal 0:

A) $f(-2) = 2(-2)^3 + 3(-2)^2 - 17(-2) + 30 = 60$
B) $f(-2) = 2(-2)^3 - 7(-2)^2 - 7(-2) + 30 = 0$
C) $f(-2) = 2(-2)^3 + 7(-2)^2 - 7(-2) - 30 = -4$
D) $f(-2) = 2(-2)^3 + 3(-2)^2 - 17(-2) - 30 = 0$

Eliminate (A) and (C), because they do not equal 0 when $x = -2$. Try another point in the remaining answers. $\frac{5}{2}$ is unpleasant to deal with, so make $x = 3$ in (B) and (D):

B) $f(3) = 2(3)^3 - 7(3)^2 - 7(3) + 30 = 0$
D) $f(3) = 2(3)^3 + 3(3)^2 - 17(3) - 30 = 0$

Ugh. Gotta try $\frac{5}{2}$:

B) $f(\frac{5}{2}) = 2(\frac{5}{2})^3 - 7(\frac{5}{2})^2 - 7(\frac{5}{2}) + 30 = 0$

D) $f(\frac{5}{2}) = 2(\frac{5}{2})^3 + 3(\frac{5}{2})^2 - 17(\frac{5}{2}) - 30 = -22.5$

The answer is (B).

7. **D**   Start by determining the expression of $f(x)$. Translate English to math. "The value of the function f at every point x" is just a fancy way of saying "$f(x)$". The word "is" represents the equals sign. "The sum of" means to add the terms that follow. "The cube of x" is x^3, and "x and 3" are, well, x and 3. This therefore translates to $f(x) = x^3 + x + 3$.

Now, you need to determine what the graph is going to look like. The degree of this function is 3 because the highest exponent on the variable is 3. The variable with the degree of 3 has a coefficient of 1. This means the graph should start out on the bottom-left and go upward as it goes right. Eliminate (C), as it goes upward both to the left and to the right (this graph likely has an even degree). Next, Plug In using the function. It's probably easiest to start with $x = 0$, because $f(0) = 0^3 + 0 + 3 = 3$. Your graph needs point $(0,3)$, so eliminate (A). Comparing (B) and (D), the graphs most obviously differ in the negative range, so choose a negative number. Make $x = -2$, so $f(-2) = (-2)^3 + (-2) + 3 = -8 - 2 + 3 = -7$. Point $(-2, -7)$ should be on the graph. Choice (B) does not have a negative value for $f(-2)$, so eliminate it and choose (D).

Drill 7

1. **A**   To find the value of $f(2)$ when given the equation of $f(x)$, you need to make $x = 2$ every time it appears in the function:

$f(2) = 0.5(2^3) - 4(2^2) + 2 - 2$
$f(2) = 0.5(8) - 4(4) + 2 - 2$
$f(2) = 4 - 16 + 2 - 2$
$f(2) = -12$

This is (A).

2. **A**   Use the two equations provided, keeping in mind that x represents the initial amount on the line of credit and y the initial amount on the credit card. The initial equation shows that $x + y = 10,000$, so the debts of the line of credit and the credit card must add up to 10,000. The second equation has the x value multiplied by 1.24. This must mean that the amount owed on the line of credit, x, is 1.24 times greater than the initial amount on the line of credit. Therefore, the amount Jerry owes on the line of credit must have increased, so choose (A).

Choice (B) cannot be true by using similar logic. Initially, Jerry owed y dollars on his credit card. After six months, the value is $0.76y$. The amount owed on the credit card after six months is 0.76 times the initial amount. Because 0.76 is less than 1, the amount owed on the credit card decreased, not increased, over the six month period.

Choices (C) and (D) require solving the system of equations. On the test, save answers like these until you've considered all the other choices, as either one of the answers is definitely true (such as (A) here), every answer but one is false (which makes the remaining answer correct), or multiple choices require some work. We can use the work for (C) to work (D) here.

To solve the system of equations, you have a few options. Often it's best to stack the equation and add or subtract to cancel out a variable. Here, you can't simply stack; you have to multiply one equation first. Cancel out the x terms by multiplying the first equation by 1.24, then stacking and subtracting:

$1.24[x + y = 10,000] \rightarrow 1.24x + 1.24y = 12,400$
Now stack and subtract:
$1.24x + 1.24y = 12,400$
$- [1.24x + 0.76y = 10,480]$
$\qquad\quad 0.48y = 1,920$

Divide both sides by 0.48 and you find that $y = 4,000$. Substitute $y = 4,000$ into the equation $x + y = 10,000$ and you find that $x + 4,000 = 10,000$, or $x = 6,000$. Therefore, initially Jerry owed 6,000 on his line of credit and 4,000 on his credit card. This disproves (C). Six months later, he owes more on his line of credit and less on his credit card, so (D) is definitely false as well.

3. **B**   The transformations represented by $g(x) = -f(x) + 1$ are as follows. The negative sign in front of $f(x)$ means that $g(x)$ is flipped upside-down from $f(x)$; eliminate (C), as it's the same direction as $f(x)$. The "+ 1" moves the whole graph up one unit. The easiest point to look for is the y-intercept. The y-intercept of $f(x)$ is at 0; the graph of $g(x)$ therefore has a y-intercept of 1. Out of the remaining answers only (B) has a y-intercept of 1.

4. **C** Plug in the values you are given. The units let you know what value goes where: 17 kg gives you m, and 19,763 is K. This makes the equation the following:

$$19,763 = \frac{1}{2}(17)v^2$$

Now you want to isolate v. Start by multiplying both sides by 2 to clear the fraction:

$$2 \cdot 19,763 = 17v^2$$

Divide both sides by 17:

$$\frac{2 \cdot 19,763}{17} = v^2$$

Finally, take the square root of both sides. Be sure to take the square root of both the numerator and denominator of the fraction:

$$\sqrt{\frac{2 \cdot 19,763}{17}} = v$$

This is (C).

5. **B** There are a couple of ways to go about this question. One way is to grab your calculator and find the value of $1 + \frac{3}{4} + \frac{9}{16} + \frac{27}{64} + \frac{81}{256}$ (stopping there and not going on forever). You find that it equals 3.05. Because you stopped the sequence early (i.e. before the infinite term), you know the answer needs to be greater than 3.05. Choice (A) equals 1.33; you can eliminate that answer. Choice (B) equals 4. That's greater than 3.05 (actually, a lot greater); it may seem too big, but it's worth keeping for now. Choice (C) equals 0.57; definitely too small, so eliminate it. Choice (D) equals 3; that's close to 3.05, but you know the answer MUST be greater than 3.05, so (D) can't be the answer. Eliminate (D) and choose (B).

Another approach is to use the equation provided and see how it applies to the second scenario. The first scenario, $1 + \left(-\frac{3}{5}\right) + \left(-\frac{3}{5}\right)^2 + \left(-\frac{3}{5}\right)^3 + \left(-\frac{3}{5}\right)^4$, has the sum of a sequence in which the terms after the first are consecutive powers of $-\frac{3}{5}$. In the equation given we see the $-\frac{3}{5}$ in the denominator being subtracted from 1. In the new scenario, $1 + \frac{3}{4} + \frac{9}{16} + \frac{27}{64} + \frac{81}{256}$, $\frac{3}{4}$ is equal to $\left(\frac{3}{4}\right)^1$, $\frac{9}{16}$ is equal to $\left(\frac{3}{4}\right)^2$, and so on. Therefore, all the terms after the first are consecutive powers of $\frac{3}{4}$. Our equation to find the sum of this sequence should therefore be $s = \dfrac{1}{1 - \frac{3}{4}}$, which is (B).

Chapter 11
Additional Topics

Additional Topics Drill 1

This section contains two types of questions. For multiple-choice questions, solve each problem and circle the letter of the answer that you think is the best of the choices given. For Student-Response questions, denoted by the grid-in icon, write your answer in the blank space provided.

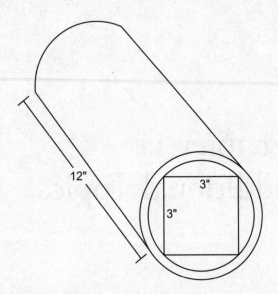

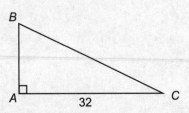

3. The figure above shows $\triangle ABC$. If $\angle ACB = 20°$, which of the following is closest to the length of $\overline{BC}$?

   A) 30
   B) 31
   C) 33
   D) 34

1. Roy has a block of wood in the shape of a rectangular solid with a width and height of 3 inches and a length of 12 inches. For the purpose of shipping, he places the block of wood in a cylindrical cardboard tube with an inside length of 12 inches, such that the four long edges of the block of wood touch the inside of the tube, as shown in the figure above. What is the inside volume, in cubic inches, of the tube before the block of wood is inserted? (Round your answer to the nearest cubic inch.)

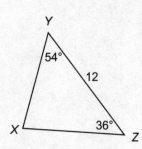

Note: Figure not drawn to scale.

2. A cylindrical water tank has a diameter of 20 meters and a height of 20 meters. If the tank currently holds 1600 cubic meters of water, what is the approximate depth of the water in the tank?

   A) 5 m
   B) 10 m
   C) 15 m
   D) 20 m

4. In $\triangle XYZ$ shown above, $\angle XYZ = 54°$, $\angle YZX = 36°$, and $\overline{YZ} = 12$. What is the length of $\overline{XY}$?

   A) 7.05
   B) 8.71
   C) 9.72
   D) 13.93

5. If $i^2 = -1$ and $(4 + 2i)(6 - ki) = 30$, what is the value of k ?

A) 3
B) 4
C) 6
D) 8

 6. What is the value of $(3 + 4i)(3 - 4i)$?

A) 1
B) 5
C) 9
D) 25

Additional Topics Drill 2

For each question in this section, solve the problem and circle the letter of the answer that you think is the best of the choices given.

1. If $0 < x < \dfrac{\pi}{2}$ and $\sin x = y$, what is the value of $\cos\left(\dfrac{\pi}{2} - x\right)$ in terms of y ?

    A) $-y$
    B) y
    C) y^2
    D) $1 - y^2$

2. Minor arc PQ in circle O below is 2π. If $\angle PQO$ is 45°, what is the area of the shaded region?

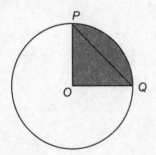

    A) 2π
    B) 4π
    C) 8π
    D) 16π

3. Points A and B lie on circle O as shown below. $\angle BOA$ is 45°. If the area of circle O is 64π, what is the length of minor arc AB?

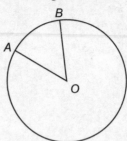

    A) 2π
    B) 4π
    C) 8π
    D) 16π

4. In the figure below, $\overline{QS}$ and $\overline{PT}$ are parallel. If $\overline{RS} = 8$, $\overline{PR} = 16$, and $\overline{PT} = 10$, what is the length of $\overline{QS}$?

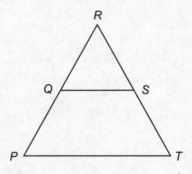

    A) 5
    B) 8
    C) 10
    D) 16

5. Right triangle *ABC*, shown below, has a base of 4 inches and a hypotenuse of 8 inches. If the height of the triangle is between 4 in and 8 in, what is the angle measure of ∠C?

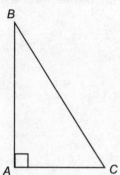

A) 30
B) 45
C) 60
D) 90

6. Lines *l* and *m*, shown below, are parallel. Lines *a* and *b* intersect as shown. If segment *DE* is 12 and *CE* is 6, which is the length of *AB* if *AC* is 18?

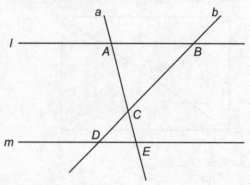

A) 9
B) 18
C) 24
D) 36

Additional Topics Drill 3

For each question in this section, solve the problem and circle the letter of the answer that you think is the best of the choices given.

1. In rectangle *PQRS*, shown below, the diagonal *PR* is 15 meters. If the sine of ∠SPR is 7/10, what is the value of *RS*?

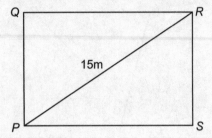

   A) 0.01
   B) 0.70
   C) 7.0
   D) 10.5

2. In the figure below, *ABC* is an isosceles triangle. The height of the triangle, *BD*, is 8 cm. *AB = BC* = 10. What is the value of tan *C*?

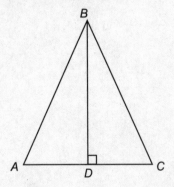

   A) 10/6
   B) 6/8
   C) 8/6
   D) 6/10

3. A child sits in a tree 9 meters off the ground. His line of sight to the ground forms a 36° angle with the tree. If he is looking at a cat on the ground, approximately how far is the cat from the base of the tree in feet?

   A) 6.5
   B) 11.0
   C) 13.8
   D) 15.0

4. In the *xy*-plane, a circle is centered on the origin and the point (p, q) lies on the circumference of the circle. What is the radius of the circle, in terms of *p* and *q* ?

   A) $p + q$
   B) $p - q$
   C) $p^2 + q^2$
   D) $\sqrt{p^2 + q^2}$

5. The diameter of the circle falls on the line $y = \frac{1}{2}x + 4$. If the radius of the circle is 4, which of the following could be the equation of the circle?

    A) $(x + 4)^2 + (y + 6)^2 = 4$
    B) $(x - 2)^2 + (y - 5)^2 = 16$
    C) $(x - 2)^2 + (y + 3)^2 = 4$
    D) $(x + 2)^2 + (y + 5)^2 = 16$

6. What is the radius of a circle represented by the equation $x^2 + y^2 - 6x + 4y = 12$?

    A) 5
    B) 4
    C) 3
    D) 2

Chapter 12
Additional Topics
Answers and
Explanations

ANSWER KEY

Additional Topics Drill 1

1. 170
2. A
3. D
4. A
5. A
6. D

Additional Topics Drill 2

1. B
2. B
3. A
4. A
5. C
6. D

Additional Topics Drill 3

1. D
2. C
3. A
4. D
5. B
6. A

ADDITIONAL TOPICS ANSWERS AND EXPLANATIONS

Drill 1

1. **170** Draw a diagonal line connecting opposite corners of the end of the rectangular solid. This diagonal divides the 3 × 3 square into a pair of 45°-45°-90° right triangles, so the diagonal is $3\sqrt{2}$. The diagonal is also the inside diameter of the tube, so the radius is $\dfrac{3\sqrt{2}}{2}$. The formula for the volume of a cylinder is $\pi r^2 h$, so the volume is $\pi \left(\dfrac{3\sqrt{2}}{2}\right)^2 (12) = 169.64$, which rounds up to 170.

2. **A** The height of the water tank doesn't matter in this problem. Simply use the formula for volume of a cylinder ($V = \pi r^2 h$) and plug in the information you have. It should look like this: $1600 = (3.14)(10^2)h$. When you solve for h, you get a number very close to 5. Since the question asks for the *approximate depth* of the water, (A) is the best answer.

3. **D** Use SOHCAHTOA to find the trig function you need. For $\angle ACB$, we have the adjacent side, and we need the hypotenuse, so $\cos 20° = \dfrac{32}{x}$. Rearrange this equation to get $x = \dfrac{32}{\cos(20°)}$, then use your calculator to find that x is just a tiny bit more than 34.

4. **A** Start by finding $\angle YXZ$. It's 90°! That makes things easier! To find $\overline{XY}$, use the sine function: $\sin 36° = \dfrac{XY}{12}$, therefore $(12)(\sin 36°) = 7.05$. Remember not to trust the figure if it's not to scale.

5. **A** Start by multiplying the equation out: $24 - 4ki + 12ki - = 30$. Since , $= -2k$, and $24 - 4ki + 12ki - (-2k) = 30$. The only way that the left side of the equation can equal 30 is if all the imaginary parts of the equation cancel out. Therefore, we can discard the remaining terms that contain i, leaving $24 + 2k = 30$. Solve this to get $k = 3$. Alternatively, if imaginary parts cancel out, we could set them equal to 0, so $-4ki + 12i = 0$, and $4k = 12$; therefore $k = 3$.

6. **D** Use FOIL to multiply the expression to get $9 + 12i - 12i - 16i^2$. Since $i^2 = -1$, and the two $12i$'s cancel out, you are left with $9+16$, which is 25.

Drill 2

1. **B**   The answer is (B). When two angles are complementary (meaning they add up to 90°), the sine of one is equal to the cosine of the other. Since $\frac{\pi}{2}$ radians = 90°, these two angles are complementary, and therefore the sine of x is equal to the cosine of $\left(\frac{\pi}{2} - x\right)$.

2. **B**   Because OP and OQ are radii, triangle POQ is isosceles. This means that if $\angle PQO$ is 45°, so is $\angle PQO$. That makes $\angle POQ$ 90°, so arc PQ is ¼ the circumference of the circle. That makes the circumference 8π. From there, you can find the radius of the circle, which is 4, making the area of the circle 16π. Since the shaded region of the circle is ¼ of the circle, the area of the shaded region is 4π.

3. **A**   You know the area is 64π, so you can solve for the radius, which is 8. That makes the circumference 16π. Since $\angle BOA$ is 45°, which is 1/8 of the 360°of a circle, the length of arc AB will be 1/8 of the circumference. 1/8 of 16π is 2π, (A).

4. **A**   Because QS and PT are parallel and both triangles share $\angle R$, you know the two triangles are similar. Therefore, the sides are proportional. Set up a proportion using similar sides: $\frac{8}{16} = \frac{x}{10}$. Solve for x and you get 5.

5. **C**   First label your figure. Since the missing side is between 4 and 8, you know $\angle C$ has to be larger than $\angle B$ but less than 90. Eliminate 90 and 30. Because the sides aren't equal, the angles will not be equal either, so you can eliminate (B). That leaves (C). You may also recognize that a right triangle with a hypotenuse twice that of one of its sides is a 30-60-90 triangle, with the 60° angle opposite the middle-length side.

6. **D** $\angle ABC$ is equal to $\angle CDE$ because they are formed by line b intersecting two parallel lines. Angles BAC and CED are equal for the same reason. The two opposite angles at point C are equal, so triangles CDE and ABC are similar. Set up a proportion: $\frac{12}{6} = \frac{x}{18}$. When you solve for x, you find that AB is 36.

Drill 3

1. **D**   If the sine of $\angle SPR$ is 7/10, that would mean the diagonal of the rectangle is 10. We know that it's 15, not 10, so we need to set up a proportion. Your proportion should look like this: $\frac{7}{10} = \frac{x}{15}$. When you solve for x, you get 10.5 meters.

2. **C**   The height of the isosceles triangle forms a right angle with the base. Because you know BD is 8 and BC is 10, you can either use the Pythagorean Theorem or Pythagorean triples to determine that CD is 6. Tan C is opposite/adjacent, which would be 8/6.

3. **A**   Draw a diagram. It should look something like this:

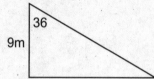

The distance between the cat and the tree is the base of triangle. Set up an equation: $\tan 36 = \frac{base}{9}$. When you solve for the base, you get approximately 6.5 meters.

4. **D**   The equation of a circle centered at the origin is $x^2 + y^2 = r^2$, where x and y are any ordered point in the circle (x, y), and r is the radius. To solve for r, all we need to do is take the square root of both sides: $\sqrt{x^2 + y^2} = \sqrt{r^2} = r$.

5. **B**   Because you know the radius is 4, you can use POE to get rid of (A) and (C). Then use the center points from the two remaining equations to see if they plug in to the original equation and give a true statement. When you plug in the point from (B), (2, 5), your equation is true. It is not true for (D).

6. **A**   In order to find the radius, you need to get the equation into the format of $(x - h)^2 + (y - k)^2 = r^2$. To do that, complete the square. First rearrange the equation so it looks like this: $x^2 - 6x +$_____$+ y^2 + 4y$ $+$_____ $= 12$. When you add the numbers to the left to complete the square, don't forget to add the same numbers to the right side. You'll get this: $x^2 - 6x + 9 + y^2 + 4y + 4 = 12 + 9 + 4$. When you factor the left and add up the right, you get $(x - 3)^2 + (y + 2)^2 = 25$. Based on the equation, you can then solve for the radius, which would be 5.

Part IV
Reading

What Can You Expect to See on the Reading Test?
13 Reading Drills
14 Reading Answers and Explanations

WHAT CAN YOU EXPECT TO SEE ON THE READING TEST?

One of the biggest changes to the SAT is that there are no more context-based Sentence Completion questions. Instead, every problem in this section is tied to one of five reading passages. (Well, six, if you account for one of those being a dual-passage set.) You may also have to take the entire section in one go, so whereas the test itself once split your work on passages across 20-25 minute chunks, you'll have to more carefully manage your timing if you choose to do all five of the Reading passages.

Moreover, if you're hoping to delve into excerpts from the latest vampire novel or the most recent stats on your favorite football hero, you may be disappointed. Instead, you'll see one U.S. or world literature passage, two history or social studies passages, and two science passages. Some of the passages—specifically one or two of the history or social studies passages, and one of the science passages—will contain charts or graphs. In other words, these can be challenging, dense passages with each of the passages being 500-750 words in length. Here are some fundamental tips to help you take advantage of the structure and nature of passage-based questions.

Staying Focused

Not surprisingly, one of the biggest complaints that students make about the Reading section is that staying focused on the passages is often difficult. Even if you enjoy reading, perusing a passage on the eating habits of Japanese mice or on the best way to translate the word "taste" from Farsi to English may cause your eyelids to begin to droop.

That said, your purpose when you read on the SAT is very different from your purpose when you read in school. When you read in school, you're hoping to learn something. You know that you may be tested on the information at some later date, and therefore you will need to remember something about what you're reading. When you read on the SAT, however, you're not trying to actually discover new information. You're unlikely, for example, to walk out of the SAT thinking, "Wow, I never knew that about phosphorescent fish!" Instead, you're merely reading so that you can answer questions about the passage, and since the SAT is an open-book test, you can always go back to the passage if you missed something. Therefore, rather than reading the whole passage before you start working the questions, try going straight to your questions and reading only what you need to read. That way, you're less likely to drift off mid-paragraph.

The Structure

Knowing how SAT Reading passages and questions are structured can help you understand how to approach the test as well. The SAT provides you with the following three key items that can help:

- **Line references.** About 80% of your SAT Reading questions will refer you to a specific line or set of lines. It's important to note, however, that you'll need to read more than just the lines referenced; to get a solid understanding of the context, read a window of about five lines above and five lines below each line reference.

- **Chronology.** While a few questions in each passage set will refer to the passage as a whole, the specific questions that follow will go in loose chronological order through the passage. Therefore, if you find the answer to question 6 in lines 20-25, and the answer to question 8 in lines 38-42, then you should find the answer to question 7 approximately somewhere in the middle—that is, somewhere between lines 25-38. Use chronology to answer questions that don't contain line references.

- **Lead words.** Lead words are words that are easy to find in the passage. These may be words that are italicized, in quotes, or have capital letters. If you're working a question that doesn't have a line reference, look for a lead word that you'll be able to easily spot in the passage.

The Approach

Once you've opened your test booklet and are looking at the Reading section, what should you do? As you work through the practice passages in the pages that follow, try out the approach below.

1. **Start with the easiest passage.** Not all passages are created equal. You may find it easier to focus on a prose fiction passage about a detective than on a science passage about causes of drought near the Colorado River, for example. Additionally, questions with line references that tell you exactly where to find the answer in the passage are often easier than those that simply refer to the passage in general, so a passage that includes many line reference questions may be easier than a passage that does not. Since you have a limited amount of time on the test, focus on the easier passages first so that you can improve your accuracy and thus your overall score. Rank your passages from easiest to hardest, and work them in that order.

2. **Read the blurb.** Once you've chosen a passage, start by reading the little italicized description at the beginning of the passage, as it will help you understand the main idea of the passage.

3. **Preview the questions.** If you examine the questions before you go to the passage, you'll get a better sense of the topic of the passage, and you'll be able to determine the order in which you'll work the questions. Put a star next to any questions that contain line references, and then go to the passage and mark the lines to which the questions refer. Circle any lead words that appear in the questions.

4. **Select and understand a question.** The first few questions in each question set will relate to the passage as a whole, while later questions will focus on specific parts of the passage. Start with the specific questions first, and save the general questions for later. Then, once you've chosen a question, take the time to actually understand what it's asking. SAT Reading questions are often not in question format. Instead, they often make statements such as, "The author's primary reason for mentioning the gadfly is to," and then the answer choices will follow. Make sure that you understand the question by turning it back into a question—that is, back into a sentence that actually ends with a question mark.

5. **Read what you need.** Many questions will refer you to a specific set of lines or to a particular paragraph, so you won't need to read the entire passage to answer those questions. If you read about five lines above and five lines below each line reference, you should have the information you need. Read carefully, however; you should be able to put your finger on the particular phrase, sentence, or set of lines that answers your question. If you save the general questions that relate to the passage as a whole for last, then by the time you begin those questions, you'll have an understanding of the passage even if you haven't read it from beginning to end.

6. **Predict the correct answer.** SAT test writers do their best to distract you by creating tempting but nevertheless wrong answers. However, if you know what you're looking for in advance, you're less likely to fall for a trap answer. Before you even glance at the answer choices, take the time to think about how you would answer each question in your own words based on the information in the passage.

7. **Use process of elimination.** Each answer has three incorrect answers, and only one correct answer, so it's much easier to find an incorrect answer than it is to find a correct answer. If you can eliminate the wrong answers, then whatever is left must be the correct answer. Physically cross off wrong answers. Incorrect answers frequently contain the following:
   - Information not mentioned in the passage
   - Extreme language that goes beyond what is stated in the passage
   - Half-right but half-wrong information

Look to eliminate these types of answers!

Chapter 13
Reading Drills

Reading Drill 1

For each question in this section, circle the letter of the best answer from among the choices given.

Questions 1-9 are based on the following passage.

This passage is adapted from Christine Amancoeur, The Rise of the Superpower States. (C) 1983 by Milleson Press.

NATO was formed in April 1949 because of a fear
by its original signatories—Belgium, Canada, Denmark,
France, Iceland, Italy, Luxembourg, the Netherlands,
Line Norway, Portugal, the United Kingdom, and the United
5 States—that the Soviet Union posed a major threat to
their security. Its central provision is Article 5, which
states: "The parties agree that an armed attack against
one or more of them in Europe or North America shall be
considered an attack against them all."

10 NATO is a grand alliance. It is, however, a grand
alliance different from earlier alliances. When grand
alliances were formed in the past—such as those that put
down Napoleon, Kaiser Wilhelm, and Adolph Hitler—they
were formed after an act of aggression occurred. The
15 purpose of NATO is twofold: deterrence and defense.
The very act of forming a peacetime alliance, it was
believed, would serve to deter aggression by the Soviet
Union. If deterrence failed, however, the alliance would be
politically united and militarily strong so as to protect its
20 members from a Soviet victory.

Certain factors underlay the formation of NATO.
These involved supremacy of the United States as
a nuclear power, the fear of Soviet policies, and the
economic conditions of the Europeans. First, in April 1949,
25 the United States had a monopoly of nuclear weapons.
The United States could carry those weapons to the
Soviet Union itself by relying on its air bases in Western
Europe and Africa. NATO members could believe that
the American nuclear forces offered a credible deterrent to
30 Soviet aggression.

Second, it seemed to NATO members that the Soviet
Union in particular and communism in general posed a
threat to Western security. The post-World War II period
was characterized by such apparent threats as a civil war
35 in Greece, communist takeover in France and Italy, a
Soviet-inspired communist takeover of Czechoslovakia in
1948, and a blockade of allied surface routes to Berlin in
1948.

Third, Western Europe was devastated by World War
40 II. It depended upon the United States for its economic
support. The Marshall Plan of 1947, in which the United
States committed nearly $15 billion of economic aid to its
Western European allies, was a reflection of that economic
bond.

45 In the more than 35 years since NATO came into
existence, there have been many changes in the conditions
underlying NATO and in the character of the alliance
itself. No longer does the United States possess a
monopoly of nuclear weapons, as it did until the 1960s.
50 During the Cuban missile crisis of 1962, the Soviet Union
had about seventy long-range missiles that took 10 hours
to fuel. This made Soviet missiles easily vulnerable to an
American attack before they could be launched. Even as
late as the Yom Kippur war of 1973, the United States had
55 a superiority of about 8 to 1 in nuclear warheads.

In addition, NATO's membership grew. Greece and
Turkey joined the alliance in 1952, and West Germany
entered in 1955. West German entrance into NATO was
the immediate cause of the establishment in 1955 of the
60 equivalent Soviet alliance defense organization—the
Warsaw Pact. In 1982, Spain became the sixteenth member
of NATO.

1. The primary purpose of the passage is to
   A) portray the Soviet Union as an aggressive force
      that could be controlled only by an alliance of
      world powers
   B) describe the influence the Marshall Plan of 1947
      had on the creation of NATO
   C) identify the conditions that led to the creation of
      NATO and outline the subsequent changes it has
      undergone
   D) question the necessity of the NATO alliance
      following the breakup of the Soviet Union

2. In line 15, the word "deterrence" refers to
   A) the discouragement of attack by other nations,
      especially the Soviet Union
   B) the strength of the NATO member nations with
      regard to the rest of Europe
   C) the possible aggressive behavior of the Soviet
      Union
   D) the high moral purpose of earlier alliances as
      opposed to the superficial purpose of NATO

3. The purpose of the second paragraph (lines 10-20) in relation to the rest of the passage is to

   A) introduce the factors underlying the formation of NATO
   B) highlight a factor distinguishing NATO from other pacts
   C) define the term "deterrence" relative to the functionality of NATO
   D) identify the aggressors prompting the formation of NATO

4. The author mentions Napoleon, Kaiser Wilhelm, and Adolph Hitler (line 13) in order to emphasize which point about the NATO alliance?

   A) It was specifically intended to stop the barbarism promoted by Adolph Hitler.
   B) It was a peacetime alliance established to deter future aggression.
   C) It was the first alliance in which both the United States and the United Kingdom were members.
   D) The military alliance was politically united and militarily strong.

5. In context, lines 21-38 suggest that the formation of NATO occurred for all of the following reasons EXCEPT

   A) democratic uprisings in France
   B) European need for monetary support
   C) apprehension about the spread of communism
   D) belief that weaker members of NATO could be defended by stronger members

6. The author uses the example of the Cuban missile crisis (lines 50-54) in order to establish that

   A) the United States' superiority in nuclear weaponry ended in the late 1960s
   B) Soviet advances in nuclear technology were considered a threat to NATO, but the United States' ingenuity saved the alliance
   C) while the United States no longer had a monopoly on nuclear weapons, it had a greater number of them than the Soviet Union
   D) the Cuban missile crisis marked the end of the United States' domination of world affairs

7. As used in line 55, "superiority" most nearly means

   A) more refined skill.
   B) arrogance.
   C) greater number.
   D) indifference

8. The Warsaw Pact is similar to NATO in that

   A) its formation was a peacetime reaction to a potential threat
   B) it was formed as a response to aggressive behavior on the part of many Western European nations
   C) Warsaw Pact member nations have a correspondingly strong commitment to democracy
   D) it too was created as a reaction to imperialistic maneuvering on the part of certain European nations

9. Which choice provides the best evidence for the answer to the previous question?

   A) Lines 16-17 ("The very act . . . Soviet Union")
   B) Lines 26-28 ("The United States . . . Africa")
   C) Lines 53-54 ("This made . . . launched")
   D) Lines 57-61 ("West German . . . Warsaw Pact")

Questions 10-19 are based on the following passage.

In 63 B.C., after losing an election for the Roman senate, the politician Catiline attempted, with the help of a band of co-conspirators, to take the office by force. When Cicero, the great Roman orator and philosopher who had defeated Catiline in election, heard of this plot, he arrested and put to death five of the conspirators. Catiline, however, had already fled. He escaped execution, but died in battle in Pistoia a month later. The first of the following passages is adapted from a speech by Catiline to his conspirators. The second is adapted from a speech against Catiline by Cicero to the Roman senate.

Passage 1

As I have, on many remarkable occasions, experienced your bravery and attachment to me, I have ventured to engage in a most important and glorious enterprise. I am
Line aware, too, that whatever advantages or evils affect you,
5 the same affect me; and to have the same desires and the same aversions is assuredly a firm bond of friendship.

My ardor for action is daily more and more excited when I consider what our future condition of life must be unless we assert our claims to liberty. For since the
10 government has fallen under the power and jurisdiction of a few, kings and princes have constantly been their tributaries; but all the rest of us have been regarded as a mere mob, without interest or authority. Hence all influence, power, honor, and wealth, are in their hands; to
15 us they have left only insults, dangers, persecutions, and poverty. To such indignities, O bravest of men, how long will you submit?

But success (I call gods and men to witness!) is in our own hands. Our years are fresh, our spirit is unbroken;
20 among our oppressors, on the contrary, through age and wealth a general debility has been produced. We have, therefore, only to make a beginning; the course of events will accomplish the rest.

Will you not, then, awake to action? Behold that liberty
25 for which you have so often wished, with wealth, honor, and glory, is set before your eyes. Let the enterprise itself, then, let the opportunity, let your property, your dangers, and the glorious spoils of war, animate you far more than my words. Use me either as your leader or your fellow
30 soldier; neither my heart nor my hand shall be wanting to you. These objects I hope to effect, in concert with you, in the character of consul*; unless, indeed, my expectation deceives me, and you prefer to be slaves rather than masters.

Passage 2

35 When, O Catiline, do you mean to cease abusing our patience? Do not the nightly guards placed on Palatine Hill— does not the alarm of the people, and the union of all good men—does not the precaution taken of assembling the senate in this most defensible place—do
40 not the looks and countenances of this venerable body here present, have any effect upon you? Do you not see that your conspiracy is already arrested and rendered powerless by the knowledge which everyone here possesses of it?

45 You ought, O Catiline, long ago to have been led to execution by command of the consul. You are summoning to destruction and devastation the temples of the immortal gods, the houses of the city, the lives of all the citizens; in short, all Italy. Wherefore, since I do not yet venture
50 to do that which is the best thing, and which belongs to my office and to the discipline of our ancestors, I will do that which is more merciful if we regard its rigor, and more expedient for the state. For if I order you to be put to death, the rest of the conspirators will still remain in the
55 republic; if, as I have long been exhorting you, you depart, your companions, will be drawn off from the city too. Do you ask me, Are you to go into banishment? I do not order it; but if you consult me, I advise it.

For what is there, O Catiline, that can now afford you
60 any pleasure in this city? For there is no one in it, except that band of profligate conspirators of yours, who does not fear you—no one who does not hate you. What brand of domestic baseness is not stamped upon your life? Is there one youth, when you have once entangled him in the
65 temptations of your corruption, to whom you have not held out a sword for audacious crime?

Since this is the case, do you hesitate, O Catiline, to depart to some distant land? Make a motion to the senate and if this body votes that you ought to go into
70 banishment, you say that you will obey. I will not make such a motion, it is contrary to my principles, and yet I will let you see what these men think of you. Do you not perceive, do you not see the silence of these men? They permit it, they say nothing; why wait you for the authority
75 of their words, when you see their wishes in their silence?

* one of the chief magistrates of the Roman Republic

10. Which of the following best describes the contrast between the portrayal of Catiline in Passage 1 and that in Passage 2 ?

    A) Passage 1 portrays him as a leader of men, while Passage 2 claims that even his co-conspirators do not subscribe to his beliefs.

    B) Passage 1 portrays him as a proponent of peaceful change, while Passage 2 portrays him as warlike.

    C) Passage 1 portrays him as a liberator, while Passage 2 portrays him as corrupt and dangerous.

    D) Passage 1 portrays him as selfless, while Passage 2 portrays him as one eager to rule.

11. Catiline's question, "O bravest . . . submit?" (lines 16-17) is most likely intended to

    A) determine how dedicated his listeners are to the rebellion

    B) diminish the aggressiveness and pride of his audience

    C) inspire his listeners to take action against their oppressors

    D) cast doubt on the bravery of his own countrymen

12. The speaker in Passage 1 advances which of the following as a reason for his belief that the rebellion he urges will succeed?

    A) The people in power have no honor or courage.

    B) Age and prosperity have weakened those who govern.

    C) A cause that is just must always prevail.

    D) The government has fallen under the power of kings.

13. What is the speaker of Passage 2 referring to when he talks about the "countenances of this venerable body" (line 40) ?

    A) The powers possessed by Cicero

    B) The intelligence of the speaker

    C) The expressions of the senators

    D) The conspiracy of Cataline and his followers

14. The measures listed by the orator of Passage 2 in lines 36-44 serve to

    A) demonstrate that the city has opposed itself to Cataline's conspiracy

    B) exploit Catiline's growing sense of isolation

    C) alert the people of the city to Catiline's subversive actions

    D) appeal to Catiline's remaining national pride

15. It can be inferred from the passage that the orator in Passage 2 chooses not to call for Catiline's execution because

    A) the execution of criminals and rebels is against his morals

    B) the senators have concluded that banishment is more prudent than execution

    C) he fears that Catiline's death could anger the senate

    D) he believes that an alternative punishment is more beneficial to the state

16. Which choice provides the best evidence for the answer to the previous question?

    A) Lines 41-44 ("Do you not . . . of it")

    B) Lines 49-53 ("Wherefore, since . . . the state")

    C) Lines 57-58 ("I do not . . . advise it")

    D) Lines 70-72 ("I will not . . . of you")

17. In line 59, "afford" most nearly means

    A) purchase

    B) spare

    C) promote

    D) provide

18. According to the orator in Passage 2, the "silence" (line 75) of the senators indicates which of the following?

    A) Their hostility toward Catiline

    B) Their unwillingness to execute Catiline

    C) Their concern with morality

    D) Their disagreement with the orator

19. The orator in Passage 1 would most likely respond to the accusation in Passage 2 that "You are summoning . . . all Italy" (lines 46-49) by

    A) claiming that his goal was justice through nonviolent revolution

    B) insisting on the right of citizens to arm themselves against oppressive rulers

    C) demonstrating that the subjugation of his people would inevitably lead to such drastic action

    D) swearing that his true allegiance lay with those having power, honor, and wealth

20. Which of the following best describes the society suggested by BOTH of the speeches?

    A) An uneasy society contemplating its current political situation

    B) A polarized society divided along economic lines

    C) A tyrannical society in which the expression of opinions is forbidden

    D) A society on the verge of sweeping political change

Questions 21-31 are based on the following passages.

Passage 1 is adapted from John Richard Alden, George Washington. *© 1984, by Louisiana State University Press. Passage 2 is adapted from James Thomas Flexner,* Washington: The Indispensible Man. *© 1974 by Little, Brown and Company.*

Passage 1

At the end of his own time and for generations thereafter, he was acclaimed at home and abroad as the founder of the American nation. He achieved sainthood in
Line the minds of the Americans who came after him. There
5 was a tendency to look upon him as an archangel who possessed the genius of Caesar, the vision of Moses, and the morals of Galahad. A change came. Later Americans gave more and more attention to their rights, less and less to the man who was the principal begetter of those
10 rights. Scholars and teachers in America offered more and more praise to men of the era of the Revolution who talked and wrote on behalf of liberty, to those who labored at European capitals for independence, to those who remodeled American institutions, to Thomas
15 Paine, Thomas Jefferson, Benjamin Franklin, Alexander Hamilton, and James Madison. There was also in the twentieth century a school of biographical "debunkers" who discovered that great men and women, American as well as European, were inconstant and incontinent,
20 addicted to profanity, and menaced by insanity. Among them were writers who sought to destroy the hallowed Washington, to reduce him to mortal or smaller proportions. They found sin in the saint. So doing, they tended to make the Father of His Country into an
25 important scamp. It was often forgotten that the sword can be more potent than the pen, that the bayonet can speak more decisively than the tongue of the diplomat, that Washington was the one man essential to the triumph of the Patriots in the War of Independence, to the creation of
30 the American union, and perhaps even to the success of the democratic revolution throughout the world.

It is no secret that Washington was not born to the imperial purple. Nor was he by birth a member of the First Families of Virginia, the fabled Virginia aristocracy. He
35 opened his eyes without fanfare of trumpets, with modest hereditary prestige, in a brick house near the junction of Pope's Creek with the Potomac River in Westmoreland County, Virginia, at 10 A.M. on February 11, 1732—a day of the month that became February 22 when Britain and
40 the British empire afterward condescended to strike eleven days from their defective calendar to match it with that of the remainder of the Western world. He was later duly baptized in the Episcopal church. He was not christened after King George III, who came into the world six years
45 later. It has been urged that he was named after a George Eskridge, a benefactor of Washington's mother. It is not unlikely that the parents had King George II in mind.

Passage 2

On April 14, 1789, Washington received formal notification of his election. He set out in his coach "with
50 more anxious and painful sensations than I have words to express."

Among the worries that now bothered him was a fear that the people might resent his return to public office after his promise that he would never do so. The
55 enthusiasm with which he was greeted on the road not only extinguished this fear but raised its opposite. As he moved, he could not see the countryside because of the dust churned up by the horsemen who in relays surrounded his carriage. At every hamlet there were
60 speeches; at every city he had to lead a parade and be toasted at a sumptuous dinner; everywhere and always people were jostling him, shaking his hand, cheering and cheering until his ears ached. Throughout the jubilations that stretched down the long days and late into the nights,
65 Washington sensed a hysteria which he found "painful." How easily and with what frenzy could this irrational emotion turn, if the government did not immediately please, "into equally extravagant (though I will fondly hope unmerited) censures. So much is expected, so many
70 untoward circumstances may intervene, in such a new and critical situation that I feel an insuperable diffidence in my own abilities."

The task which he was now approaching was both more uncertain and infinitely more important than that
75 which had lain before him when in 1775 he had ridden north to take command of the Continental Army. His duty then had been to win military victory. Since such victories had been won ten thousand times, there was no philosophical reason to doubt that success was possible.
80 And, if he did fail, the result would be sad for America, catastrophic perhaps for himself and his companions, but no more than a tiny footnote in the history of mankind.

Washington's present mission might change all history. As he himself put it, "the preservation of the sacred fire
85 of liberty and the destiny of the republican model of government are justly considered as deeply, perhaps as finally, staked on the experiment entrusted to the hands of the American people." He was on his way to lead an enterprise which, if it succeeded, would prove to all the
90 world, and for the future to time immemorial, the falsity of the contention that men were "unequal to the task of governing themselves and therefore made for a master." That contention had, down the ages, been accepted by many of the greatest thinkers. Supposing the failure of
95 the American experiment should seem to prove them right? How long would it be before this "awful monument" to the death of liberty would be forgotten, before the experiment was tried again? And if, through inability or misunderstanding, Washington contributed to the
100 catastrophe, how deep and eternal would be his personal guilt?

21. As used in line 9, "begetter" most nearly means

    A) owner.
    B) procreator.
    C) reformer.
    D) procurer.

22. The author of Passage 1 objects to the attitudes of certain "Later Americans" (line 7) for which of the following reasons?

    A) Their admiration for Caesar, Moses, and Galahad was unjustified.
    B) They tended to ignore the achievements of Washington.
    C) Their misconceptions of Washington could have been easily avoided.
    D) They took their personal rights for granted.

23. According to the author of Passage 1, the "biographical 'debunkers'" described in lines 17-20 were responsible for

    A) discovering the greatness of American and European men and women
    B) expanding awareness of such historical figures as Jefferson and Franklin
    C) writing inaccurate portrayals of Washington's patriotism
    D) reducing Washington to a less than heroic status

24. Which choice provides the best evidence for the answer to the previous question?

    A) Line 7 ("There was . . . Galahad")
    B) Lines 10-16 ("Scholars . . . Madison")
    C) Lines 20-23 ("Among them . . . proportions")
    D) Lines 25-31 ("It was often . . . world")

25. In lines 59-73, the author of Passage 2 implies that the wildly supportive crowd

    A) could help Washington succeed by supporting his policies
    B) could quickly turn on Washington if he did not satisfy their needs
    C) would ignore Washington's shortcomings because of their overwhelming allegiance
    D) would not endorse a president about whom they knew so little

26. In line 71, the phrase "insuperable diffidence" refers to

    A) Washington's lack of self-confidence
    B) the disparity between Washington's own beliefs and the beliefs of his constituents
    C) Washington's unwavering self-assurance in the face of adversity
    D) Washington's firm convictions about how the country must be run

27. The distinction between Washington's potential success in his "task" (line 73) and his command of the Continental Army might be best expressed in which of the following ways?

    A) The first had historical precedent, the second did not.
    B) The first was more easily accomplished than the second.
    C) The first was as yet untried by Washington, the second was familiar and possible.
    D) The first was Washington 's responsibility, the second was not.

28. Which pair of words best describes the author's view in Passage 2 of Washington's "duty" (line 77) in the continental Army and Washington's presidency?

    A) Abrasive and contentious
    B) Impartial and disinterested
    C) Unremarkable and momentous
    D) Uncertain and doubtful

29. According to the author of Passage 2, which of the following is true about the statement that men "were 'unequal to the task of governing themselves and therefore made for a master'" (lines 91-92) ?

    A) It was not a commonly held belief.
    B) It was believed only by pessimistic philosophers.
    C) It would be disproved if Washington was successful.
    D) It was Washington's credo.

30. Which of the following best describes the primary difference between Passage 1 and Passage 2 ?

   A) Passage 1 describes the myths surrounding Washington's life, while Passage 2 presents Washington's view of his place in history.

   B) Passage 1 presents an objective view of Washington, while Passage 2 attempts to show Washington as a perfect leader.

   C) Passage 1 focuses on Washington's achievements after the Revolutionary War, while Passage 2 discusses his military successes.

   D) Passage 1 gives a personal view of Washington, while Passage 2 shows how academics have recently changed their opinion of Washington's success as president.

31. With which of the following statements would the authors of BOTH passages agree?

   A) Washington's failure may have caused the United States to abandon a democratic system of government.

   B) Although not without flaw, Washington was indispensable to the success of world democracy.

   C) Washington, like other great men and women, was often inconstant and incontinent.

   D) Washington played a formative role at a pivotal point in the history of the United States.

Reading Drill 2

For each question in this section, circle the letter of the best answer from among the choices given.

Questions 1-11 are based on the following passages.

Passage 1 is adapted from Dwight McCabe, Little Boxes and Big Boxes. *© 2007 by Dwight McCabe. Passage 2 is adapted from John Vespa,* The Garden State Fights Sprawl. *© 2011 by John Vespa.*

Passage 1

Pull up to a traffic light in Anytown, U.S.A. and look around. On one side sits a franchised burger joint or a national clothing retailer; on the other, an expansive set of cookie-cutter homes separated by perfectly trimmed lawns and wide streets named for bucolic features of the landscape long since obliterated. In front and behind lie endless streams of red brake lights and bright white headlights emanating from blue, silver, and red hunks of steel.

Welcome to Suburbia. While suburbs offer their residents convenient shopping and generally comfortable standards of living, they concomitantly promote a uniformity that is a disservice to all. American suburbs arose in the 1940s as a way to effectively utilize large tracts of land needed to house a booming population.

While the suburban building frenzy did make home ownership more accessible to the average American, the resulting communities are mainly characterized by hyper-organization and uniformity. But at what cost? Suburban culture and its principles of residential planning, instead of improving our condition of life as intended, have in fact diminished our standing as an inquisitive, expressive people.

Identical-looking, prefabricated houses have robbed us of hundreds of years of original and beautiful home design; simple, efficient construction has trumped all. Suburban sprawl has engulfed the natural landscape, a practice that has laid the groundwork for a hotbed of consumerism made manifest in strip malls, gas stations, fast-food restaurants, and chain music and video stores. Family-owned businesses and independent merchants who specialize in the sale of handcrafts and locally made products have been swept away, unable to compete economically against national and multinational corporate conglomerates. The ultimate results of such rampant growth are communities with no center, no soul, few social bonds, and no reason to exist other than to consume.

It is perhaps too much of a stretch to claim the growth of suburbia is responsible for all of today's problems; crime, pollution, and other social problems constitute more immediate and pervasive threats. Nevertheless, suburban culture, with its emphasis on standardization and ubiquity, has proven to be a sore spot for a culture hungry for individual expression in the way it shops, dresses, lives, and dreams.

Passage 2

Difficult problems call for creative answers. Critics of suburban growth point to a variety of problems caused by the seemingly quickening pace of so-called "sprawl," a derisive term that refers to the spread of suburban housing developments onto farms and unused plots of land. While many of these complaints border on the histrionic, one must concede that sprawl does detract from the beauty of the landscape and decrease the amount of open space available for public use.

Despite alarming forecasts enumerating the damage to be wrought if growth is not stemmed, sprawl has shown few signs of relenting, primarily because of the public's appetite for big suburban homes and easy access to shopping centers. In an attempt to address the problem of sprawl, the state of New Jersey proposed a program intended to stem the tide of sprawl before it was too late. The plan would allow the state to use taxpayer money to protect remaining open land—for years and years to come—from mall builders, three-bedroom house owners, or anyone else, for that matter.

Through a statewide referendum, the state successfully earned the support of its citizens to buy back up to one million acres of land; the measure passed in 1998 with 66 percent voter assent and was signed into law in June 1999. For 10 years from the signing of the Garden State Preservation Trust Act, the state promised to spend $98 million a year to repurchase land. Residents, eager to maintain the beauty of their areas, voted for the referendum, despite the eventual increase in their own taxes required by the act.

The "Garden State," known as much for its boundless suburban tracts as its beautiful beaches, farms, and pinelands, has demonstrated that it is possible to control sprawl without unduly hurting economic growth or the fiscal health of the state. Homeowners are reminded through green-and-blue road signs that their tax dollars are preserving the beauty of the state. The tourism industry has a new draw for visitors. And all residents of the state may now rest assured that the state's natural charms will not soon disappear.

1. In the first paragraph of Passage 1, the author uses the term "Anytown, U.S.A." (line 1) to

   A) indicate that the described conditions are commonly found in the United States
   B) introduce the reader to a specific place
   C) suggest that the description of the suburban condition is mostly imaginary
   D) imply that suburbia is common only in the United States

2. In the context of Passage 1, "concomitantly" (line 11) most nearly means

   A) simultaneously
   B) in a widespread way
   C) with greedy intent
   D) ostentatiously

3. The first sentence in the final paragraph of Passage 1 (lines 36-39) serves to

   A) clarify the extent to which the author believes suburbs are a problem
   B) exemplify the primary argument of suburbia's effects
   C) summarize the collection of prior points about suburban sprawl
   D) modify a previously made argument about standardized housing

4. As used in line 39, "pervasive" most nearly means

   A) narrow.
   B) physical.
   C) widespread.
   D) intrusive.

5. The author of Passage 1 asserts that, to some degree, suburban sprawl is responsible for

   A) a desire for individuality
   B) an increase in conformity
   C) air pollution
   D) a million acres of farmland and open space

6. Which of the following relationships is most similar to that between the government of New Jersey and suburban sprawl legislation as described in Passage 2?

   A) An adult lion protecting her cub
   B) A homeowner purchasing a fence to keep out destructive animals
   C) A man depositing money into his bank account
   D) A locksmith changing the lock on a door

7. According to Passage 2, all of the following statements about the "Garden State" are true EXCEPT

   A) Its governor authorized the repurchase of land through executive order.
   B) It is well known for topographical features such as pinelands.
   C) Its implementation of an anti-sprawl effort has been considered a success.
   D) Evidence of a land repurchase program is visible to the state's residents.

8. The author of Passage 1 and the author of Passage 2 are similar in that both

   A) argue the construction of typical suburban houses has no benefit to homeowners
   B) agree suburban sprawl has a negative impact on the aesthetics of an area
   C) feel efforts to curb suburban sprawl have been effective
   D) feel suburban sprawl has been detrimental to American culture

9. What would the author of Passage 2 most likely say about the arguments posed in the third paragraph of Passage 1?

   A) They rely too heavily on a faulty premise.
   B) They make too many false assumptions.
   C) They ignore the underlying problems associated with the topic.
   D) They are excessively dramatic or emotional.

10. Which choice provides the best evidence for the answer to the previous question?

    A) Lines 48-52 ("While many . . . public use")
    B) Lines 60-63 ("The plan . . . matter")
    C) Lines 70-73 ("Residents . . . the act")
    D) Lines 81-83 ("And all . . . disappear")

11. Which best describes the relationship between Passage 1 and Passage 2 ?

    A) Passage 2 argues for changes described in Passage 1.
    B) Passage 2 debunks the arguments made in Passage 1.
    C) Passage 2 describes one solution to a problem described in Passage 1.
    D) Passage 2 provides a theoretical argument that offsets the practical argument provided in Passage 1.

Questions 12-22 are based on the following passage.

This passage is adapted from Joachim-Ernst Berendt and Günther Huesmann, The Jazz Book: From Ragtime to the 21st Century. *© 2009 by Lawrence Hill Books.*

Duke Ellington's Orchestra is a complex configuration of many spiritual and musical elements. To be sure, it was Duke Ellington's music that was created here, but it
Line was just as much the music of each individual member of
5 the band. Many Ellington pieces were genuine collective achievements, but it was Ellington who headed the collective. Attempts have been made to describe how Ellington recordings have come into being, but the process is so subtle that verbalization appears crude. Duke, or
10 his alter ego, the late arranger and jazz composer Billy Strayhorn, or one of the members of the band would come to the studio with a theme. Ellington would play on the piano. The rhythm section would fall in. One or another of the horn men would pick it up. Baritone saxophonist Harry
15 Carney might improvise a solo on it. The brass would make up a suitable background for him. And Ellington would sit at the piano and listen, gently accenting the harmonies—and suddenly he'd know: This is how the piece should sound and no other way. Later, when it was
20 transcribed, the note paper only happened to retain what was, in the real meaning of the word, improvised into being.

The dynamic willpower with which Ellington stamped his ideas on his musicians, while giving them the
25 impression that he was only helping them to unfold and develop their hidden powers, was one of his many great gifts. Owing to the relationship between Duke and his musicians, which can barely be put into words, everything he had written seemed to be created for him and his
30 orchestra—to such a degree that hardly anyone can copy it.

When Ellington was eighteen, he wanted to become a painter. By becoming a musician he only seemed to have abandoned painting. He painted not in colors but in sounds. His compositions, with their many colors of
35 timbre and harmony, are musical paintings. Sometimes this is revealed by the titles: "The Flaming Sword," "Beautiful Indians," "Portrait of Bert Williams," "Sepia Panorama," "Country Girl," "Dusk in the Desert," "Mood Indigo," and so forth. Even as a conductor, Ellington
40 remained the painter: in the grand manner in which he confronted the orchestra and, with a few sure movements of the hand, placed spots of color on a canvas made of sounds.

It may be due to this that he perceived his music as
45 "the transformation of memories into sounds." Ellington said, "The memory of things gone is important to a jazz musician. I remember I once wrote a sixty-four-bar piece about a memory of when I was a little boy in bed and heard a man whistling on the street outside, his footsteps
50 echoing away."

Again and again Ellington has expressed his pride in the color of his skin. Many of his larger works took their themes from black history: "Black, Brown, and Beige," the tone painting of the American Negro who was "black"
55 when he came to the New World, became "brown" in the days of slavery, and today is "beige"—not only in his color, but in his being as well; "Liberian Suite," a work in six movements commissioned by the small republic on the west coast of Africa for its centennial; "Harlem," the
60 work in which the atmosphere of New York's black city has been captured; "Deep South Suite," which reminds us of the locale of the origins of jazz, or "New World A-comin'," the work about a better world without racial discrimination.

65 Many critics have said that Ellington often comes too close to European music. They point to his concern with larger forms. But in this very concern is revealed an insufficiency in the molding of these forms which is certainly not European: an astonishing, amiable naïveté.
70 This naïveté was also present in those medleys—long series of his many successful tunes—with which Duke again and again upset many of his more sophisticated fans at his concerts. Ellington simply failed to see why the idea of the hit medley should be alien to an artistic music.

75 The jungle style is one of the four styles identified with Duke Ellington. The other three are (in a somewhat simplistic but synoptically clear grouping) "mood style," "concerto style," and "standard style," which came rather directly from Fletcher Henderson, the most important
80 band leader of the twenties, and initially did not contribute much that was new. What it did have to offer, though, was clothed in typically Ellingtonian colors and sounds. In addition, of course, there is every imaginable mixture of these styles.

85 The history of Duke Ellington is the history of the orchestra in jazz. No significant big band—and this includes commercial dance bands—has not been directly or indirectly influenced by Duke. The list of innovations and techniques introduced by Ellington and subsequently
90 picked up by other orchestras or players is unrivaled.

12. Which of the following best describes the working relationship between Ellington and his band members?

    A) Ellington's primary concern was to help his band members realize their full potential as composers.
    B) Ellington and his band collaborated as equals in the development of new compositions.
    C) Ellington used his band's improvisations as inspiration for his compositions.
    D) Ellington based his compositions on early recordings by his band members.

13. Which choice provides the best evidence for the answer to the previous question?

    A) Lines 9-12 ("Duke, or . . . theme")
    B) Lines 15-19 ("And Ellington . . . other way")
    C) Lines 34-35 ("His compositions . . . paintings")
    D) Lines 81-82 ("What it did . . . sounds")

14. In line 17, "accenting" most nearly means

    A) fashioning
    B) emphasizing
    C) enunciating
    D) reworking

15. The descriptions given in lines 52-64 provide the reader with which of the following?

    A) an understanding of Ellington's youth
    B) a sense of the momentum behind Ellington's earlier work
    C) a history of Ellington's social conscience
    D) the inspirations for some of Ellington's compositions

16. According to the author, which of the following is true of "Black, Brown, and Beige" (line 53) ?

    A) It tells the story of several major black historical figures.
    B) Its title refers to color both literally and metaphorically.
    C) It is comprised of three distinct sections.
    D) It was written on commission for a national celebration.

17. In the context of the sixth paragraph (lines 65-74), "larger forms" most nearly means

    A) songs played by an entire symphony orchestra.
    B) upright basses, trombones, and tubas.
    C) long songs made up of the melodies of many shorter songs.
    D) the most sophisticated European music fans.

18. Which of the following attributes does the author mention in response to the criticisms leveled in lines 65-66 ?

    A) Ellington's pride in the color of his skin
    B) Ellington's European sensibility
    C) Ellington's genuine innocence
    D) Ellington's ability to write hit songs

19. According to the passage, some "fans" (line 72) of Ellington were

    A) critical of one of Ellington's presentation formats
    B) unfamiliar with more classical forms of music
    C) lacking in the naïveté required to understand Ellington's medleys
    D) dismayed by Ellington's use of European musical forms

20. The author mentions all of the following as sources of inspiration for Ellington's work EXCEPT

    A) famous paintings
    B) ethnic heritage
    C) orchestral improvisations
    D) regional ambiance

21. It can be inferred from the passage that "Fletcher Henderson" (line 79)

    A) was a stylistic influence on Duke Ellington
    B) composed in a style that was inspired by the work of Duke Ellington
    C) was a contemporary of Duke Ellington
    D) wrote music that had much in common with Ellington's jungle style

22. Which of the following questions could be answered based on information in the passage?

    A) At what age did Ellington achieve success as a musician?
    B) By what process did Ellington develop his orchestral compositions?
    C) What are the characteristics of Ellington's jungle style?
    D) What is considered Ellington's best-known composition?

Questions 23-33 are based on the following passage.

This passage is adapted from a book published in 2012.

Google, Yahoo!, Bing, and other search engines are all over the internet, seeming to promise us all the information we could ever need. With such a profusion of information at our fingertips, we wonder how previous generations of scholars slaved away at libraries, pulling dusty books from the shelves and hoping that those books could reveal all the world's secrets.

Because the internet search has become such an essential part of our daily routines—because we can do it on our phones and TVs as well as our computers—we can finally begin to assess how this information saturation has affected our minds. Now that we have all this information at our behest, are we smarter? Or, as one writer in the *Atlantic Monthly* asked, "Is Google Making Us Stoopid?"

In many ways, our informational field has reflected our understanding of the universe: where we once thought of the "heavens" as the things that we could see in the sky, we now theorize the universe as infinite, containing literally countless numbers of worlds like our own in literally countless figurations. Just as the universe is too large to conceptualize, there's now too much information available for anyone ever to know. In the days of traditional library research, the search for the appropriate sources was itself part of the process. Researchers did the selecting themselves and assimilated a good deal of peripheral knowledge into the bargain. A scholar like James Frazer, author of *The Golden Bough* (1890), could be fairly certain that he was assembling all of the world's myths and folklore in a single book.

Now, we know that Frazer's project was a very limited one. A single Google search for the word "myth" will show us how many billions of things he missed. In fact, projects like Frazer's must necessarily have changed. Because we know how much information is out there, we can't possibly dream of trying to assemble it all into anything as manageable as a single book. We instead generate theories to support our impossible positions, as if to say that because there is too much information, nothing can be knowable in any real depth.

Indeed, this shift from the finite to the infinite is another version of the globalization that we experience every day: cars from Japan, electronics from Korea, and furniture from Sweden are parts of our daily lives, which we no longer experience as foreign. Ours is truly a world community, where the lines between nations have become blurred and where people have more in common than ever before.

Because the whole world and all its information are at our fingertips, how can we possibly begin to understand this new world that has grown up around us? How do we evaluate something that we can hardly understand? The researcher of a century ago spent many hours poring over a single text, and often had to learn entirely new languages to do so. The computer-savvy researcher of today, by contrast, can have that information instantaneously and can even search within it for whatever bits of information seem relevant.

To ask the question in the most simpleminded of ways, are we smarter? All this information is now at our fingertips, but can we really be said to have it? Those older scholars and thinkers may have known what they knew more intimately. They may have worked harder to acquire it. But there was simply less for them to know, and it's no mistake that scholars from our own era are constantly improving upon and refining what those older scholars have done. They may have known everything there was to know, but that was a very limited everything indeed. Still, our own omniscience is not without its limitations. Rather than delving more deeply into this or that topic, we are much more likely to throw up our hands, to say that if we can't know everything, then it's not worth it to try to know anything at all. How can we take seriously any attempt at knowing when the remainder of all that we don't know is there as a constant reminder? It is at the very least my hope—and the hope, I suspect, of many others—that there must be some way between the two extremes. We don't want to return to the era of the very small world, nor can we allow ourselves to drift off into the infinite immensity of the informational world that is available now.

23. The first paragraph (lines 1-7) most directly focuses on the

A) death of true research in contemporary scholarship.
B) distinction between topics of old scholarship and new.
C) reduction of intelligence in the modern age.
D) contemporary availability of large amounts of information.

24. In context, the reference to previous generations of scholars (lines 22-26) is significant in that it

A) demonstrates the contrast between old and new methods of research.
B) states that people from earlier eras had more time to spend reading.
C) emphasizes the contemporary scholar's contempt for libraries.
D) indicates the accuracy provided by basic internet searches

25. In context, the phrase "information saturation" (line 11) describes the

 A) mode of thinking that has crippled contemporary research methods.
 B) contrast between effective and ineffective methods of acquiring information.
 C) moment at which an intelligent human being can no longer learn new information.
 D) emerging situation in which information becomes too much for one person to know.

26. As used in line 13, "at … behest" most nearly means

 A) under our control.
 B) in our books.
 C) available to us.
 D) within our grasp.

27. In line 16, "our understanding" represents a shift away from

 A) online databases.
 B) universal knowledge.
 C) faith-based interpretations.
 D) a knowable world.

28. The author mentions researchers (line 24) and a scholar (line 26) primarily to

 A) underline the importance of traditional modes of study.
 B) warn against the dangers of traditional research.
 C) compare the researchers of previous ages unfavorably to those of today.
 D) demonstrate instances of one type of study.

29. In context, the book cited in line 27 supports the notion that

 A) the scope of contemporary research has changed.
 B) scholars no longer have ambitious research goals.
 C) the study of mythology has disappeared from contemporary scholarship.
 D) one particular book answers more questions than the internet can.

30. The author suggests that "Now" (line 30) scholars have become

 A) hopeless.
 B) collaborative.
 C) inundated.
 D) smarter.

31. In lines 40-44 ("Indeed … foreign"), the author notes a parallel between

 A) contemporary research and the makeup of mall food courts.
 B) the amount of information and the excesses of consumerism.
 C) trends in research and preferences for foreign goods.
 D) the range of available information and economic globalization.

32. The example of the computer-savvy researcher (line 54) is primarily used to illustrate

 A) rampant procrastination.
 B) technological sophistication.
 C) deep knowledge.
 D) informational availability.

33. The primary purpose of the last paragraph (lines 53-79) is to

 A) doubt that the new modes of acquiring information will ever generate important discoveries.
 B) suggest that some compromise is possible between old and new ways of acquiring information.
 C) long for an earlier mode of research that relied on the deep study of long printed books.
 D) outline the differences between those who use computers to access information and those who do not.

Reading Drill 3

For each question in this section, circle the letter of the best answer from among the choices given.

Questions 1-12 are based on the following passage.

Passage 1

Music in Peril confirms most of our worst suspicions. The 2011 survey gives an interesting but ultimately saddening assessment of the state of music in schools. In
Line a span of only thirty years, the number of children playing
5 musical instruments has been cut in half. If you care about sustaining cultural life in this country, you are probably as worried now as many of the rest of us are.

Music in Peril is not the collection of urban legends that most of its critics will accuse it of being. It is a set
10 of data collected from elementary and middle schools all over the country. With schools represented from each of the 50 states, it accounts for all the great diversity in this country—not merely race and gender diversity, but class and regional diversity as well. Given the broad reach of the
15 survey, and the fact that it has collected its data in at least the five most populous towns in each state, *Music in Peril* is a statistically sound document. Although the survey covers a wide range of topics relating to music education, the basic results go something like this: music education
20 and instrument-playing have decreased dramatically among all children aged 6-18, regardless of race, gender, or region, and this decrease is occurring at a higher rate than in the past.

Even if the data in the report are potentially disturbing
25 these data are hardly unexpected, unless we did not realize just how widespread music education was in the past. *Music in Peril* has simply put what everyone knows—that state and federal governments have cut music out of public schools at an alarming rate—into the language of statistics.
30 The ability to play a musical instrument and to appreciate music is not inborn, even if some people seem to have "natural" talents. True musical proficiency is the result of many years of encouraging musical education, and not only for those who eventually become musicians. Ours is
35 a dire world indeed when not only have our musicians lost the ability to play but also the broader populace has lost the discernment and ability to hear them.

Passage 2

Music in Peril is hardly surprising in our era of apocalyptic surveys, yet more evidence that all the bad
40 things we suspect are worse than we even knew. These surveys are the bread and butter of cultural critics, who are always looking for social-scientific support for their own suspicions. These critics were already speaking of "decline" and "death," and now these surveys just give
45 more fodder to their calls for "reinvention" and "change." Now, for the first time in history, the story goes, fewer children are learning instruments than ever before.

Nevertheless, *Music in Peril* misses the important fact that music is as interesting as it has ever been, even if the
50 average teen doesn't know a Beethoven symphony from a Chopin étude. In the age of the iPod, people are listening to music all the time, even if they're not doing it in quite the ways or the places that musical conservatives want them to.

55 It would be naïve, however, to say that *Music in Peril*'s findings are completely wrongheaded. Music programs have been slashed at many public schools, and less than half as many children today are learning instruments than were the generations of forty or fifty years earlier. And
60 this statistical certainty is not limited to the less fortunate areas of the country: "Indeed," write the statisticians, "the 50 percent reduction is only the median. While some schools have seen more modest declines, many schools have cut out their music education and appreciation
65 programs almost entirely."

So what is the lesson of the survey? The musical landscape is changing, yes, but not in the distressing way that *Music in Peril* wants to suggest. The survey can't capture the fact that classical music is not the only place
70 to find interesting, complex music anymore, except by the most conservative, crustiest definitions. Listen to any of the new experimental music in genres like post-rock, math rock, and tech-noire, and you'll see that classical music no longer has an exclusive hold on musical virtuosity. You'll
75 see that, in surveys like *Music in Peril*, the only real decline is in musical categories that don't apply anymore. All that is happening is that the institutions of old are trying to hold on for dear life and actually belong in the same irrelevant pile as studies on the decline of cursive or
80 telephone conversations.

1. Lines 3-5 ("In a ... half") suggest that the situation described should be considered

   A) rapid.
   B) suspicious.
   C) inevitable.
   D) essential.

2. The author of Passage 1 suggests that a set of data (lines 9-10) should ideally be

   A) taken from the same set as previous surveys.
   B) diverse enough to reflect the group it represents.
   C) made up of elementary-school-aged children.
   D) comprised of equal numbers from each race.

3. The author of Passage 2 would most likely argue that the reach of the survey (Passage 1, lines 14-15) is

   A) less representative of racial diversity than the author of Passage 1 promises.
   B) less relevant to the study than the author of Passage 1 believes.
   C) drawn from a group that does not represent the diversity that the author of Passage 1 assumes.
   D) more similar to the reach of previous studies than the author of Passage 1 knows.

4. The final paragraph of Passage 1 (lines 24-37) serves primarily to

   A) discount the survey's findings by showing that they are already well-known.
   B) argue for a new approach that the survey's results show is inevitable.
   C) take issue with the statisticians who collected the data for the survey.
   D) suggest the cultural implications of the trend it is describing.

5. The author of Passage 2 would most likely consider the final two sentences of Passage 1 (lines 32-37) to be

   A) overstated.
   B) ironic.
   C) shrewd.
   D) dishonest.

6. Which of the following would the author of Passage 2 most likely consider another apocalyptic (line 39) idea?

   A) An editorial that argues that the trend toward text messaging has led to a decline in the number of E-mails sent per year
   B) An article that shows that reading among teenagers has increased since the popularization of e-readers
   C) A slideshow that details the 20 most environmentally conscious cities in the United States
   D) A sociologist who argues that the use of smartphones among teenagers will lead to a significant increase in driver fatalities

7. Lines 55-65 ("It would ... entirely'") focus on which aspect of the statistical certainty?

   A) Its obviousness
   B) Its range
   C) Its conservatism
   D) Its bias

8. The author of Passage 2 indicates that the landscape referenced in line 67 is

   A) characterized by a lack of expertise.
   B) based on regional preferences and racial identity.
   C) shifting and thus not possible to describe.
   D) no longer defined by its traditional parameters.

9. As used in line 71, "crustiest" most nearly means

   A) most ineffective.
   B) cruelest.
   C) most inflexible.
   D) filthiest.

10. The author of Passage 1 would most likely respond to the last statement in Passage 2 (lines 77-80) by asserting that

    A) a survey of musical-education programs has broader cultural importance.
    B) classical music is as essential to well-rounded citizens as cursive.
    C) *Music in Peril* is one of the first studies of school-aged children.
    D) surveys like the one in *Music in Peril* are run by respected statisticians.

11. Which best describes the tone of the first paragraph of Passage 1 and the tone of the first paragraph of Passage 2, respectively?

- A) Morose vs. elated
- B) Sensitive vs. offensive
- C) Conservative vs. dismissive
- D) Concerned vs. skeptical

12. Which best conveys the primary relationship between the two passages?

- A) Passage 2 discusses some of the findings that undermine the survey described in Passage 1.
- B) Passage 2 takes issue with some of the premises that shape the argument made in Passage 1.
- C) Passage 2 offers the cultural context that adds support to the conclusions drawn by the author of Passage 1.
- D) Passage 2 uses the predictions offered in Passage 1 as a way to argue for a revolutionary change.

The following excerpt is adapted from a 1985 book on the role of storytelling in human understanding.

We love to spin yarns, to tell tales, to chronicle events.
If we get even a few details about someone, we'll start to
connect those details into some kind of narrative about
Line   that person. We want any nearby dots to be connected.
5   Effect with no cause, correlation with no causation: we
can't assimilate these ideas because they don't have that
narrative structure. Our minds want stories, even if those
stories need to be twisted and mangled into existence.

This is how we give order to the chaotic world
10 around us. Take any messy, complicated historical event,
something like the American Civil War: a bloody and long
conflict, and hopelessly complex when taken in isolation.
Historians and onlookers alike have spent over a century
debating the causes, the effects, and the place of this event
15 in the ongoing plot of American history. Neuroscientists
have referred to a "need for narrative," both as an
explanation for the popularity of fiction and for how
people interact with one another. In the grander scheme,
the need for narrative may inform the way we understand
20 ourselves. We'll take anything conclusive as long as it's
consistent.

Personality is one of life's great mysteries. It is too
large; it has too many components; it has too many
omissions. It changes all the time, from day to day or
25 hour to hour, and there are times that it can seem we've
got multiple personalities at once. Because it is too
many things to manage, we turn personality into a single
narrative, a single "me" or "you." I need my friend Jack to
be the brainy one; I need my husband to be the comforting
30 one; I need my parents to be my sources of strength.
Understanding them as I do, as the stories that they are, I
simply forget whenever they do something that doesn't
make narrative sense. It makes sense that in the earliest
literary and historical texts we have, the main characters
35 are defined by their cardinal attributes. Whether Odysseus
is characterized by his bravery, Penelope by her devotion,
or Oedipus by his tragic love, these complex characters are
made into simpler, more consistent wholes on the strength
of narrative.

40   In all eras of history, literature and art have been
filled with "characters," whether the symbolic, allegorical
characters of the Bible or the subjects of contemporary
biographical film. In the early twentieth century, the very
notion of "consistent" stories broke down, and characters
45 became less rigidly defined as a result. Suddenly, amid
a cultural shift away from religious certainty, one's
environment, one's historical era, one's family history
could all come to bear on the maze of human personality.
Psychologists began to spend entire careers studying
50 human personalities, but for all these changes, the goal
was still the same: contain the human experience, find the
story that can encapsulate all of human complexity. If the

human personality seems more complex, then the method
of storytelling needs to be changed accordingly. Our need
55 for narrative will not allow us to abandon storytelling
altogether. Because after all that has come before us, and
all that will come later, if we're not part of the big story,
what are we?

13. As used in line 1, "yarns" most nearly means

A) strings.
B) tapestries.
C) narratives.
D) tails.

14. The author implies that "nearby dots to be connected"
(line 4) are details that

A) are part of the simplicity of the meaning of life.
B) do not exist in the real world.
C) different personalities understand in different
ways.
D) may not be connected outside the human mind.

15. The author uses the phrase "twisted and mangled"
(line 8) in order to

A) chastise readers for accepting simple solutions.
B) show the historical roots of a human response.
C) identify why humans prefer certain types of
personality.
D) underline the need for a particular preference.

16. In context, the reference to the "ongoing plot" (line
15) serves to emphasize the

A) historical interest in conspiracy theories.
B) challenge in uncovering historical mysteries.
C) perceived relatedness of historical events.
D) human talent for creating fictional stories.

17. The phrase "In the grander scheme" (line 18) serves
as a transition between a discussion of

A) historical events and literary texts.
B) a contested theory and scientific certainty.
C) a neuroscientist's view and a psychologist's
critique.
D) a general theory and a specific application.

18. Based on information presented in lines 22-26, which of the following would most likely be the title of a study of human personality in the twentieth century?

    A) The Tragic Flaw in Human Personality
    B) Who We Are In Three Easy Steps
    C) The Mirror and the Labyrinth of Personality
    D) The Role of the American Civil War in History

19. The author refers to a "cultural shift" (line 46) to help account for

    A) the historically consistent understandings of personality.
    B) psychologists' desires to do away with storytelling.
    C) a general human distrust of psychological theories.
    D) the broad historical change in attitudes toward personality.

20. As used in line 51, "contain" most nearly means

    A) hold.
    B) understand.
    C) imprison.
    D) restrain.

21. Which of the following best captures the main idea in lines 56-58 ("Because … we?")?

    A) Our historical era is just as important as other past eras.
    B) People in the future will tell themselves different stories from the ones we tell ourselves.
    C) History is ultimately very similar to writing fiction or poetry.
    D) Life as we know it would be much different without the need for narrative.

Questions 22-33 are based on the following passage.

In this passage, a literary critic discusses some of the issues he encountered while researching the life of Jean Toomer (1894-1967), an author from the early to mid-twentieth century. Most famous as the author of the seminal book Cane (1923), Toomer was also a deeply private individual, whose views of race were often in conflict with those of others from his time.

Though lauded as a central figure in the Harlem Renaissance, Jean Toomer the man has remained a mystery to literary historians. In an article published in
Line *The Crisis* in 1924, race leader W.E.B. DuBois pointed to
5 the mystery surrounding Toomer: "All of his essays and stories, even when I do not understand them, have their strange flashes of power, their numerous messages and numberless reasons for being." Essayist William Stanley Braithwaite is unreserved in his praise for Toomer's major
10 book, *Cane* (1921): "*Cane* is a book of gold and bronze, of dusk and flame, of ecstasy and pain, and Jean Toomer is a bright morning star of a new day of the race in literature." Toomer gained huge accolades from the white literary world as well, and well-known authors such as Sherwood
15 Anderson and Waldo Frank considered him one of their own. But Toomer's full connection to the white world remains a mystery, and critics have begun to wonder whether Toomer is the paragon of racial representation that he was initially represented, by Braithwaite especially,
20 to be.

For many black artists in the 1930s and 1940s, Jean Toomer was an inspiration. He helped to broaden the definition of what "race literature" could be. He was not constrained, as many other black authors of the time were,
25 to writing only about race oppression and race conflict. He could incorporate influences from white as well as black artists, and he melded them into an innovative style that mixed poetry, prose, jazz, folklore, and spiritualism. He showed that an African American author didn't have to
30 be defined by his race but could enjoy, and even surpass, the artistic freedom enjoyed by white artists. Furthermore, he was able to cross over the color line to reach white audiences, who, in the 1920s especially, remained widely uninformed about cultural production by African
35 Americans.

Still, his relationship to civil rights and the African American community has been difficult to determine. After the success of *Cane*, Toomer contributed only a few more essays before withdrawing from the literary world
40 altogether. In the 1930s, he had nearly disappeared from the literary scene, and his two marriages, in 1931 and 1934, were interracial, both to white women. Although intermarriage between blacks and whites was still socially vilified at the time, Toomer's attitude toward this social
45 restriction is vague. Toomer himself may not have thought of these marriages as interracial: particularly by the 1940s, Toomer insisted that his race was "American" and by the end of his life, he may have even identified as a white man. These scraps are all historians have.

50 By the 1960s, race activism reached its apex with such figures as Martin Luther King, Jr., and Malcolm X. Black and white artists alike joined together in the fight that became known as the Civil Rights movement. By that time, however, Jean Toomer was nestled in a deeply
55 private life in Doylestown, Penn., and was not one of the voices in the fight for black equality. By then, and until his death in 1967, Toomer was much more taken with local issues, and his main concern was with his church, the Society of Friends (Quakers), and the high school students
60 whom he taught there.

If Toomer's early literary output can be more thoroughly understood than his later personal life, or his later racial identification, it can only be because Toomer himself wanted it to be so. His own sense of race and
65 personality was so complex that he likely did not want to become embroiled in debates that were literally so black and white. In a 1931 essay, Toomer announced that "the old divisions into white, black, brown, red, are outworn in this country. They have had their day. Now is the time of
70 the birth of a new order, a new vision, a new ideal of man." Whether we consider Toomer's view naïve or not, there can be no question that he thought himself a part of this "new order." Because Toomer was such a truly great artist, literary historians will always long for more information
75 about his life. Unfortunately, there's little hope more information will emerge, and Jean Toomer the man must remain an inscrutable piece in our understanding of Jean Toomer the artist. Perhaps such inscrutability is good for us, too. We should be wary of the rigid categories that
80 Toomer fought against all his life, and if anything, perhaps Toomer's refusal to fit into these categories can help us to modify our own.

22. The author suggests that Toomer's relationship with the black community has remained a mystery to literary historians (lines 2-3) because

A) details of Toomer's later life are insufficient to explain his personal attitudes.
B) Toomer's fame in literary circles was not acknowledged by white authors.
C) Toomer's essays provide inconsistent representations of his views.
D) evidence shows that Toomer worked against the Civil Rights movement.

23. In lines 3-16, the author's discussion of Toomer's contemporaries and later artists is used to

A) show how one particular era viewed the role of race in art.
B) give evidence of their views of Toomer's influence on black artists and thinkers.
C) provide examples of Toomer's literary mastery and experimentation.
D) list the challenges faced by black artists in contemporary society.

24. As used in line 9, "unreserved" most nearly means

A) vacant.
B) available.
C) garrulous.
D) complete.

25. The author mentions Waldo Frank and Sherwood Anderson (lines 14-15) as indications of the

A) urgency with which Toomer courted a white readership.
B) limited supply of published reviews of Toomer's first novel.
C) types of influences upon which Toomer drew in writing *Cane*.
D) appeal that Toomer had to both black and white readers.

26. The author most directly supports the statement in lines 21-22 ("For many … inspiration") by citing

A) influences from which Toomer drew inspiration.
B) the reception of Toomer's work by contemporary black critics.
C) lists of Toomer's most famous published works.
D) aspects of Toomer's art that showed a new way.

27. "These scraps" (line 49) most directly refer to evidence that

A) gives actual details of Toomer's biography.
B) paints a complete picture of Toomer's life.
C) frees literary historians to speculate.
D) reaffirms the messages found in Toomer's work.

28. In lines 50-53, the author discusses race activism primarily to

A) demonstrate that Toomer's racial attitudes were atypical.
B) praise the achievements of the Civil Rights movement.
C) refer to a major equality movement in American history.
D) state that Toomer had no interest in contemporary race relations.

29. The word "taken" (line 57) most directly emphasizes which aspect of Toomer's approach to race issues?

A) His disapproval of broad social changes
B) His ability to play both sides of an issue
C) His focus on smaller matters
D) His eagerness to fight for broader causes

30. In lines 61-67, the author emphasizes which point about Toomer?

A) His contemporaries disparaged him for his cowering attitude toward social equality
B) His attitude toward race was rooted in private and philosophical concerns
C) His public attitude toward race differed sharply from his private views
D) His commitment to racial equality influenced his political views on race

31. As used in lines 66-67, "black and white" most nearly means

A) faintly tinged.
B) socially progressive.
C) racially complex.
D) reductively simple.

32. Which resource, if it existed, would be most helpful for the task described in lines 75-78 ("Unfortunately … artist")?

A) Accurate information about the progress of social equality in the United States
B) Toomer's personal diary or autobiography
C) Records of household income kept by Toomer's wives
D) Statements from later authors about the importance of Toomer's influence

33. The final phrase in lines 80-82("if … own") primarily emphasizes which of the following points?

A) Toomer identified as white at the end of his life to distance himself from Civil Rights.
B) Those in the Civil Rights movement were correct to dismiss Toomer as a counterproductive force.
C) Toomer had more advanced views than most African American authors from the 1920s.
D) Toomer's personal views on race remain complex even in our own day.

Reading Drill 4

For each question in this section, circle the letter of the best answer from among the choices given.

Questions 1-12 are based on the following passage.

This passage is adapted from a 2009 book looking at Western (that is, European and American) attempts to modernize the Middle East and other regions.

The international history of the twentieth century is overflowing with Western projects to modernize the Middle East. The United States, and England to a
Line lesser degree, have tried to bring freedom to oppressed
5 peoples throughout the region, and as the word "freedom" implies, this was a philanthropic mission. President Bill Clinton, for example, is still praised for his role in Israeli-Palestinian peace talks, even as his other failures and accomplishments gained front page news in the mid-
10 1990s. His even-handed, mediating role helped to save these warring states from total destruction. This attitude toward non-Western regions, the belief that the West's systems of government can help save the people of the Middle East, Africa, or Latin America, is a holdover from
15 an imperial moment, when European nations conquered these regions with militaries rather than diplomats. It may be time to start asking, however, whether Western systems of government are universally applicable. That is to say, perhaps the Western value of "freedom"—as it relates to
20 markets, speech, and behaviors—is not one that is shared by people outside the West. Unrest in the Middle East and other non-Western regions can only continue until new systems of governance begin to emerge from the regions themselves.

25   These modernization projects bear an eerie resemblance to the "civilizing missions" of European nations in the nineteenth century. These missions always begin with the premise that those in non-Western nations are unable to govern themselves. In most cases,
30 the result is little more than a large-scale, prolonged clash of cultures, in which prejudices toward the "poor souls" who can't take care of themselves only become that much firmer in the minds of the un-self-conscious interlopers. The native peoples who are then forced to
35 live under the new government's rule become extremely skeptical of it, as its supposed successes are measured by seemingly irrelevant metrics. Many ancient and historical societies come from these regions, but since the seventeenth century, these regions have been considered
40 almost universally backward. This notion persists in contemporary politics, and in the United States, the idea that the U.S. is making the world safe for democracy is common among both major political parties. As recently

as 2003, in a war that was billed as one of self-defense,
45 George W. Bush was promising Americans, "Helping Iraqis achieve a united, stable, and free country will require our sustained commitment."

Bush is the inheritor of a long tradition of this belief in the power of Western influence. This influence, though,
50 has not been a pure force for good. While Western systems of government were created as responses to nation-states and royal traditions, non-Western nations have their own set of foundations and traditions. The earliest colonial governments in these non-Western regions were run by
55 Westerners. But now that the colonial governments have been kicked out, a system of rule by the actual people who live in these non-Western nations must be something else.

To take one example, the name "Iraq" is not quite as applicable to all its citizens as the names "France,"
60 "Portugal," or "The United States" are in their own regions. For many Westerners, nationality is a given and ultimately trumps the more local identifications of town, city, or state. In Iraq, as the Bush administration learned, religious distinctions are more meaningful than
65 national similarities. Approximately 65 percent of those living in Iraq are Shia Muslims, but does this make it a Shia country? To an extent, maybe, but Sunni Muslims represent a powerful and vocal minority, and the northern regions of Iraq comprise a semiautonomous region of a
70 third group, the Kurds. The Western notions of nation-above-all and religious coexistence can't maintain in this and other countries because the value systems have developed so independently of these notions.

As in many other parts of the world, "Iraqi freedom"
75 was defined by someone other than the Iraqis themselves. Western civilizing efforts have always been based on the unfortunate premise that non-Westerners cannot govern themselves, often on no other evidence than Westerners' firm belief in the success of their own political
80 systems. The refusal to accept that the basic principles of democracy and free-market capitalism may not be universally applicable has always compromised efforts at Western modernization because these efforts have lacked the appropriate local perspectives. Certainly, Western
85 nations are today more sensitive to cultural differences than they have ever been. It remains to be seen, however, whether this new multicultural stance is a genuine change or a simple repackaging of an old product.

1. In the context of lines 1-3 ("The international … East"), the phrase "overflowing with" suggests that

   A) modernization is a common subject of conversation for Middle Eastern visitors to the West.
   B) some Middle East countries have been subject to more modernization efforts than others.
   C) there have been many attempts by Western countries to modernize the Middle East.
   D) there are simply too many countries in the Middle East for historians to describe accurately.

2. The author mentions Bill Clinton (line 7) primarily in order to

   A) cite one person who represents a certain perspective.
   B) describe the rewards of one person's courage against difficult odds.
   C) state that those who have contributed to peace in the region come from a variety of backgrounds.
   D) show that Middle East peace was only one of Clinton's minor accomplishments.

3. According to the passage, it is worth asking whether Western systems of government are universally applicable (line 18) because they

   A) are too reliant upon ancient forms of non-Western government.
   B) refuse to recognize the accomplishments of diplomats like Bill Clinton.
   C) have as their only goal the introduction of Western goods into non-Western markets.
   D) may not be the most appropriate forms of government for those outside the West.

4. Which of the following best states how the peoples mentioned in line 34 feel about West-influenced governments?

   A) They despise the governments because they are hopelessly corrupt.
   B) They question the ability of their fellow citizens to govern them.
   C) They doubt that the governments have delivered on all that they have promised.
   D) They support the new regime because it represents a change from old ways.

5. According to the author, what has changed since the seventeenth century (line 39)?

   A) Native citizens are now in open conflict with Western-style governments.
   B) Middle Eastern government officials look to the West for models of how to govern.
   C) Regions that were once considered model civilizations are no longer thought of as ideals.
   D) People in non-Western countries are not willing to compromise in a way that supports democracy.

6. The statement that Western influence has not been a pure force for good (line 50) suggests that the author, in general, believes that

   A) people in the Middle East would prefer to have their fellow citizens in high government positions.
   B) people in the Middle East have not necessarily benefited from Western-style governments.
   C) voters in Middle East elections wish there were more candidates from the West.
   D) forms of democracy in the Middle East are more advanced than those in the West.

7. As used in line 62, "trumps" most nearly means

   A) kicks out.
   B) defeats by force.
   C) beautifies.
   D) is more important than.

8. As used in line 71, "maintain" most nearly means

   A) work.
   B) repair.
   C) hang.
   D) build.

9. Which of the following, if true, would refute the claim made in lines 74-75 ("As … themselves")

   A) The Western influence in the Middle East has not been able to overcome internal divisions among groups within Iraq.
   B) Many representatives from the Middle East have been crucial to developing the government systems that exist in the Middle East today.
   C) Contemporary styles of government in the Middle East can be traced back to principles developed in Europe in the late 1700s.
   D) Famous diplomats such as Bill Clinton have continued to offer guidance to those in the Middle East and elsewhere.

10. Which of the following best describes the sentence in lines 84-86 ("Certainly … been")?

   A) A response to critics of the author's own argument
   B) An idea developed further in other works by the author
   C) A tangent that the author considers necessary for his main point
   D) A concession that contemporary trends are not exclusively negative

11. The author uses the phrase "repackaging of an old product" (line 86) primarily to

   A) outline an analogy for an ideal approach.
   B) suggest the type of reformulation necessary for success.
   C) express skepticism toward a certain transformation.
   D) criticize the financial interests of Western governments.

12. The author would most likely consider which approach to be a new strategy for the formation of governments in the Middle East?

   A) Allowing Western governments to shape government policy in the Middle East
   B) Breaking down cultural barriers within countries to promote national unity
   C) Increasing the authority of government officials to implement Western democracy
   D) Collaborating with local representatives to determine which style of government is best for a particular country

Questions 13-22 are based on the following passage.

This passage is adapted from Jennifer O'Sullivan, Reflection or Reimagining: Examining Authorial Intent in Twentieth Century Fiction.© 2013 by The Gazette of Literary Criticism.

The Irish author James Joyce (1882-1941) created some of the most unique and personal, yet controversial and inaccessible, literature of the last century. With
Line his modernist, experimental narrative style, his close
5 attention to the details of ordinary life, his novel technical innovations, and his recurring themes of isolation and exile, Joyce created fictional worlds at once stark and foreign, yet simultaneously rich and familiar.

In order to better decipher the seemingly endless
10 conundrum of Joyce's meanings and messages, it is worth turning one's attention to events in Joyce's life that may help the reader understand some of the sources of his creative inspiration. While studies of Joyce have considered the importance of Joyce's years in exile to
15 his writing, few have made explicit the connections between Joyce's writing and the specific contexts of his time abroad; Richard Ellman's definitive 1959 treatment and John McCourt's more recent work are the exceptions rather than the rule in this regard. The parallels between
20 the reality of Joyce's life and the fictional worlds he created are too frequent to ignore.

Joyce first fled Dublin in 1904 with his lifelong love, Nora Barnacle, for reasons both personal and professional. Joyce and Barnacle were then unmarried, and their
25 relationship was the target of social condemnation. So, too, was Joyce driven out of Ireland by the Catholic Church's harsh criticism of his early writings in which he clearly rejected what he felt to be the Church's oppressive spiritual controls. For eleven years, the couple
30 lived in the major Mediterranean seaport of Trieste, then an Austrian imperial city. Trieste was a melting pot of mercantile, religious, and cultural activity, and its language, Triestino (which Joyce came to speak beautifully) was an amalgamation of blended words
35 and sounds from many languages. Joyce's exposure to Triestino directly influenced Joyce's fashioning of his own potpourri language for his final novel *Finnegan's Wake*; the composite dialect of the work harkened back to its English origins, but also incorporated diverse elements of
40 many tongues.

As Joyce's most famous biographer, Ellman, notes, every moment of an author's waking life may manifest itself in the author's work, and Joyce himself encouraged his audience to read his works autobiographically.
45 However, ferreting out the autobiographical elements from Joyce's work involves much more than such a superficial survey of literary images. The relationship between an author's writings and the author's life experiences is not as transparent as it may seem. A writer's life may be
50 reflected in his work, but this reflection is almost always distorted to some degree, sometimes purposefully, and sometimes inadvertently.

This situation leaves both the reader and the critic at an intriguing impasse: when can we know when a
55 seemingly autobiographical image in a fictional work is actually meaningful? When, in *Ulysses,* Joyce's literary alter ego Stephen Dedalus muses on whether Shakespeare's characters were all based on actual people that he knew, is this an example of Joyce commenting
60 indirectly on Shakespeare, or of Joyce alluding to his own work? Regardless of how tempting it may be for the reader to read *Ulysses* or *A Portrait of the Artist as a Young Man* solely through the biography of Joyce, such a technique is fraught with danger, since we can ultimately never be sure
65 exactly what any author means to express through his or her art.

13. The author mentions Joyce's viewpoint ("Joyce himself . . . autobiographically") in lines 43-44 to emphasize

   A) how tempting it may be to read Joyce's work as a reflection of his life
   B) that Joyce intended to fool the reader all along
   C) that Joyce had to fight with his critics to have his work interpreted this way
   D) that Joyce always spoke directly through one of the characters in his books

14. The author most nearly believes that *Ulysses*

   A) is autobiographical in nature, and that Stephen Dedalus can be understood to represent Joyce himself.
   B) is pure fiction, and that nothing in the book represents anything that ever happened to Joyce.
   C) probably reflects elements of Joyce's life, but that it is difficult to say exactly which details are autobiographical.
   D) is the most unique example of autobiographical fiction written in the Twentieth Century.

15. Which choice provides the best evidence for the answer to the previous question?

   A) Lines 1-3 ("The Irish author . . . last century")
   B) Lines 19-21 ("The parallels . . . ignore")
   C) Lines 41-44 ("As Joyce's . . . autobiographically")
   D) Lines 61-66 ("Regardless of . . . her art")

16. It can be inferred that Joyce left Dublin and went into exile to

   A) find literary inspiration
   B) attain greater artistic and personal freedom
   C) accept a job as a writer
   D) escape Nora's parents' disapproval

17. The description of Joyce's work in the first paragraph provides information about all of the following EXCEPT

   A) when Joyce wrote his first novel
   B) the style in which Joyce wrote
   C) the degree of critical acclaim Joyce has received
   D) when Joyce lived

18. In line 10, "conundrum" most nearly means

   A) conception
   B) intuition
   C) parody
   D) puzzle

19. Which of the following best describes the organization of the passage?

   A) The author makes a specific claim, offers evidence to support this claim, and ends by expanding the discussion to a more general, but related, idea.
   B) The author states the main point, offers three theories that may support this point, and ends by selecting the theory that provides the best evidence.
   C) The author makes a claim, shows that other writers also make this claim, and ends by criticizing the others' research methods.
   D) The author summarizes scholarly literature about James Joyce, then concludes that Joyce isn't as great a writer as originally claimed.

20. The comment in lines 51-52 ("sometimes purposefully, and sometimes inadvertently") suggests that

   A) writers are usually writing about themselves
   B) writers may misrepresent an actual event in a fictional work without realizing it
   C) readers should not trust writers who write autobiographically
   D) readers don't always interpret a novel the way the author intended

21. According to the ideas presented in the final paragraph, which of the following is the most appropriate interpretation of Dedalus's claim regarding Shakespeare?

   A) The character of Dedalus was a literary critic.
   B) Joyce expressed this controversial belief through Dedalus to protect his career.
   C) Joyce may have believed Shakespeare's characters were based on real people.
   D) Dedalus was based on a person Joyce knew personally.

22. All of the following could be considered autobiographical elements in Joyce's writing EXCEPT

   A) themes of isolation and exile
   B) a character who worked as a sailor in Trieste
   C) a character who is persecuted for his religious beliefs
   D) the character of Stephen Dedalus

Questions 23-32 are based on the following passage.

This passage is adapted from Arthur Loman, Life of a Salesman. © 2007 by Arthur Loman.

William was completely lost, that much he knew. Unfortunately, that was all he knew.

Of course, he hated to admit it when he was lost, so
Line much so that when he did get lost, it would inevitably
5 create a tragic episode of the grandest proportions, rather than a minor inconvenience. In a way, that made it easier for him to explain his tardiness to others. It was certainly easier to evade responsibility for a huge, unforeseeable mishap than for a series of small, yet obvious, errors.

10 These situations always started out the same way. William would be setting out to drive to a business appointment. Before leaving he would verify that he had everything he needed for the day. First he checked to see that he had his briefcase. He then checked and rechecked
15 the contents of the briefcase to see that every possible document he might need was there, not to mention extra pens, notepads, a calculator, spare calculator batteries, his cell phone, and spare cell phone battery.

He even insisted upon carrying a miniature tape
20 recorder, and spare batteries for that, as well. The inclusion of this last item was particularly perplexing to his coworkers, as there was no possible use for it in his work. When casually queried about the tape recorder, William merely responded, "I might need it." That much,
25 certainly, was evident, and they let the matter drop. To be sure, his insistence on traveling with a tape recorder for which he had no need was not the oddest thing about William, as far as his coworkers were concerned. Although his hygiene and grooming were impeccable, his
30 clothing seemed remarkably similar, if not identical, from one day to the next. His coworkers surmised that he owned several suits and ties, all of the same cut, in just two colors, navy blue and brown.

As he began his trip, William would have the
35 directions to his destination neatly written out in his own, extremely precise handwriting (the only handwriting he could dependably read, he would say). The directions would be hung on the dashboard within easy view, on a miniature clipboard. William didn't actually need the
40 directions at that point, since he had already committed them to memory. In fact, if you were in the car with him on such occasions (a practical impossibility since William would never drive with anyone in the car during business hours, not that anyone was anxious to, of course), you
45 would hear him muttering a litany of lefts and rights; chanting his mantra, street names and route numbers in their proper order.

Everything would be going fine until something would distract William, perhaps a flock of birds flying
50 in formation, or an out-of-state license plate he didn't recognize. Several minutes would pass, and he would slowly realize that he might have lost command of his directions and missed a turn. He would remain, however, in relatively calm denial of this possibility, until he had
55 driven many more miles and passed several other turns. "This road doesn't look like it goes the right way," he would grumble. "Too many other people are turning off here; I don't want to get stuck in traffic." And maybe, just maybe, he *hadn't* missed his turn, and it was going to
60 appear around the next bend in the road. "No way to find out but to keep on going." Obviously, the sensible thing to do would be to pull over, and consult a map, or perhaps use the cell phone to call for assistance. Neither of these things was an option as far as William was concerned.
65 The cell phone, as he put it, "should be used only in emergencies." Since nothing that ever happened to him constituted an "emergency" in his mind, he never once actually used the phone.

As to maps, he never carried one. He claimed that most
70 of them were useless to him, as they were "organized and planned so badly." In any event, what need did he have for maps when he always had his directions written out so carefully?

So on and on he drove, hoping that some type of
75 resolution would eventually reveal itself to him, that it would suddenly occur to him where to turn around, what to do. On one occasion, he drove through three different states before finding his way back to the office, well after dark, his suit rumpled, but his blue necktie still flying
80 proudly.

23. The primary purpose of the passage is to

A) recount the mishaps of a man driving to a business meeting
B) chronicle the idiosyncrasies of a traveling businessman
C) provide a detailed description of a day in the life of a salesperson
D) explain a man's lateness to his co-workers

24. The list of items in William's briefcase (lines 15-18) serves to

A) give an indication of the compulsive nature of William's preparations.
B) illustrate the stupidity of William's behavior.
C) show that William was a conscientious planner.
D) describe all the items William might need while at a business appointment.

25. The attitude of William's coworkers toward him can best be described as

    A) mildly curious
    B) coldly indifferent
    C) overtly condescending
    D) deeply intrigued

26. Which choice provides the best evidence for the answer to the previous question?

    A) Lines 7-9 ("It was certainly . . . errors")
    B) Lines 25-28 ("To be sure . . . concerned")
    C) Lines 53-55 ("He would remain . . . turns")
    D) Lines 77-80 ("On one occasion . . . proudly")

27. William's answer to his coworkers' questions about his tape recorder (lines 19-25) implies that he

    A) knows much more about the applications of technology in business than they do
    B) records business conversations in order to have proof of what was discussed
    C) believes it is best to be prepared for any contingency
    D) feels that their questions are rude and intrusive

28. William's preparations for his business meetings are best described as

    A) professional
    B) careless
    C) useful
    D) fruitless

29. As used in line 44, "anxious" most nearly means

    A) nervous.
    B) eager.
    C) uneasy.
    D) stressed.

30. As used in lines 51-53 "command" most nearly means

    A) power.
    B) authority.
    C) leader.
    D) control.

31. The reference to maps (line 69) implies that William

    A) has much to learn about navigation
    B) relies more on instinct than reason
    C) questions the mapmaker's eye for detail
    D) does not trust the orderliness of most maps

32. The author refers to William's "blue necktie" (line 79) in order to suggest

    A) the importance William places on his hygiene and grooming
    B) his ability to display dignity despite his mistakes
    C) the lack of variety in his wardrobe
    D) his obliviousness to the fact the he caused his own tardiness

Reading Drill 5

For each question in this section, circle the letter of the best answer from among the choices given.

Questions 1-11 are based on the following passage.

This passage is adapted from Marcantonio Raimondi,
From Reproduction to Objet: Printmaking in America. ©
2011 by Art History Quarterly.

"Printmaker!" The connotation of this word, curiously
absent from other languages, began to have some meaning
only after World War II. Surely, before the war, and often
Line in the long, splendid history of prints, there had been
5 artists who created nothing but prints. However, in most
cases the artists drew a composition before going to the
plate or block of stone, rather than working directly on
these materials exclusively. Even this is not the entire
distinction between earlier artists like Callot and Meryon
10 and those followers of Hayter who could be called
only "printmakers." Callot and Meryon made prints that,
following the original object of working in a multiple
medium, were meant to be printed in large numbers for
wide distribution of the image. Indeed, many painters
15 made prints for this sole reason. But the printmakers of
the second half of the twentieth century have found that
creating in a print medium is itself totally satisfying;
they often care not at all if no more than a few copies
are made before they go on to the next image. It is the
20 complex techniques of printmaking that entrance them. In
the words of Sylvan Cole, former Director of Associated
American Artists (AAA, the largest print gallery in
America and publisher of over 1,500 prints since 1934),
"The change that was taking place was the breakup with
25 the artist/painter (or Abstract Expressionist) who was not
interested in printmaking, and out of this came a man
called a printmaker, people like Karl Schrag, Peterdi,
Lasansky, Misch Kohn—who built their reputations as
printmakers."
30 Before the war, artists made considerable numbers of
prints. This was their only work; no doubt it was often a
matter of survival, not preference. Dozens of prints in a
relatively new medium, silkscreen, were turned out for the
adornment of schools and other government buildings.
35 The G.I. Bill filled the colleges, universities, and art
schools of post-war America during a period of prosperity
that encouraged such institutions to enlarge their facilities
or open new ones, particularly those devoted to the arts.
Many veterans who would never have had the opportunity
40 to attend college if they had not been drafted had little
direction—were "lost," so to speak—and found that the
unrestrained atmosphere of the post-war art schools and
art departments represented just the sort of freedom they
needed after years of military conformity. (Many others,
45 of course, had profited from the organized lifestyle of the
military and sought it in more disciplined fields such as
law, medicine, and business. The famous "Organization
Man" could hardly have had such success if this less
independent group had not also made a major contribution
50 to post-war society.) In the late 1940s, then, one could
observe the beginnings of a phenomenal expansion of
art education in institutions of higher learning, where art
departments attracted returning G.I.s who had completed
their undergraduate work before the war, and in older,
55 established art schools that were filled to capacity with
those who had finished only high school. Students who fell
under the spell of Lasansky during his first years at the
State University of Iowa went on to found print workshops
in other universities. Soon students of these workshops
60 pioneered others, so that in a very short time there were
facilities for the study of printmaking in most universities
in the United States.
The proliferation of places where printmaking was
taught and the subsequent increase in the number of
65 printmakers led to the birth of ancillary institutions: the
Brooklyn Museum's annual National Print Exhibition,
an open exhibition, in contrast with the traditional
invitational showings of the Society of Etchers (note
that these artists referred to themselves as etchers, not
70 printmakers) or the other one-medium groups such as
the National Serigraph Society; the International Group
Arts Society, a membership/subscription organization the
purpose of which was to publish and sell prints by new
artists of less conservative nature than those sponsored
75 by AAA; and regional and international exhibitions
devoted exclusively to prints, such as the Northwest
Printmakers Society, the Philadelphia Print Club, and
international biennials of prints in Cincinnati, Ljubljana,
and Tokyo. Thus, in the United States and elsewhere, the
need to show and distribute the outpourings of the print
80 workshops produced new organizations that in turn further
encouraged the creation of prints.

1. Which of the following could be expected of a
   disciple of Lasanky?

   A) Viewing the intricacies of print production as a
      necessary but uninteresting part of their art
   B) Focusing on the mass production or distribution
      of new prints
   C) Forgoing the composition stage in the creation
      of new art
   D) Advocating that artists work in multiple medium
      formats

2. Which choice provides the best evidence for the answer to the previous question?

   A) Lines 5-8 ("However, in most . . . exclusively")
   B) Lines 19-20 ("It is the . . . entrance them")
   C) Lines 32-34 ("Dozens of prints . . . buildings")
   D) Lines 55-58 ("Students who fell . . . universities")

3. In lines 11-14, the author asserts that Callot and Meryon

   A) collaborated with Hayter in pioneering the role of "printmaker"
   B) were more concerned with producing large numbers of prints than Hayter's disciples had been
   D) found complete satisfaction in the creating art through a print medium
   E) were difficult to distinguish from earlier artists, like Hayter

4. The author contends that "printmakers of the . . . twentieth century" (lines 15-16)

   A) were more concerned with the quantity of their prints than with the intricacy of their work
   B) were often distracted from their primary intention by the complexity of printmaking
   C) were fulfilled by the act of printmaking itself, while mass production was a secondary concern
   D) wanted to achieve international recognition for their groundbreaking work

5. The author quotes Sylvan Cole in lines 24-29 in order to

   A) demonstrate how Cole changed the art of printmaking during the turn of the century
   B) introduce the term "Abstract Expressionist" and examine its place in the art movement
   C) explain the relationship between printmaking and painting
   D) provide support for his assertions about the new developments in printmaking

6. The purpose of the second paragraph (lines 30-34) in relation to the passage is to

   A) provide support for the idea that modern printmaking emerged only after World War II
   B) acquaint the reader with the long established history of printmaking as a distinct art form
   C) question the originality of such artists as Callot and Meryton who claimed to have invented modern printmaking
   D) argue for the recognition of artists who were forced to create prints for the government

7. In line 34, "adornment" most nearly means

   A) inundation
   B) decoration
   C) enjoyment
   D) construction

8. The purpose of the G.I. Bill, mentioned in line 35, was to

   A) allow veterans to bypass college in order to concentrate on artistic pursuits
   B) allow veterans to attend colleges or specialized schools by offering assistance after the war
   C) provide the "lost" veterans with a place to study
   D) open new facilities or strengthen already established art institutions

9. In line 41, "lost" most nearly means

   A) unfound
   B) desperate
   C) aimless
   D) aberrant

10. The author attributes the "phenomenal expansion of art education" (lines 50-51) primarily to

    A) increased membership in the military
    B) the appeal of art departments both to veterans who had graduated from college and to those who had not
    C) the State University of Iowa's groundbreaking work in recruiting students
    D) the influence in the late 1940s of the famous "Organization Man"

11. In the final paragraph, the author cites which of the following effects of the "proliferation of places where printmaking was taught" (line 63) in the United States?

    A) The increased opportunities to display printmakers' work encouraged the production of more prints.
    B) The financial success of the AAA encouraged many businesses to establish their own institutions.
    C) Attempts to expose the public to the works of less conservative artists produced a backlash against all printmakers.
    D) Increased publicity spurred a rise in public appreciation and financial support.

Questions 12-21 are based on the following passage.

Adapted from Bradley J. Phillips, Coronal Mass Ejections: New Research Directions. *Journal of Solar Research, 2009.*

The idea that the sun has an almost unambiguously benign effect on our planet appears, on the surface, to be an incontrovertible one. Few people realize, however, that certain events on the sun can have disastrous
Line
5 consequences for life here on Earth. The geomagnetic storm is one such phenomenon. These storms begin on the surface of the sun when a group of sunspots creates a burst of electromagnetic radiation. These bursts thrust billions of tons of ionized gas, known as plasma, into
10 space; scientists refer to these solar projections as coronal mass ejections (CMEs). After this initial explosion, the CME gets caught up in a shower of particles, also known as a "solar wind," that continuously rains down on the Earth from the sun.
15 The last recorded instance of a major CME occurred in 1989, when the resulting geomagnetic storm knocked out an entire electrical power grid, depriving over six million energy consumers of power for an extended period. As we become increasingly dependent on new
20 technologies to sustain ourselves in our day-to-day activities, the potential havoc wrought by a major CME becomes even more distressing. Scientists conjecture that a "perfect storm" would have the potential to knock out power grids across the globe and create disruptions in the
25 orbit of low-altitude communication satellites, rendering such satellites practically useless.

What troubles scientists most about these "perfect storms" is not only their potential for interstellar mischief, but also the fact that they are so difficult to forecast. For
30 one thing, remarkable though these solar occurrences might be, they are still a relatively rare phenomenon, and the few existing records regarding major CMEs provide researchers with scant information from which to draw conclusions about their behavior. Solar storm watchers
35 are frustrated by yet another limitation: time. CMEs have been known to travel through space at speeds approaching 5 million miles per hour, which means they can cover the 93 million miles between the sun and the Earth in well under 20 hours. (Some have been known
40 to travel the same distance in as little as 14 hours.) The difficulties created by this narrow window of opportunity are compounded by the fact that scientists are able to determine the orientation of a CME's magnetic field only about 30 minutes before it reaches the atmosphere, giving
45 them little or no time to predict the storm's potential impact on the surface.

Some world governments hope to combat this problem by placing a satellite in orbit around the sun to monitor activity on its surface, in the hopes that this will
50 buy scientists more time to predict the occurrence and intensity of geomagnetic storms. In the meantime, many energy providers are responding to the CME threat by installing voltage control equipment and limiting the volume of electricity generated by some power stations.

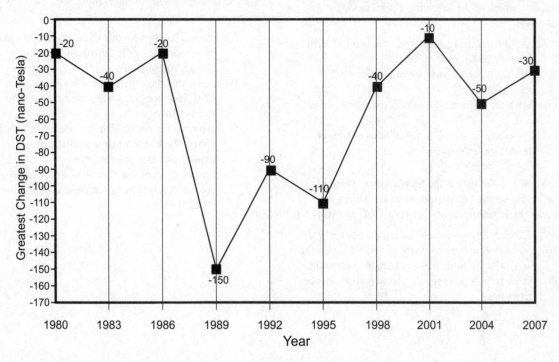

Geomagnetic Storm Activity as Measured by Change in Disturbance Storm index (DST)

12. With which of the following statements would the author of this article be most likely to agree?

   A) CMEs are a subject of interest but little practical importance, because there is nothing that can be done to minimize their impact.
   B) In the next decade, a perfect storm will interrupt power supplies and cause extensive inconvenience and loss of services.
   C) We should learn more about the potential dangers of CMEs, but few steps can be taken to alter such storms' effects.
   D) Each of us should view a significant CME as a real possibility but should also expect that leaders will have effective protective measures in place before such an event.

13. Which of the following can most reasonably be inferred about the significant CME that took place in 1989?

   A) Because of the hysteria caused by this storm, scientists and world leaders are more fearful of future storms than they are willing to express publicly.
   B) The next geomagnetic storm that occurs will be much worse.
   C) Its effects were limited to knocking out a power grid, depriving customers of power for a week.
   D) A geomagnetic storm of similar magnitude could easily cause more extensive damage and hardship in today's society.

14. The information presented in the graph above supports which of the following claims made by the author?

   A) CMEs can travel between the sun and the earth in under 20 hours.
   B) The last recorded instance of a major CME occurred in 1989.
   C) A perfect storm has the power to disrupt power grids.
   D) Geomagnetic storms thrust billions of tons of ionized gas into space.

15. According to the data in the graph above, which of the following can be inferred about the pattern in geomagnetic storm activity between 1980 and 2007?

   A) Geomagnetic storm activity increased each year.
   B) Geomagnetic storm activity decreased each year.
   C) Geomagnetic storm activity remained constant.
   D) No pattern in geomagnetic storm activity can be determined.

16. As used in line 33, "scant" most nearly means

   A) limited.
   B) exhaustive.
   C) excessive.
   D) appropriate.

17. The author first mentions geomagnetic storms in order to illustrate which of the following claims?

   A) Many energy companies are installing voltage control equipment and limiting the amount of power used by power stations.
   B) Despite the widespread notion that the sun has apparently limited effects on Earth, certain events on the sun can in fact have serious consequences for our planet.
   C) It is an incontrovertible fact that the sun has virtually no effect on our planet.
   D) Major CMEs are a relatively rare phenomenon, despite the fact that they have been known to travel between the sun and the Earth in under 20 hours.

18. Which choice provides the best evidence for the answer to the previous question?

   A) Lines 6-8 ("These storms . . . electromagnetic radiation.")
   B) Lines 8-11 ("These bursts . . . coronal mass ejections.")
   C) Lines 11-14 ("After this . . . the sun.")
   D) Lines 15-18 ("The last . . . extended period.")

19. The author uses the term "compounded by" (line 41) to

   A) emphasize the fact that these researchers face even more stringent time limits than those already mentioned.
   B) assert that the scientists working to predict CMEs are not given adequate time to do so successfully.
   C) disprove the notion that the orientation of CMEs affects the length of time available for scientific inquiry into this phenomenon.
   D) caution readers that speculations of energy providers might heighten the uncertainty raised by CMEs.

20. Which of the following were mentioned as factors contributing to the difficulty of forecasting CMEs?

    I.   Limited available reaction time in which to determine orientation

    II.   The tendency of voltage controls to be overridden by electrical surges

    III. Insufficient data upon which to base assessments of past behavior

    A) I only
    B) I and II
    C) I and III
    D) II and III only

21. The primary purpose of this passage is

    A) to describe the chilling potential effects of a perfect storm.
    B) to inform readers about CMEs and their effects on electrical circuitry on Earth.
    C) to persuade readers that CMEs are a problem that both governments and individual citizens need to combat.
    D) to inform readers about a potentially dangerous phenomenon and the difficulties in addressing that danger.

Questions 22-32 are based on the following passage.

Adapted from Maxwell Foltz, Stellar Bodies: An Introduction. *St. James Press, 1994*

Passage 1

The concept of black holes is not new; it also arises in Newtonian gravity. Laplace pointed out in 1824 that if a star contains enough mass in a small enough package, the velocity needed to escape from its surface is greater than that of light. No light can get out, though light and matter can enter. Simply add the speed limit of c from special relativity, and you have a one-way ticket into the universe; nothing that goes in can ever get out.

In general relativity, unlike Laplace's case, the light does not just fall back. It simply travels on curved paths smaller than the size of the star. The star is thus plucked out of space-time.

The density of matter required is phenomenal. Our sun would have to be only a few miles in diameter to become a black hole. The pressure generated by the nuclear "flame" in its heart prevents it from collapsing. Even when the sun finally exhausts its fuel, we do not expect it to become a black hole but simply to collapse to a form called a white dwarf.

A star 5 to 10 times heavier than our sun would have gravity enough to pull it through the white-dwarf stage to the black-hole stage. Whether heavy stars actually do this is anyone's guess. Stellar collapse usually leads to an explosion. The greater part of the star's mass is blown away, and whether enough remains to make a black hole is hard to say. We do know that enough often remains to form a neutron star; there is one in the center of the Crab Nebula, the debris of a supernova recorded in 1054. Since the minimum mass for a black hole is not much greater than for a neutron star, it is likely that they do sometimes form.

For obvious reasons, a black hole is nearly impossible to detect. Our best bet is to catch one that is absorbing matter at a substantial rate. This can happen if the black hole has a nearby binary partner and draws in hot gases from its companion's atmosphere. As they fall, the acceleration makes the gases radiate light; the higher the acceleration, the greater the frequency. A black hole has strong enough gravity to make x-rays come out.

Passage 2

Astrophysicist Stephen Hawking has suggested the existence of mini black holes. There is no observational evidence for a mini hole, but they are theoretically plausible. Hawking has deduced that small black holes can seem to emit energy in the form of elementary particles (neutrinos, etc.). The mini holes would thus evaporate and disappear. This may seem to contradict the concept that mass can't escape from a black hole, but when we consider effects of quantum mechanics, the picture of black holes that we have discussed thus far is insufficient. Hawking suggests that a black hole so affects the space near it that a pair of particles—a nuclear particle and its antiparticle—can form simultaneously. The antiparticle disappears into the black hole, and the remaining particle reaches us.

Emission from black holes is significant only for the smallest ones, for the amount of radiation increases sharply as we consider less and less massive back holes. Only mini black holes up to the mass of an asteroid would have had time to disappear since the origin of the universe. Hawking's ideas set a lower limit on the size of black holes now in existence, since we think the mini black holes were formed only in the first second after the origin of the universe.

On the other extreme of mass, we can consider what a black hole would be like if it contained a very large number of solar masses. Thus far, we have considered only black holes the mass of a star or smaller. Such black holes form after a stage of high density. But the more mass involved, the lower the density needed for a black hole to form. For a very massive black hole, the density would be fairly low.

Thus if we were traveling through the universe in a spaceship, we couldn't count on detecting a black hole by noticing a volume of high density. We could pass through a high-mass black hole without even noticing. We would never be able to get out, but hours on our watches could pass before we would notice that we were being drawn into the center at an accelerating rate.

22. According to Passage 1, all of the following are reasons our own sun will not become a black hole in the immediate future EXCEPT

    A) its diameter is too large.
    B) when it collapses, it will become a white dwarf instead.
    C) the "nuclear flame" at its core prevents it from collapsing.
    D) its gravitational pull is too strong.

23. As used in line 17, the word "exhausts" most nearly means

   A) uses up.
   B) squanders.
   C) fatigues.
   D) emits.

24. The author of Passage 1 refers to the Crab Nebula in order to

   A) discuss relevant Chinese astronomers.
   B) prove the existence of black holes.
   C) give an example of what leftover star mass can form.
   D) describe the process a star goes through to become a black hole.

25. It can be inferred from Passage 1 that the best way to find a black hole is to

   A) measure the density of a star.
   B) search for x-ray emissions.
   C) locate a white dwarf.
   D) find two planets next to each other.

26. Which choice provides the best evidence for the answer to the previous question?

   A) Lines 5-6 ("No light . . . can enter.")
   B) Lines 15-16 ("The pressure . . . from collapsing.")
   C) Lines 24-26 ("The greater . . . to say.")
   D) Lines 38-39 ("A black . . . come out.")

27. The primary purpose of Passage 2 is to

   A) discuss the theoretical existence of black holes of extreme sizes.
   B) explain the ratio of mass to density within mini black holes.
   C) describe Stephen Hawking's significance as a premier physicist.
   D) cite the many different mini black holes observed by astronomers.

28. As used in line 44, the word "elementary" most nearly means

   A) basic.
   B) scholastic.
   C) theoretical.
   D) electric.

29. It can be inferred that the emission from mini black holes is significant only for the smallest black holes (lines 57-58) because

   A) the amount of radiation released by mini black holes is minuscule compared to that emitted by larger black holes.
   B) nearly all notable astronomers have attempted to disprove the trend.
   C) emissions from black holes are inversely proportional to the size of black holes.
   D) larger black holes disappear before they have a chance to emit radiation.

30. The last paragraph of Passage 2 uses the spaceship scenario in order to

   A) prove the existence of a much-discussed hypothetical phenomenon.
   B) illustrate an abstract theory with some concrete details.
   C) warn future theorists of the danger of tenuous evidence.
   D) add credence to an otherwise flimsy hypothesis.

31. The authors of Passage 1 and Passage 2 would probably agree that which of the following is an identifying factor of a star capable of becoming a black hole?

   A) The number of asteroids nearby
   B) The pathway of the emitted light
   C) The presence of quasars
   D) Its mass and density

32. With which of the following statements would the author of Passage 2 most likely dispute the statement put forth in lines 6-8 of Passage 1?

   A) It is possible for only extraordinarily powerful energy emissions to escape black holes.
   B) While nothing can escape a black hole, it is unlikely that any matter can go in.
   C) Hawking theorized that matter can, in fact, escape a mini black hole.
   D) Black holes do exist, but it is impossible to theorize about their gravitational pull.

Chapter 14
Reading Answers
and Explanations

ANSWER KEY

Reading Drill 1	Reading Drill 2	Reading Drill 3	Reading Drill 4	Reading Drill 5
1. C	1. A	1. A	1. C	1. C
2. A	2. A	2. B	2. A	2. A
3. B	3. A	3. B	3. D	3. B
4. B	4. C	4. D	4. C	4. C
5. A	5. B	5. A	5. C	5. D
6. C	6. B	6. D	6. B	6. A
7. C	7. A	7. B	7. D	7. B
8. A	8. B	8. D	8. A	8. B
9. D	9. D	9. C	9. B	9. C
10. C	10. A	10. A	10. D	10. B
11. C	11. C	11. D	11. C	11. A
12. B	12. C	12. B	12. D	12. C
13. C	13. B	13. C	13. A	13. D
14. A	14. B	14. D	14. C	14. B
15. D	15. D	15. D	15. D	15. D
16. B	16. B	16. C	16. B	16. A
17. D	17. C	17. D	17. A	17. B
18. A	18. C	18. C	18. D	18. D
19. B	19. A	19. D	19. A	19. A
20. A	20. A	20. B	20. B	20. C
21. D	21. A	21. D	21. C	21. D
22. B	22. B	22. A	22. B	22. D
23. D	23. D	23. B	23. B	23. A
24. C	24. A	24. D	24. A	24. C
25. B	25. D	25. D	25. A	25. B
26. A	26. C	26. D	26. B	26. D
27. C	27. D	27. A	27. C	27. A
28. C	28. D	28. A	28. D	28. A
29. C	29. A	29. C	29. B	29. C
30. A	30. C	30. B	30. D	30. B
31. D	31. D	31. D	31. A	31. D
	32. D	32. B	32. B	32. C
	33. B	33. D		

ANSWERS AND EXPLANATIONS FOR READING

Drill 1

1. **C** The passage as a whole is informative and provides a description of how NATO was formed. Choice (A) is too strong. Choice (B) indicates that the main focus is the *Marshall Plan*, not *NATO*. In (D), *question* does not reflect the informative tone of the passage. Choice (C) is the best match.

2. **A** After line 15, the passage describes *deterrence* in that forming a *peacetime alliance* would *deter aggression by the Soviet Union*. So we need an answer that means "to preserve peace" or "prevent fighting." Only (A) *the discouragement of attacks* and specifically mentions *the Soviet Union*. The other answers are not supported by the passage.

3. **B** The second paragraph overall describes what makes NATO different from other alliances that came before. This is paraphrased in (B) *highlight a factor distinguishing NATO from other pacts*. Choice (A) is mentioned in the next paragraph, but does not answer the question asked. The rest of the answers are not supported by the paragraph or the passage as a whole.

4. **B** In the passage, the three men are cited as leaders *put down* by a *grand alliances* that differed from NATO in that the *grand alliances* were formed specifically *after an act of aggression* to get rid of those leaders, whereas the NATO alliance was to form in peacetime to prevent any aggressive acts from occurring. This is paraphrased best in (B). Choice (A) is contradicted by the passage, and there is no evidence for (C) or (D) in the passage.

5. **A** Go through each answer choice, and eliminate those supported by evidence in the passage. Choice (A) is not a reason for the formation of NATO. While France is mentioned, it was not *democratic uprisings* but *communist political strength in France* that served as a reason that NATO was formed. The rest of the answers are paraphrases of the reasons listed in lines 21–38.

6. **C** Choice (A) is not true: While the U.S. *no longer had a monopoly*, the passage states that the U.S. *had a superiority of about 8 to 1*. Choice (C) gives a paraphrase of this, and is the correct answer. There is no evidence for (B), and (D) is too strong.

7. **C** Go back to the passage and use the context to come up with a word or phrase to replace *superiority*. The sentence indicates the *number* of nuclear warheads the United States had in relation to the Soviet Union. Only (C) refers specifically to numbers, so it is the correct answer. Choices (A) and (B) are alternate meanings of the word *superiority*, but do not work in context. Choice (D) is irrelevant to the sentence.

8. **A** Choice (B) is not true: there was no *aggressive behavior*: both were established in peacetime. Choice (C) is incorrect because the Warsaw Pact was a *Soviet alliance defense organization*, and so communist, not democratic. Choice (D) is out: there is no evidence for *imperialism*.

9. **D** The Warsaw Pact is mentioned in the last paragraph. Lines 54-57 describe a peacetime event, *West German entrance into NATO, that was the immediate cause of the establishment of . . . the Warsaw Pact*, so (D) is the correct answer. While (A) and (C) mention the Soviet Union or its missiles, they do not mention the Warsaw Pact. Choice (B) also does not mention the Warsaw Pact.

10. **C** Both passages describe Catiline; to find the difference, or *contrast*, between them, look for the main idea of the passages. Passage 1 is by Catiline, and he speaks of wanting to bring people to liberty and freedom. Passage 2 describes Catiline as someone who is alarming the people (line 37) and should be executed (lines 45-46) and whose followers are considered *worthless dregs*. This is best paraphrased in (C). The other answers do not have the correct relationship to the ideas expressed in the passage.

11. **C** The question is rhetorical, and not meant to be answered, so eliminate (A). The purpose of a rhetorical question is to emphasize the speaker's main point. The speech as a whole is an attempt to rally followers to rebel against the people in charge. Just before the question, Catiline mentions how those in the government have all the *power, honor, and wealth*, while the common people that he is trying to gather to fight have only *insults, dangers, persecutions, and poverty*. The question is supposed to inspire the people to fight the unjust situation he described. This is best paraphrased in (C).

12. **B** In the third paragraph, the speaker tells why he thinks they will *succeed*: his side is *fresh* and *unbroken* while the other side has a *debility* caused by *age* and *wealth*. This is paraphrased in (B). In lines 18–19 the speaker mentions that success *is in our own hands*. Choices (A) and (C) are extreme. Choice (D), *kings,* is mentioned in the passage, but not in relation to the success of Catiline and his followers.

13. **C** The *venerable body* mentioned in line 40 are the senators in *the senate* that the speaker in Passage 2 describes as a place that Catiline has the freedom be in despite his personal beliefs and actions. The clue *looks and countenances,* mentioned in the passage just before the quote in the question, helps explain what is referred to. The look on a person's face is a clue to their emotions, such as an angry look or a pleased look. It turns out that the word *countenance* actually does have the meaning of "face," but *look* may be enough to identify that we are talking about emotion or *expressions* as in (C).

14. **A** In lines 36–44 the orator lists the things that should be convincing Catiline that he is in the wrong and has been defeated by those in charge of the city. This is best paraphrased in (A). There is no evidence of *isolation,* for the orator to *exploit* in (B). In fact, later, the orator even mentions the freedoms that Catiline is allowed. There are *alarmed people* mentioned in the passage but the measures listed are not meant to *alert* them. The list is about things that should be making Catiline feel remorseful for his actions, not to *appeal to his national pride* as in (D).

15. **D** The evidence for why the orator is against executing Catiline is in lines 49–53: The speaker states that he will do that which is . . . *more expedient for the state,* which best matches (D). Choice (A) is not true: the blurb mentions that Cicero had previously ordered executions. There is no evidence that the reason involved the *senators* in (B), or angering the senate as in (C). Cicero is concerned about the followers staying in town after Catiline died.

16. **B** The second paragraph of passage 2 is where the speaker discusses his reasons for not calling for Catiline's execution. Choices (A) and (D) are in the wrong parts of the passage. In the sentence in (B), the speaker says he *will do that which is more expedient for the state*, which directly supports (D) in the previous question. In the sentence in (D), the speaker indicates what he wants Catiline to do, but not why.

17. **D** Go back to the passage and use the context to come up with a word to replace *afford*. In the passage, the orator is implying that nothing could "give" Catiline any pleasure, because everyone in the city hated him. Only (D) *provide* has a meaning close to give. Choice (A), *purchase,* is a word that connects with a different meaning of *afford* and does not fit into the context of the sentence in the passage.

18. **A** In lines 72–75, the orator points out the silence of the senators to show that they agree with him in his condemnation of Catiline and his activities. The orator's speech is pretty harsh on Catiline, so the correct answer indicates that the senators feel negatively toward Catiline. Choice (A) is the best match. Although (B) also mentions Catiline, the silence had nothing to do with their willingness to execute him. There is no evidence for (C), and (D) is the opposite of what is presented in the passage.

19. **B** The orator in Passage 1 is pro-Catiline (he *is* Catiline) and would respond in way that agrees with the main idea of Passage 1. Passage 1 was about how the people were being unfairly treated by those in power, and the people needed to rise up and claim their liberty and right to wealth and power. Violence is advocated in Passage 1, so (A) is not true. Choice (B) invokes the unfairness (*oppressiveness*) of the situation and mentions the rights of citizens, so it is a good match. Choice (C) is out because *inevitably* is too strong and impossible to *demonstrate* in the situation described. Choice (D) is the opposite of what is expressed in Passage 1.

20. **A** See what you can eliminate. Only Passage 1 brings up the point in (B). Choice (C) is shown to be untrue in the second paragraph of Passage 2, in which the freedoms that are allowed even to those who express disagreement are mentioned. Choice (D) is not correct because it is impossible to say if things will change drastically or if the current situation will simply be strengthened or stabilized.

21. **D** Go back to the passage and use the context to come up with a word to replace *begetter*. The word describes George Washington's position in relation to Americans' rights. In the first sentence, Washington is described as the *founder of the American nation*, so look for a word that means something similar to *founder*. He was not the owner of anyone's rights, so eliminate (A). Because Americans did not have legal rights before the nation was established, Washington could not have been the *reformer* of those rights, so eliminate (C). Although *procreator* is an alternate definition of *begetter*, it is usually used in the context of having children. *Procurer* means a person who obtains things. Washington helped obtain legal rights for Americans, so (D) is the correct answer.

22. **B** The sentence that begins with *Later Americans* describes them as people who enjoy their rights but forget about the person (Washington) who established some of those rights. This is best paraphrased in (B). *They tended to ignore* Washington. There is no evidence in the passage for any of the other answers.

23. **D** The *debunkers* are people who tried to find out improper things about the people we hold up as examples of goodness in order to *destroy* or *reduce* them. This is expressed in (D), *reducing to a less than heroic status*. Choice (A) is the opposite of what the debunkers are doing. Chocie (B) is not negative enough to describe the debunkers' activities. Choice (C) is incorrect because the focus is not about Washington's *patriotism* but his very character.

24. **C** The *biographical 'debunkers'* are described as finding *sin in the saint*, or questioning a purely positive view of an important figure. Choice (A) is incorrect because it describes the opposite viewpoint. Choice (B) describes scholars whose attention strayed from Washington, but not the *biographical 'debunkers'* themselves. Choice (C) accurately describes what the 'debunkers' did, so it is the correct answer. Choice (D) describes a reason they may have thought as they did, but not what they were responsible for.

25. **B** In the paragraph that mentions the *wildly supportive crowd* the author describes their *hysteria* and then asks *How easily and with what frenzy could* the *emotion turn* if the *government did not please*. So he's worried that the crowd could *turn* on him, and be the opposite of supportive if the government doesn't do what the people want. Only (B) reflects this.

26. **A** Go back to the passage where *insuperable diffidence* is mentioned. This is the end of the paragraph in which Washington is worrying about whether he'll do a good enough job as president to keep the people from turning on him. He's worried he won't measure up to his duties, so a good word for the spot that *insuperable diffidence* is taking up is "insecurity." In (A) *lack of self-confidence* is a good match for insecurity. There is no difference in belief mentioned in the paragraph. Eliminate (C) and (D) because they are the opposite of what we're looking for.

27. **C** The *task* is described in the passage as *more uncertain* and *important* than his Continental Army command. He felt about the Continental Army role that there was no *reason to doubt that success was possible*. Only (C) indicates that Washington was *untried* or uncertain about the first situation and that the second was *possible*. Choice (A) is the opposite of what we're looking for. Choice (B) is not mentioned in the passage. Choice (D) is not true because the responsibility in both cases definitely belonged to Washington.

28. **C** The pair of words that best describes Washington's Continental Army *duty* and the presidency that Washington is about to assume in the passage is (C), *Unremarkable and momentous*. The Army duty described in lines 76–77 *had been won ten thousand times*, which supports *unremarkable*. The author describes the presidency in line 83 as *Washington's present mission* as something *that might change all history*, which supports *momentous*. None of the other answers are supported by the passage.

29. **C** In Passage 2, the quote is mentioned as something that Washington will prove untrue if his presidency is a success. Choice (A) is unrelated to Washington proving anything. Choice (B) is out because the passage mentions that the idea had been accepted by *many of the greatest thinkers*, not just pessimistic ones. Choice (C) mentions that the quote *would be disproved* if he was *successful*, so it is a very good match. There is no evidence that the quote was Washington's *credo* as in (D): in fact, it was something that he wanted to disprove.

30. **A** Choice (A) best describes the main difference between the passages. The most striking thing in the second passage is that it tells about the beginning of the American presidency in a reflective way from Washington's view of the event. Looking just at the descriptions of Passage 2 in the answers, eliminate any that are not close to the main point of Passage 2. We can keep (A) for *Washington's view of his place in history*. In (B), *perfect* has no support from the passage. Choice (C) is incorrect because Passage 2 is about worries at the time of becoming president, not *military successes*. Choice (D) is wrong because there is no mention of academics changing their position in Passage 2. This leaves only (A), and the first part of the answer, *describes the myths*, does actually reflect what is happening in Passage 1.

31. **D** Both passages support the statement in (D): Passage 1 mentions that *Washington was the one man essential to the triumph...to the creation* of America, and *the success of the democratic revolution* (lines 28–31). Passage 2 mentions that *Washington's present mission might change all history* (line 83). Choice (B) is extreme, and there is no support in the passage for any of the other answers.

Drill 2

1. **A** The term *Anytown, U.S.A.*, implies that the conditions described could be found in practically any town in the United States. Choice (A) captures exactly what the term implies, while (B) expresses the opposite. For (C), while *Anytown* may be imaginary, this is not the author's point. Choice (D) is incorrect because the author does not discuss whether suburbs are common outside the United States.

2. **A** If we cross out the word we're trying to understand, what word could we put in its place? The sentence suggests that suburbs offer some good things, but also offer some bad things at the same time. Thus, we're looking for a word that means "also or at the same time." Choice (A) means "at the same time"—keep it! Choices (B), *widespread,* and (C), *greedy,* may describe suburbia, but they don't mean "also or at the same time," so eliminate them. Choice (D) means "in a showy fashion"—not what we're looking for, so eliminate it.

3. **A** The author uses the phrase *too much of a stretch* (line 36) to show his or her belief that all modern problems are not caused by suburbia. Choice (A) captures the meaning for which we are looking. Choice (B) is wrong because nothing in this answer is reflected in the author's statements. Choices (C) and (D) are incorrect, since the list of problems on these lines was not mentioned before, so the list isn't a summary or a modification of a previous argument.

4. **C**   Go back to the passage and use the context to come up with a word to replace *pervasive*. The sentence indicates that the threats described are *more immediate* than the growth of suburbs, so look for a word that agrees with that idea. *Narrow* means the opposite of *pervasive*, so eliminate (A). Not all social problems are *physical*, so eliminate (B). *Pervasive* means *widespread*, so (C) is correct.

5. **B**   Choice (B), suburban conformity, is what Passage 1 is all about. Choices (A), (C), and (D) are mentioned in the passage, but not as results of *suburban sprawl*.

6. **B**   A homeowner spends money to limit property damage, just as the government spends money to protect state land from the potential damage of suburban sprawl, so (B) is correct. A mother lion protects her cub out of instinct; the New Jersey government is not acting on instinct, so eliminate (A). The New Jersey government is trying to save something but not in the sense of putting money in a safe place to earn interest that can be spent later; eliminate (C). The government's action is not like changing a lock; rather, it is like putting a lock on where none existed. Therefore, eliminate (D).

7. **A**   Four of the answer choices are mentioned in the passage; we're looking for the one that is not. Choice (A) is wrong because, as line 64 shows, New Jersey residents voted for the measure in a referendum; it was not implemented through executive order. Choice (B) is incorrect because the pinelands are mentioned in line 76. Choice (C) is wrong since lines 76-77 states the anti-sprawl effort *has demonstrated that it is possible to control sprawl*. We can eliminate (D) based on lines 78–80.

8. **B**   The author of Passage 1 laments that suburban sprawl has *robbed us of hundreds of years of original and beautiful home design* (lines 22–23) and the author of Passage 2 *must concede that sprawl does detract from the beauty of the landscape* (lines 50–51). Choice (B) best sums up these concerns. Choice (A) is extreme—neither author argues that there's no benefit whatsoever to suburban construction. The author of Passage 1 would disagree with (C), and the author of Passage 2 would disagree with (D).

9. **D**   The author of Passage 2 says that complaints about sprawl—like the ones in Passage 1—*border on the histrionic* (line 49), which means "excessively emotional or dramatic." Choices (A), (B), and (C) are not specifically mentioned in Passage 2, and don't describe the criticism we're looking for.

10. **A**   The third paragraph of Passage 1 criticizes suburban sprawl. The sentence in (A) indicates the opinion of the author of Passage 2 towards critics of suburban growth: *many of these complaints border on the histrionic*, which supports (D) in the previous question. None of the other choices refer to the author's opinion of critics of sprawl.

11. **C**   Passage 1 outlines, in vivid detail, the problem posed by suburban sprawl. Passage 2 describes how New Jersey fought back. This is most like (C). Passage 1 doesn't advocate specific changes, so strike (A). While Passage 2 contradicts parts of Passage 1, it doesn't *debunk*, or "expose the falseness or ridiculousness of," Passage 1, so eliminate (B). Choice (D) is wrong because it reverses the two arguments (Passage 1 is more *theoretical* while Passage 2 is more concrete and *practical*).

12. C The *process* was one of collaboration, with different people bringing in ideas until the song is *improvised into being*, although *it was Ellington who headed the collective*. Only (B) and (C) come close to the description in the passage, and (B) can be ruled out because the members band were not *equals*—Ellington was definitely the leader.

13. B The *working relationship* between Ellington *and his band members* is described in the first paragraph. Choice (B) best describes how Ellington would decide what to use from an improvisation session with the band when writing his compositions. Choice (A) describes how the composition of a new song would begin, but does not fully describe the process. Choices (C) and (D) are in the wrong part of the passage.

14. B Go back to the passage and use the context to come up with a word to replace *accenting*. In the passage, Ellington is "bringing out" the melodies of the piece from the *background*. This is closest to (B), *emphasizing*. More to the point, there is no evidence for the rest of the answers in the passage.

15. D The description in the fifth paragraph provides some of the ideas behind some of Ellington's works. This is best paraphrased in (D). The rest of the answers are not supported by the passage.

16. B The paragraph describes the colors of the title in two ways, as the colors of people's skin and *not only in color, but in his being as well*, using color describing the state of the world as a *metaphor*. This is reflected best in (B).

17. C Go back to the passage and use the context to come up with a phrase to replace larger *forms. Larger forms* are introduced in the context of Ellington's *critics*. Later in the fourth paragraph, Ellington's *medleys—long series of his many successful tunes* are mentioned as the thing that *upset many of his more sophisticated fans*. Therefore, the *larger forms* are the same as the *medleys*, as in (C). A *symphony orchestra*, as in (A), is never mentioned in the passage. Choice (B) describes large instruments, but not the songs discussed in the passage. Choice (D) recycles some words from the fourth paragraph, but also does not refer to the songs.

18. C The author follows the description of the *criticisms* with a discussion about Ellington's *astonishing, amiable naïveté* and gives examples of how Ellington *failed to see* that his choices were not sophisticated. This sense of *naïveté* is best captured in the *innocence* in (C). Choice (A) is not mentioned in the correct part of the passage to answer this question. Choice (B) is the actual criticism, not the author's response to it.

19. A Always go back to the passage: we need to find out how the attitude of the *fans* is described. The fans were *upset* by Ellington's use of *medleys of his successful tunes*. This is best summarized in (A). There is no evidence for (B), (C) is extreme and attributes *naïveté* to the wrong individuals, and (D) is the attitude of the *critics*, not the *fans*.

20. A Only (A), *famous paintings,* is not mentioned in the passage. Choice (B) is in lines 53–57, (C) is in lines 9–18, and (D) is in 59–62.

21.   A   *Fletcher Henderson* is mentioned as the person from whom Ellington *rather directly* got three of his four styles. So Henderson was an inspiration or model for Ellington. This is best captured in (A), *influence on*. Choice (B) reverses the relationship. It is clear that Henderson came first, so they were not *contemporaries* as in (C). Choice (D) is not supported by the passage.

22.   B   While the passage mentions Ellington's age at the time he wanted to become a painter, it does not give the age at which he became a musical success: eliminate (A). The *jungle style* is mentioned, but not described in detail: eliminate (C). The passage does not provide the title of Ellington's best-known composition; eliminate (D). Only the question in (B) could be answered by information in the passage.

23.   D   Each sentence in the first paragraph refers to something about the new wealth of information available. The first sentence mentions all the information we could ever need. The second mentions the profusion of information. Although the author does go on to say that our approach to this information has changed, he does not speak of it disparagingly, as (A) and (C) suggest. And although the author discusses distinctions between old and new methods of research, he doesn't discuss distinctions between old and new topics, which eliminates (B).

24.   A   The previous generations of scholars is described as slav[ing] away at libraries, pulling dusty books from the shelves and hoping that those books could reveal all the world's secrets. This information is given in contrast to the first sentence of the first paragraph, which shows that now that information is all more readily available. The author does not indicate a preference in these lines for either method, which eliminates (D). And while (B) may be true, the author does not state it, and it is not his main point.

25.   D   The term information saturation refers back to all the information we could ever need and the profusion of information mentioned in the previous paragraph. The term does not refer to a mode of thinking, which eliminates (A). Nor does the author suggest that contemporary human beings are unable to learn any new information, eliminating (C). The author writes only that there is too much available information for any single human being to know, as in (D).

26.   C   The author continually refers to the new wealth of information as available (as in (C)), but he does not indicate that we have a complete grasp or understanding of that information, which eliminates (A) and (D).

27.   D   Pay close attention to the question. It does not ask the meaning of the phrase "our understanding," which might lead one to pick (A) or (B). Instead, it asks from what this understanding is a shift away. Note the next line: where we once thought of the 'heavens' as the things that we could see in the sky. In other words, the universe used to be knowable because it was something we could see, as in (D).

28. **D** The researchers and scholar mentioned in this part of the passage are given as examples of the older mode of study. While they might be contrasted with newer scholars, they are not being contrasted with newer researchers in these lines, eliminating (C). Choices (A) and (B) can be eliminated because the author is either not warning against this mode of study or emphasizing its importance; he is merely describing it. Only (D) can work because, while it is less specific than the others, it does not contain any errors.

29. **A** Note the contrast between (A) and (B). These two answers have some similarities, but (B) is more extreme and should therefore be eliminated. Choice (A) is supported in the transition between the third and fourth paragraphs: A scholar like James Frazer, author of *The Golden Bough* (1890), could be fairly certain that he was assembling all of the world's myths and folklore in a single book. Now, we know that Frazer's project was a very limited one.

30. **C** Read the fourth paragraph carefully: Because we know how much information is out there, we can't possibly dream of trying to assemble it all into anything as manageable as a single book. We instead generate theories to support our impossible positions. The author's use of hyperbole here is used to underline the extent to which contemporary researchers are overwhelmed or "inundated," as in (C), by the wealth of information available.

31. **D** In this part of the passage, the author discusses goods from different countries and then goes on to say that ours is truly a world community, where the lines between nations have become blurred and where people have more in common than ever before. As with all the information that is constantly at our fingertips, so too is the world constantly at our fingertips. This agrees with (D). Choice (A) is not supported by the passage. Choice (B) refers to consumerism as "excess," a value judgment that the author does not place on consumerism. Choice (C) refers to a preference for foreign goods, where the author refers only to their availability.

32. **D** The mention of the "computer-savvy researcher" appears in the following line: "The computer-savvy researcher of today, by contrast, can have that information instantaneously and can even search within it for whatever bits of information seem relevant." In other words, this researcher has an abundance of information available to him at all times, as (D) suggests.

33. **B** The crucial line appears near the end of the final paragraph: "It is at the very least my hope—and the hope, I suspect, of many others—that there must be some way between the two extremes." This "way" agrees with the "compromise" mentioned in (B). The author is dismissive of neither the new nor the old modes of research, which eliminates (A) and (C). Choice (D) can be eliminated because the differences between users is not discussed here.

Drill 3

1. **A** The full lines read as follows: *In a span of only thirty years, the number of children who play musical instruments has been cut in half.* The word "only" indicates the quickness with which this transformation has occurred, lending support to (A). The author goes on to list the troubling aspects of this trend, so none of the other choices work in this context.

2. **B** The author of Passage 1 discusses the survey in the first part of the second paragraph: Music in Peril *is not the collection of urban legends that most of its critics will accuse it of being. It is a set of data collected from elementary and middle schools all over the country. With schools represented from each of the 50 states, it accounts for all the great diversity in this country.* From this statement, it can be inferred that the author disapproves of *urban legends* and approves of data collected from *all over the country that accounts for all the great diversity in this country.* The author is most concerned with span and diversity, as (B) suggests. While (C) does partially describe *Music in Peril*'s data, it does not account for all the data, so it can be eliminated. Choice (D) addresses the issue of race, but not the other types of diversity described in the passage.

3. **B** The author of Passage 2 does not dispute the methods employed by the statisticians described in Passage 1. She instead thinks the criteria should be changed. As she writes in the last paragraph, *The survey can't capture the fact that classical music is not the only place to find interesting, complex music anymore, except by the most conservative, crustiest definitions.* In this sense, the author of Passage 2 would likely consider the diversity of the groups surveyed irrelevant because the survey is based on faulty premises, as suggested in (B). The author of Passage 2 does not take issue with Passage 1's data but more with its premises and conclusions.

4. **D** The main point of the final paragraph of Passage 1 comes through in the last two sentences: *True musical proficiency is the result of many years of encouraging musical education, and not only for those who eventually become musicians. Ours is a dire world indeed when not only have our musicians lost the ability to play but also the broader populace has lost the discernment and ability to hear them.* In other words, musical education does not only affect schoolchildren but affects society as a whole, as (D) paraphrases. While (B) may be implied in the passage, it is never directly stated, so this answer choice has to be eliminated.

5. **A** The author of Passage 2 refers to Passage 1's conclusions as *apocalyptic* and *evidence that all the bad things we suspect are worse than we even knew.* Passage 2's sarcastic, dismissive language suggests that the author thinks Passage 1's conclusions are a bit dramatic, or overstated, as (A) suggests. Although she disagrees with these conclusions, she does not refer to the author of Passage 1 as *dishonest*, merely misguided, eliminating (D).

6. **D** The author of Passage 2 refers to these *apocalyptic surveys as providing evidence that all the bad things we suspect are worse than we even knew*. The survey in the answer choices must therefore describe a negative trend, eliminating (B) and (C). Choice (A) describes a trend, but it is one that is simply true. It does not contain within it the value judgment that (D) does. Only (D) remains, as exactly the kind of *apocalyptic survey* she considers commonplace.

7. **B** The third paragraph of Passage 2 states the following: *Music programs have been slashed at many public schools, and less than half as many children today are learning instruments than were the generations of forty or fifty years earlier. And this statistical certainty is not limited to the less fortunate areas of the country.* Words like *many* and *limited* refer to the *range* of the problem, as (B) suggests. The author of Passage 2 does accuse *Music in Peril* of both *conservatism* and *bias*, but in these lines, she is conceding that the study describes a wide-ranging trend, eliminating (C) and (D).

8. **D** The word *landscape* is used in the beginning of the fourth paragraph: *The musical landscape is changing, yes, but not in the distressing way that* Music in Peril *wants to suggest. The survey can't capture the fact that classical music is not the only place to find interesting, complex music anymore.* In other words, the typical definition suggests that *classical music* is the only *interesting, complex* type of music—a claim that the author disputes, lending support to (D). Choice (C) is correct to say *shifting*, but the trend is not *impossible to describe*, as the author does try to describe it.

9. **C** Throughout the fourth paragraph, the author uses terms like *most conservative, traditional, musical categories that don't apply anymore, institutions of old*, and *irrelevant*. In other words, the categories are still being used even though they have not changed to reflect current realities and are therefore *inflexible*, as (C) suggests. Other terms may provide alternate meanings for the slangy word crusty, but they do not apply here.

10. **A** The last sentence of Passage 2 says the following: *All that is happening is that the institutions of old are trying to hold on for dear life and actually belong in the same irrelevant pile as studies on the decline of cursive or telephone conversations.* The key word here is *irrelevant*, and the author of Passage 1 would likely respond by noting the larger relevance of the project, as (A) does. There is no support in Passage 1 for (B) and (C). Choice (D) may be true, but it would not respond to Passage 2's criticism.

11. **D** Compare the first sentences of both passages. Passage 1 states, Music in Peril *confirms most of our worst suspicions*, suggesting a concerned or saddened tone. Passage 2 states, Music in Peril *is hardly surprising in our era of apocalyptic surveys, yet more evidence that all the bad things we suspect are worse than we even knew*, which is far more sarcastic and dismissive. Choice (A) is correct only for Passage 1, and (C) is correct only for Passage 2. The only choice that correctly identifies the tone in each of the passages is (D).

12. **B** Passage 2 is primarily a critique of the ideas in Passage 1, which eliminates (C) and (D). Passage 2 does not, however, provide new findings or new data, which eliminates (A). Only (B) remains, and it correctly identifies Passage 2's issue with the premises of Passage 1's argument, namely that classical music is the main outlet for interesting, important music.

13. **C** The phrase to *spin yarns* appears in the first sentence, and it is reiterated in the later sentences in the paragraph, which refer to *some kind of narrative* and our minds wanting stories. While (A), (B), and (D) offer alternate meanings of the word *yarns*, only (C) works in this context.

14. **D** The metaphor of connecting dots appears in this context: *We want any nearby dots to be connected. Effect with no cause, correlation with no causation: we can't assimilate these ideas because they don't have that narrative structure.* In other words, even if these dots aren't connected, our minds want them to be and thus connect them, as (D) suggests. Although the connections may not exist in the real world, the passage does not imply that the details themselves do not exist, thus eliminating (B).

15. **D** The full sentence reads as follows: *Our minds want stories, even if those stories need to be twisted and mangled into existence.* In other words, we can have a difficult time creating stories, but we have the need nonetheless, as (D) suggests. The author does not reflect on whether this is a good or bad trait, thus eliminating (A). The discussion of history does not come until later in the passage, thus eliminating (B).

16. **C** The phrase appears in this context: *Historians and onlookers alike have spent over a century debating the causes, the effects, and the place of this event in the ongoing plot of American history. Neuroscientists have referred to a "need for narrative."* The passage as a whole is about narrative, and the word plot relates to narratives, suggesting that the history of the American Civil War is another one of these narratives, full of related events, as (C) indicates. Choice (B) cannot work because the *plot* referred to here is not that of a *mystery*, nor are any historical mysteries discussed. The author does not refer to this need for narrative as a special *talent*, thus eliminating (D).

17. **D** The first two paragraphs discuss the *need for narrative* in a general way, even citing the findings of neuroscientists and the work of historians. The third and fourth paragraphs focus more specifically on *personality*, which can be explained with a specific application of the general theory of the need for narrative. Choice (D) best captures this transition. The latter half does discuss literary texts, but not exclusively, and the first half is focused on much more than historical events, so (A) can be eliminated. Choice (C) cannot work because the "need for narrative" is ultimately a psychological concept that is discussed throughout the passage, and it is not critiqued.

18. C The early twentieth century is discussed in these lines: *In the early twentieth century, the very notion of "consistent" stories broke down, and characters became less rigidly defined as a result. Suddenly, amid a cultural shift away from religious certainty, one's environment, one's historical era, one's family history could all come to bear on the maze of human personality.* In other words, this era was characterized by complexity rather than simplicity, so any discussion of personality must be more complex than the titles in (A) and (B). Choice (D) is off-topic. Only (C) adequately captures the complexity described in the passage.

19. D This shift *away from religious certainty* is discussed in these lines: *In the early twentieth century, the very notion of "consistent" stories broke down, and characters became less rigidly defined as a result. Suddenly, amid a cultural shift away from religious certainty, one's environment, one's historical era, one's family history could all come to bear on the maze of human personality.* In other words, personality had become a newly complex object with many things influencing it, as (D) suggests. Choice (A) cannot work because understandings of personality have not been consistent throughout history. Choice (C) does not work because there is no evidence in the passage that non-psychologists critique the theories of psychologists.

20. B The word *contain* appears in this sentence: *Psychologists began to spend entire careers studying human personalities, but for all these changes, the goal was still the same: contain the human experience, find the story that can encapsulate all of human complexity.* Use the second part of the sentence as a clue. The word *contain* must mean something like *find the story that can encapsulate*, and the closest approximation from this list of answer choices is (B). The other choices offer synonyms for the word *contain*, but they do not work in this particular context.

21. D The last sentence of a passage will typically offer some kind of summary of a passage, and this sentence does just that. The passage as a whole discusses the *need for narrative* in many aspects of life, including how we understand ourselves. The last sentence asks, rhetorically, *Because after all that has come before us, and all that will come later, if we're not part of the big story, what are we?* Choice (D) captures this basic idea well in suggesting that without the big story, our lives would be different. Although the last sentence does look to the future a bit, it does not make any claims about the stories that people in the future will tell themselves, thus eliminating (B). Also, while there are some implied comparisons between the "narrative" of history and that of fiction, these comparisons are not addressed in this final sentence, eliminating (C).

22. A Although the first few paragraphs detail Toomer's importance during the Harlem Renaissance, the end of the passage states that *Toomer's early literary output can be more thoroughly understood than his later personal life.* Choice (B) is disproven in the first paragraph, and (D) is disproven in the fourth paragraph. Choice (C) is also slightly off: it cannot be said that Toomer's essays were inconsistent, only that there were so few of them.

23. **B** Because these two paragraphs are particularly about Jean Toomer, (A) and (D) can be eliminated. Both paragraphs are concerned with how other artists and thinkers thought of Toomer, however, so the best answer must be (B).

24. **D** Because Braithwaite's review of *Cane* is so glowing, his praise can be described as *total* or *complete*, as in (D). All other choices provide alternate meanings of the word "unreserved," but they do not work in this context.

25. **D** The first paragraph states, *Toomer gained huge accolades from the white literary world as well, and well-known authors such as Sherwood Anderson and Waldo Frank considered him one of their own.* In this context, Sherwood Anderson and Waldo Frank are used as representatives of the white *literary world*, lending support to (D). Choice (A) cannot work because there is no indication that Toomer was courting this white readership, particularly not with any urgency.

26. **D** The sentence in question is the topic sentence of the second paragraph. It introduces the ideas that are to come. The paragraph goes on to say that Toomer *could incorporate influences from white as well as black artists, and he melded them into a new, innovative style that mixed poetry, prose, jazz, folklore, and spiritualism.* As in (D), these are aspects of Toomer's art that showed black and white artists alike a new *artistic freedom*.

27. **A** The sentence that directly precedes "These scraps" is as follows: *Toomer himself may not have thought of these marriages as interracial: particularly by the 1940s, Toomer insisted that his race was "American" and by the end of his life, he may have even identified as a white man.* The repetition of the word *may* shows the author's uncertainty as to Toomer's exact attitudes. "These scraps" must then refer to the scant biographical evidence that literary historians have in piecing together Toomer's later life, as suggested by (A).

28. **A** The fourth paragraph discusses the increase in race activism, though it says of Toomer, *By then, and until his death in 1967, Toomer was much more taken with local issues, and his main concern was with his church, the Friend's Society of Quakers, and the high school students whom he taught there.* In other words, Toomer was not as interested in race activism as were many of his African American contemporaries. In this sense, his views were atypical, as suggested by (A). Choice (D) offers a similar answer, but it is too extreme and is disproven by the quotation in the following paragraph. It was not that he had *no* interest in contemporary race relations but more that his interest was different.

29. **C** Pay careful attention to the sentence that contains the word in question: *By then, and until his death in 1967, Toomer was much more taken with local issues, and his main concern was with his church, the Friend's Society of Quakers, and the high school students whom he taught there.* "Taken with" in this context means "occupied with" or "interested in," and as the sentence then states, Toomer was much more interested in smaller, local problems than in national race problems.

30. **B** The topic sentence of this paragraph reads as follows: *If Toomer's early literary output can be more thoroughly understood than his later personal life, or his later racial identification, it can only be because Toomer himself wanted it to be so.* This sentence suggests that the paragraph itself will discuss Toomer's own attitudes, eliminating (A). We learn in earlier paragraphs that Toomer did not have a typical "commitment to racial equality," eliminating (D), and he did not contradict himself in public and private, eliminating (C). Only (B) reflects the actual content of the paragraph.

31. **D** As the quotation from Toomer demonstrates, he saw race as a more complex thing than mere black and white. We can deduce, then, that he would've found the contemporary debates far too simple, as (D) suggests. His own views were "racially complex," but "black and white" refers to the contemporary debates in which Toomer was not a participant, eliminating (C). We may consider his views "socially progressive," but the passage does not state that they are, so (B) must also be eliminated.

32. **B** The sentence before the one cited in the question reads as follows: *Because Toomer was such a truly great artist, literary historians will always long for more information about his life.* In other words, literary historians would like more information about his life. Among the answer choices, (B) would best supply this information.

33. **D** The full sentence in question reads as follows: *We should be wary of the rigid categories that Toomer fought against all his life, and if anything, perhaps Toomer's refusal to fit into these categories can help us to modify our own.* This sentence is a reference to our own contemporary views on race, which, the sentence suggests, Toomer might be able to help us modify, as paraphrased in (D). Although we may consider his views more advanced, the passage does not refer to them in this way, eliminating (C).

Drill 4

1. **C** The word "overflowing" suggests that there have been many *Western projects to modernize the Middle East.* This is a fairly general statement, so the specifics in (A) and (B) cannot be supported. Choice (D) does not address these *Western projects* at all, so it too can be eliminated.

2. **A** The sentence in which Bill Clinton appears reads as follows: *President Bill Clinton, for example, is still praised for his role in Israeli-Palestinian talks,* and a few sentences later, the author goes on to say, *This attitude toward non-Western regions, the belief that the West's systems of government can help save the people of the Middle East....* Therefore, it can be inferred that Bill Clinton is a representative of this attitude, as (A) suggests. The author goes on to criticize this attitude, so (B) and (D) can be eliminated. Choice (C) can also be eliminated because Clinton is the only example given.

3.   **D**   Another way of saying *universally applicable* would be "appropriate to all." The author is stating in these lines that Western styles of government may not be appropriate for all people, especially those outside the West, as (D) indicates. The author goes on to suggest a need for more non-Western perspectives, therefore eliminating (A) and (B). Choice (C) is too extreme in its use of the word *only*, so it can be eliminated. Choice (D) remains as the correct answer.

4.   **C**   The relevant lines state the following: *The native peoples who are then forced to live under the new government's rule become extremely skeptical of it, as its supposed successes are measured by seemingly irrelevant metrics.* The key words here are *extremely skeptical*, which agree most closely with (C) and disagrees with (D). The information in the passage is not specific enough to support (B). Choice (A) is too extreme in its use of the word *despise*, so it can be eliminated.

5.   **C**   The relevant lines state the following: *Many of the great ancient and historical societies come from these regions, but since the seventeenth century, these regions have been considered almost universally backward.* In other words, these regions were once considered "great" but are now considered "backward," as (C) suggests. These lines do not address contemporary governments, which eliminates all other choices.

6.   **B**   This paragraph discusses the influence of George W. Bush and others, suggesting that this influence has not been a good one, as (B) suggests. The lines do not contain specific support for the other choices, so (A), (C), and (D) can be eliminated.

7.   **D**   Cross out the word in the context and replace it with your own: F*or many Westerners, nationality is a given and ultimately _____ the more local identifications of town, city, or stat*e. A word like *supersedes* or *replaces* would work here, in which case only (D) comes close. The other choices may represent other meanings for the word *trumps*, but they do not work in this context.

8.   **A**   Cross out the word in the context and replace it with your own: *The Western notions of nation-above- all and religious coexistence can't _____ in this and other countries because the value systems have developed so independently of these notions.* Some word like *apply* or *function* would work here, in which case only (A) comes close. The other choices may represent other meanings for the word *maintain*, but they do not work in this context.

9.   **B**   This question asks for a statement that would *refute* the author's claim in the lines, *As in many other parts of the world, "Iraqi freedom" was defined by someone other than the Iraqis themselves.* Any statement that would suggest that Iraqis or some other Middle Eastern group had a role in defining their own government systems would refute this claim, so (B) provides the best refutation. Choices (A), (C), and (D) all support the author's central claim that the West has had a too-powerful influence in the region.

10. **D**   The author writes for the most part about the negative effects of Western influence in the Middle East, but the lines, *Certainly, Western nations are today more sensitive to cultural differences than they have ever been*, suggest that this influence may be improving. Choice (D) reflects this concession and slight change of tone. It does not reflect the author's broader point, however, which eliminates (B) and (C). Finally, there is no evidence that the author is writing these lines in response to his critics, which eliminates (A).

11. **C**   The relevant sentence says the following: *It still remains to be seen, however, whether this new multicultural stance is a genuine change or a simple repackaging of an old product.* In this case, the *simple repackaging* is contrasted with a *genuine change*. The author is therefore skeptical that this new approach is a *genuine change*, as suggested in (C). The author does not hope for this *simple repackaging*, eliminating (A) and (B). Choice (D) takes the word product too literally.

12. **D**   The author argues throughout the passage that the influence of the West has been too strong in the Middle East and that there needs to be more local influence in government policy. Choice (D) best reflects this main idea. Choices (A) and (C) go against this goal. Choice (B) is also an example of a Western ideal, so it too can be eliminated.

13. **A**   Choice (B) is not indicated and is too extreme. There is no mention that Joyce's critics were against an autobiographical interpretation of his work, so eliminate (C). Joyce may have spoken through the character of Dedalus, but it is too extreme to say this always occurred, so (D) is wrong.

14. **C**   The author states towards the beginning of the passage that *it is worth turning one's attention to events in Joyce's life that may help the reader understand some of the sources of his creative inspiration*, but ends the passage by saying that reading his books *solely through the biography… is fraught with danger*. Choice (C) best reflects this two-sided attitude towards the extent to which one can read *Ulysses* as an autobiography. Choices (A) and (B) each only represents one aspect of the author's opinion. Choice (D) is too strong; since this passage is only about Joyce, we don't know how the author views *Ulysses* in relation to other books.

15. **D**   The author believes that understanding Joyce's biography *may help the reader understand some of the sources of his creative inspiration*, but warns that reading *Ulysses solely through the biography… is fraught with danger*. Choice (D) provides the best support for this double-sided attitude, as the word *solely* in line 58 indicates that the biography is still useful to some degree. Choice (A) describes Joyce in general, but not *Ulysses* in particular. Choices (B) and (C) each only support one side of the author's argument.

16. **B**   Choice (B) is correct, as Joyce fled for *reasons both personal and professional* (line 22). Choice (A) is wrong because while Joyce did find inspiration abroad, the passage offers other reasons for his leaving. Choices (C) and (D) are wrong because they are not mentioned in the passage. Choice (B) is the best paraphrase of the two reasons.

17. **A** Choice (A) is not mentioned. Eliminate (B) because Joyce wrote in a modernist, experimental narrative style. Choice (C) is incorrect because the passage tells us that Joyce is regarded as one of the greatest writers ever. Eliminate (D) because Joyce lived between 1882 and 1941.

18. **D** A *conundrum* is a predicament or a puzzling statement. The word *inaccessible* in the first sentence supports this idea. Choice (D), *puzzle,* is closest to this meaning.

19. **A** The author of the passage claims that the reader can understand a writer's work by studying that person's biography. Then he or she describes elements from James Joyce's life in Trieste that are reflected in his writing. Lastly, the author moves from a discussion of Joyce's work to pose a more general question about how to interpret autobiographical elements in a writer's work. This structure most closely agrees with (A). Choice (B) is incorrect because three theories are not mentioned. Choice (C) is wrong; the author doesn't criticize other writers. Finally, eliminate (D), since the author never says this.

20. **B** The word *inadvertently* means the author may misrepresent reality without meaning to do so. Choice (A) is not mentioned. Both (C) and (D) are about readers, but the statement at issue is about writers.

21. **C** Choice (C) may be one way to interpret Dedalus's claim. Choice (A) is wrong because the author states we can't know for sure exactly what Joyce meant here, and we aren't given any information about Dedalus's profession. For (B), even if Joyce used Dedalus to voice an opinion, nowhere does it say that he had reason to fear making this claim. There is no evidence in the passage for (D).

22. **B** Joyce was not a sailor (the passage says he's an author), so such a character would not be autobiographical. Choices (A) and (C) are described in the passage as characteristics of Joyce's life. As for (D), Stephen Dedalus is described as Joyce's *literary alter ego* (line 52), meaning the character through whom Joyce speaks in this book.

23. **B** The primary purpose of a passage is what the author is trying to accomplish in his or her writing. This is a fictional piece, written to tell a story and the focus from the very first sentence is about how an individual with odd habits is always lost and late. Choice (A) does not mention how weird some of William's behavior is. Choice (B) is good because *chronicles* means to tell a story, and it mentions *idiosyncrasies* of a *salesman.* Choice (C) does not mention any weirdness about the day or the salesperson. The passage is not directed to William's coworkers as in (D)—they're fictional!

24. **A** The list of items in William's briefcase is part of a description of the detailed preparations that William makes for a business trip. The passage indicates that *he would verify that he had everything he needed for the day,* and also that some of the items he felt he needed were *perplexing to his coworkers.* Choice (A) best describes these two ideas, that William paid a lot of attention to his preparations, but that they were also a bit odd. Choice (B) is too strongly worded. Choices (C) and (D) lack any sense of the strange nature of William's behavior.

25. **A**   William's *coworkers* are mentioned in line 22 and find William's behavior *perplexing*. In the next mention of the coworkers in line 28, it states in the coworkers' viewpoint that the tape recording is *not the oddest thing* about William. Since the *coworkers surmised* (line 31) the reason for his dressing in identical clothes every day indicates that they have been interested enough to discuss his behavior and want to understand why he does things in his peculiar way. The coworkers seem *mildly curious*, (A). The emotion in (B) *coldly indifferent* is not supported by the passage. There is no evidence of the coworkers being condescending, (C). Choice (D) *deeply intrigued* is too strong compared to the level of interest expressed in the passage.

26. **B**   Choice (B) indicates that William's *coworkers* found some things about him *odd*, which indicates mild curiosity. Choices (A), (C), and (D) all describe William, without mentioning his coworkers.

27. **C**   William's answer is that he *might need* the tape recorder. There is no mention of knowledge of *technology* in (A). Choice (B) is incorrect because the passage states that *there was no possible use for it in his work*. Bringing something that one *might need* is a way of being prepared, so hold on to (C) and check the other two answers. There is no evidence that William feels the questions are rude as in (D).

28. **D**   William's preparations are painstaking: he *checks and rechecks* his possessions, his directions are *neatly written out*, but it's all for nothing. William has packed useless items, and he never gets to use any of his meeting supplies because he doesn't make it to the meeting; his neatly written directions get him lost. The useless energy put into preparations "all for nothing" situation is best described by *fruitless,* (D), which means "useless or unproductive." Choice (A), *professional* is incorrect, because William's coworkers wouldn't think he was *odd* if he were acting professionally. While William does not pay attention on his way and gets lost, his *preparations* themselves are not *careless,* (B). The preparations are not *useful,* (C), because William has unnecessary items and doesn't get where he plans to go. There is no evidence that William or anyone else thought his preparations were *tiresome,* or "annoying."

29. **B**   Go back to the passage and use the context to come up with a word to replace *anxious*. The sentence indicates that the possibility of someone riding in the car with William is a *practical impossibility*, and the phrase containing the word *anxious* agrees with the idea that no one would be in the car with him. Look for a word that means something like *excited*. Choices (A), (C), and (D) are all alternate meaning of the word *anxious*, but don't work in this context. Choice (B) is the closest to meaning *excited*, so it is the correct answer.

30. **D**   Go back to the passage and use the context to come up with a word to replace *command*. The sentence in question describes William realize that he stopped following his direction, so look for a word that means he *lost track* of the directions. Only (D), *control*, gives the appropriate meaning. Choices (A) and (B) gives alternate definitions of *command* that do not work in context. Choice (C) is a person who might hold *command*, but also does not work in context.

31. **A** The best supported answer is (A). Although William *says* that he doesn't use maps because they lack organization, it is implied that the actual reason is that William doesn't understand how to use them—it seems unlikely that all the map-makers are wrong and William is right. William also states that he doesn't need maps because he has the directions written down. These directions end up getting him lost, so it is further evidence that William *has much to learn about navigation.*

32. **B** The *blue necktie* is still flying proudly despite William's disastrous day and the poor state of the rest of his clothes. Just as in a sentence completion, the word *but* indicates the opposite of what comes before. In this case, the necktie is a positive symbol in contrast to the other aspects of William's behavior. Choice (C) is too literal: this isn't about the variety of his wardrobe.

Drill 5

1. **C** Lasanky is used in the passage as an example of the new, post-World War II, type of printmaker, who built their reputations as *printmakers*. Choices (B) and (D) both describe the older, pre-war printmakers. Choice (A) is the opposite of how the new printmakers felt: *It is the complex techniques of printmaking that entrance them.* The idea of *drawing a composition before going to the plate or block of stone* describes how the older printmakers worked, specifically in contrast to the newer printmakers such as Lasanky, so (C) is the best answer.

2. **A** Choice (A) describes how the older, pre-World War II printmakers worked, and is used specifically as a contrast between them and the newer, post-war printmakers like Lasanky, so it provides the best support for (C) above. Choice (B) describes the post-war printmakers, but is unrelated to any answer choices for the above question. Choice (C) describes the pre-war printmakers, not Lasanky. Choice (D) describes what some of Lasanky's students did, but is also not related to any answer choices for the above question.

3. **B** The assertion is that *Callot and Meryon made prints that…were meant to be printed in large numbers.* Eliminate (A): the term *printmakers* represents the "other side" in a distinction between *Callot and Meyron* and *those followers of Hayter.* Choice (B) is correct because it addresses the *large numbers* of prints. The *complete satisfaction* in (C) is extreme. Choice (D) is incorrect: a distinction is provided in lines 8–14.

4. **C** In the passage in lines 14–17, the *printmakers* are described as having *found that creating in a print medium is…totally satisfying.* This is best paraphrased in (C), *fulfilled.* There is no evidence for the other answers in the passage.

5. **D**   In lines 24–29, the quote of Sylvan Cole describes *the change that was taking place,* which was from printmaking for mass production, and the artistic printmaking practice of making few prints. The pronoun *this* (*...and out of this came a man...*) indicates that the change was mentioned previously, and in fact the whole paragraph has been discussing how printmaking changed between one era and another. The passage does not indicate that *Cole,* in (A), changed anything; he just explains it. Choice (B) is incorrect because *Abstract Expressionism* is mentioned only in line 23, not *examined.* There is a relationship between painting and printmaking described in the quote, but the question asks why the author includes it. The reason is that it is support from an expert about the changes in printmaking that the whole essay so far has been discussing. This is paraphrased in (D).

6. **A**   The question asks what the second paragraph does to help the passage. The short paragraph discusses that *Before the war* printmakers made only prints, and made lots of them. In the first paragraphs, the point was made that there was a big change from prolific printmaking for mass distribution to smaller runs of prints as art. The third paragraph discusses how the number of people studying printmaking changed drastically because of programs for those who fought in the war. We need an answer that mentions both *war* and that printmaking changed. Choice (A) mentions both of these and seems reasonable, but take a quick look at the rest of the answers: (B) is the opposite of what we are looking for. *Callot and Meryon* in (C) were only discussed in the first paragraph. Choice (D) is not mentioned in the passage.

7. **B**   Go back to the passage and use the context to come up with a word to replace *adornment.* In the passage, *adornment* describes the use of artwork in schools and government buildings. While many of the answers could refer to prints, in this case, these visual artworks are more for *decoration* than just for *enjoyment* so (B) is closest.

8. **B**   The passage states that the G.I. Bill gave veterans *the opportunity to attend college* (lines 39–40). This is stated to be *during a period of prosperity* (line 36), so it meant that *opportunity* was that the government paid the schools the money for the veterans' education. Choice (B) is the best paraphrase of these elements. The opposite of (A) is true. The G.I. Bill was not just for *lost* veterans. Choice (D) has the wrong chronology: students using the GI Bill directed money to institutions that used the funds to expand.

9. **C**   Go back to the passage and use the context to come up with a word to replace *lost.* In lines 40–41 of the passage, the *"lost"* are described as those that *had little direction*—they didn't know what to do with themselves. The word *aimless* in (C) describes this quality best. While *lost* can have the meaning of some of the other words in the answers, these do not fit in the context of the passage.

10. **B** The *phenomenal expansion* in the passage is that of *art education*. One reason mentioned is that the *atmosphere* of art departments was appealing, and in lines 51–55, the *expansion* is described at two levels: new and advanced programs for those with college degrees at *institutions of higher learning*, and older, established schools for beginning students that were *filled to capacity*. This is all addressed in the education experiences listed in (B). The membership of the army (A) is not a reason, but the number of those using the G.I. Bill to obtain art education. Choice (C) is not mentioned, and (D) does not refer to art at all.

11. **A** The best supported answer is (A). The effect of the *proliferation* is mentioned in lines (62–78) the passage as causing an increase in the number of printmakers, which in turned caused more *institutions* whose purpose was to *exhibit* and *publish and sell* prints. To fill all this demand, more organizations were created in order to *encourage the creation of prints*. There is no evidence for (B) or (D), and (C) is extreme due to the use of *all*.

12. **C** The author of this passage shows an interest in informing readers about CMEs, but the author also explains that scientists (and, implicitly, readers can do little to predict these storms or prevent the damage they cause. Choice (A) is extreme: the author cites countermeasures in the final paragraph, so there are some things that can be done to minimize impact. Choice (B) is also extreme: the author has not provided evidence that identifies so precisely the time or effects of future CMEs. The first half of (D) is reasonable, but the second half overstates the author's view of how prepared our society will be.

13. **D** The 1989 storm is described as a major CME. The author also states that since our society is increasingly dependent on technology, the potential havoc wrought by a major CME becomes even more distressing. Choices (A), (B), and (C) are not supported by any information in the passage.

14. **B** In lines 15-16 of the passage, the author claims that the *last recorded instance of a major CME occurred in 1989*. According to the graph, the biggest change in the Disturbance Storm Index occurred in 1989, when the line drops to its lowest point. This data supports the author's claim. The claims listed in (A), (C), and (D) are mentioned in the passage, but are not supported by the data in the graph.

15. **D** The data points on the graph do not follow any discernably predictable pattern, and thus no trend can be identified, (D).

16. **A** The researchers have *scant information* about the CMEs because there are few *existing records*. Therefore, we're looking for a word that means only a few, or not enough. Choice (A) is a good match. Choices (B) and (C) are opposite (and distracting). Choice (D) simply doesn't have the meaning that we're looking for.

17. **B** In the first paragraph, the author notes that while few people realize it, certain phenomena originating on the sun can, in fact, have serious consequences on Earth, (B). The author cites geomagnetic storms as one such phenomenon.

18. **D**   The answer to the previous question, the author's claim that certain events on the sun can have serious consequences on Earth, is best supported by the example of the results of the 1989 geomagnetic storm, which knocked out a power grid and thus deprived millions of people of electricity, (D).

19. **A**   *Compounded* means "increased or added to." Scientists' inability to *determine the orientation of a magnetic field* more than *30 minutes before it reaches the atmosphere* increases, or adds to, the *difficulties* of prediction. Choice (A) best expresses this problem. Choice (B) is close but not quite right. The author already says that there is little time to predict CMEs, and just uses *compounded by* to show that the situation is even worse than previously asserted. Choice (C) is incorrect because the author does not try to *disprove* this idea. There is nothing in the passage to support (D).

20. **C**   To answer this question, we must determine the truth of the given statements and rely upon Process of Elimination. The second-to-last paragraph discusses how rare CMEs are, and therefore, how little data exists that would allow scientists to predict future occurrences. III is therefore true, so eliminate (A) and (B). The same paragraph also mentions how little time there would be to react to and study a CME, so I is true. This eliminates (D), leaving (C) as the only possible answer.

21. **D**   Choice (D) accurately reflects both the author's effort to inform and warn readers about CMEs and the author's explanation of the challenges researchers are facing. Choices (A) and (B) accurately describe only one part of the passage. Choice (C) is wrong because most of the passage is not persuasive in style.

22. **D**   There is evidence for three of the choices in the passage: (A), lines 13-15, *Our sun would have to be only a few miles in diameter to become a black hole*. It isn't, therefore it won't become a black hole; (B), lines 20-21; and (C), lines 15-16. Choice (D) is correct because it is the only one NOT in the passage. Indeed, the opposite of this is true: the sun would have to be heavier to have enough gravity to pull it down into a black hole, suggesting that its gravitational pull is not enough to make a black hole.

23. **A**   Try replacing the word *exhausts* with what would make sense in the sentence. A good phrase to replace *exhausts* is "uses all." Choice (A), "uses up," comes closest to this meaning. None of the other answer choices comes close. Choice (B) means "to spend or use up senselessly." Choice (C) means "to tire or make weary." Choice (D) means "to give off or send out."

24. **C**   Choice (A) is mentioned in the passage, but is not the reason that the author mentions the Crab Nebula. Choice (B), *prove*, is extreme (and not the focus). There is no evidence for (D) in the passage. The author mentions the Crab Nebula in conjunction with the *neutron star* (lines 26-31).

25. **B**   There is no evidence for any of the answer choices in the passage except (B). Choice (B) is correct because of evidence in the last paragraph of the passage. Lines 38-39 state that black holes have *enough gravity to make x-rays come out*.

26. D   The answer to the previous question, that the best way to find a black hole is to look for evidence of x-ray emissions, is best supported by the information In the final paragraph; in particular, in lines 38-39 the author states that *a black hole has strong enough gravity to make x-rays come out,* (D). This statement indicates that while black holes are nearly impossible to detect, the best way to do so is to look for x-rays.

27. A   Choices (B) and (C) are mentioned in the passage, but are both too narrow to accurately reflect the main idea of the whole passage. Choice (D) contradicts the passage; the mini black holes have not been observed. Choice (A) is correct because Passage 2 is primarily about the theory that mini black holes exist.

28. A   The clue to the meaning of *elementary particles, neutrinos,* refers to the smallest, or most basic (A) units that make up neutrons, protons, and electrons. Choices (B), (C), and (D) can thus be eliminated. (Think elementary school, which is basic compared to high school or college).

29. C   Choices (A), (B), and (D) take bits and pieces from the passage, so they all "sound" pretty good. However, we're asked to select what can be *inferred*; that is, what do we know for a fact passed on the passage? Choice (C) is correct because the passage states in lines 55-56 that *the amount of radiation increases sharply as we consider less and less massive black holes.* This is an inverse relationship, since the more radiation, the smaller the size.

30. B   Choice (B) is correct because the paragraph describes the experience you would have on the edge of a black hole, incorporating such mundane details as checking the time. Choice (A) is too strong—scientific proof takes more than an analogy. There is no evidence of warning, as in (C). Choice (D) is insulting to the author, and thus cannot be correct.

31. D   Lines 3-4 of Passage 1 state that *mass in a small enough package* is a black hole, and go on to discuss why our sun is not likely to become a black hole because of its density. The second paragraph of Passage 2 also discusses mass and density. There is no evidence in either passage that (A), (B), or (C) are factors enabling us to identify a star that is capable of becoming a black hole. Choice (D) matches the statements noted.

32. C   In lines 7-8, the author of Passage 1 states that black holes are a *one-way ticket*—matter goes in, but doesn't come out. There is no evidence for (A) in the passage. Choices (B) and (D) are contradicted by information in the passage. Choice (C), Hawking's theory of mini black holes, does the most to dispute the statement.

NOTES

NOTES

NOTES